NATIONAL
GEOGRAPHIC
KiDS

ALMANAC
2025

Monarch butterflies fly around the Monarch Butterfly Biosphere Reserve in Michoacan, Mexico.

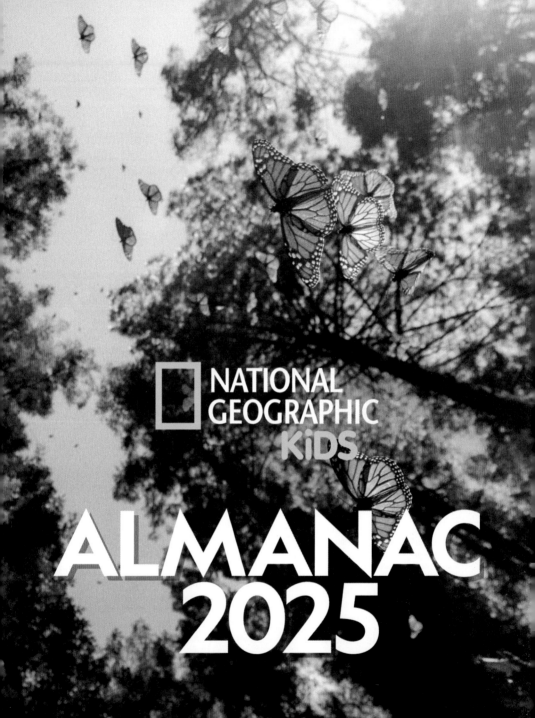

NATIONAL GEOGRAPHIC KiDS

ALMANAC
2025

NATIONAL GEOGRAPHIC
WASHINGTON, D.C.

National Geographic Kids Books
gratefully acknowledges the following people for their help with the *National Geographic Kids Almanac*.

Stacey McClain of the
National Geographic Explorer Programs

Amazing Animals

Suzanne Braden, Director, Pandas International

Dr. Rodolfo Coria, Paleontologist,
Plaza Huincul, Argentina

Dr. Sylvia Earle, National Geographic
Explorer in Residence

Dr. Thomas R. Holtz, Jr., Senior Lecturer,
Vertebrate Paleontology,
Department of Geology, University of Maryland

Dr. Luke Hunter, Executive Director, Panthera

Nizar Ibrahim, National Geographic Explorer

Dereck and Beverly Joubert,
National Geographic Explorers in Residence

"Dino" Don Lessem, President, Exhibits Rex

Kathy B. Maher, Research Editor (former),
National Geographic magazine

Kathleen Martin, Canadian Sea Turtle Network

Barbara Nielsen, Polar Bears International

Andy Prince, Austin Zoo

Julia Thorson, Translator, Zurich, Switzerland

Dennis vanEngelsdorp, Senior Extension Associate,
Pennsylvania Department of Agriculture

Space and Earth
Science and Technology

Tim Appenzeller, Chief Magazine Editor, *Nature*

Dr. Rick Fienberg, Press Officer and Director of Communications,
American Astronomical Society

Dr. José de Ondarza, Associate Professor,
Department of Biological Sciences, State University
of New York, College at Plattsburgh

Lesley B. Rogers, Managing Editor (former),
National Geographic magazine

Dr. Enric Sala, National Geographic Explorer in Residence

Abigail A. Tipton, Director of Research (former),
National Geographic magazine

Erin Vintinner, Biodiversity Specialist,
Center for Biodiversity and Conservation at the
American Museum of Natural History

Barbara L. Wyckoff, Research Editor (former),
National Geographic magazine

Culture Connection

Dr. Wade Davis, National Geographic
Explorer in Residence

Deirdre Mullervy, Managing Editor,
Gallaudet University Press

Wonders of Nature

Anatta, NOAA Public Affairs Officer

Dr. Robert Ballard,
National Geographic Explorer in Residence

Douglas H. Chadwick, Wildlife Biologist and Contributor
to *National Geographic* magazine

Susan K. Pell, Ph.D., Science and Public Programs Manager,
United States Botanic Garden

History Happens

Dr. Sylvie Beaudreau, Associate Professor,
Department of History, State University of New York

Elspeth Deir, Assistant Professor, Faculty of Education,
Queens University, Kingston, Ontario, Canada

Dr. Gregory Geddes, Professor, Global Studies,
State University of New York–Orange,
Middletown-Newburgh, New York

Dr. Fredrik Hiebert, National Geographic Visiting Fellow

Micheline Joanisse, Media Relations Officer,
Natural Resources Canada

Dr. Robert D. Johnston,
Associate Professor and Director of the
Teaching of History Program, University of Illinois at Chicago

Dickson Mansfield, Geography Instructor (retired),
Faculty of Education, Queens University,
Kingston, Ontario, Canada

Tina Norris, U.S. Census Bureau

Parliamentary Information and Research Service,
Library of Parliament, Ottawa, Canada

Karyn Pugliese, Acting Director, Communications,
Assembly of First Nations

Geography Rocks

Dr. Kristin Bietsch, Research Associate,
Population Reference Bureau

Carl Haub, Senior Demographer,
Conrad Taeuber Chair of Public Information,
Population Reference Bureau

Dr. Toshiko Kaneda, Senior Research Associate,
Population Reference Bureau

Dr. Walt Meier, National Snow and Ice Data Center

Dr. Richard W. Reynolds, NOAA's National Climatic Data Center

United States Census Bureau, Public Help Desk

Contents

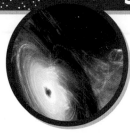
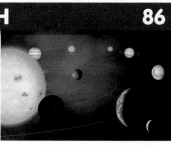

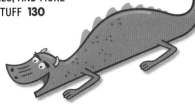

SCIENCE AND TECHNOLOGY 188

WONDERS OF NATURE 212

HISTORY HAPPENS 236

GEOGRAPHY ROCKS 268

YOUR WORLD 2025

A "trashion" show in Nigeria showcases clothing made by teens from plastic waste.

ORANGE SKIES

Wildfires don't just affect Earth's surface—they impact the sky, too. For example, when fires burned throughout Canada in the summer of 2023, the skies stretching along the U.S. East Coast shifted from blue to a hazy reddish orange, a direct result of the massive amount of smoke being released into the environment. Why? The sky gets its color from tiny particles in the air, plus the wavelengths of light these particles refract, or bend. Blue light has shorter wavelengths and scatters easily, creating the blue sky you see on normal days. But when smoke particles are in the atmosphere, they block blue wavelengths and scatter orange and red wavelengths. That creates an eerie haze that can be seen far away from the fires.

Mount Everest Cats

Talk about sky-high living!
In 2019, a team of scientists ascended more than 16,000 feet (4,877 m) above sea level on Mount Everest on the side in Nepal. Their mission: to learn more about the animals that live there. To do it, the team collected poo droppings from the ground, then analyzed the DNA inside them. Surprisingly, researchers discovered that two of the samples belonged to Pallas's cats, a house cat–size species that had never been seen on the mountain. The discovery has researchers wondering how many more of these cats could be living in the area.

Stone of Destiny

The Stone of Destiny might sound like something straight out of a fantasy movie, but this oblong slab of sandstone is, in fact, very real. The ancient symbol of Scotland's monarchy, this 335-pound (152-kg) sacred object was featured in King Charles III's 2023 coronation, where it sat beneath his chair as he was crowned.

So what's the significance of the stone? To start, it's old—although its earliest origins are still unknown. And it's been used in coronations of kings and queens since the 14th century. Because the stone's origins are murky, both England and Scotland have claimed ownership of it, and it was even stolen from Westminster Abbey by a group of Scottish students in 1950. England eventually got it back before returning it to Scotland's Edinburgh Castle, where it remains—unless it's being used in a coronation.

HEAD-SPINNING SCIENCE

FACT: Even astronauts get motion sickness. To find ways to combat nausea during spaceflights, NASA is using a disorientation device to study what happens to your brain and body when it tumbles around at speeds up to three times the force of gravity.

In a partnership with the U.S. Navy, NASA is employing the Kraken, a device typically used for jet pilots. The Kraken takes occupants on a dizzying 60-minute ride, after which their head and eye movements, as well as their heart rates, are tracked. After the ride, the participants' balance, speed, and ability to climb over obstacles are tested. NASA's goal? To figure out what, if anything, might ease astronauts' motion sickness during and after flights, as well as how they can restore their sense of balance quickly. That way, astronauts can efficiently do their jobs—without having to reach for the barf bag.

RAINFOREST CRANES

Going up! A new experience at a rainforest eco-lodge is giving visitors a unique, bird's-eye view of Ecuador's Yasuní National Park. After boarding a specialized cabin dangling from the extended arm of a crane, visitors are lifted 150 feet (45 m) off the Amazon rainforest floor. Inside the crane's cabin, forest-goers can take in 360-degree views of the rainforest canopy for a closer look at the monkeys, birds, and other incredible creatures that live in the treetops.

The crane is also open to researchers studying the Amazon's canopy creatures, which are estimated to make up more than half of all species in the Amazon. By studying these animals from the sky, researchers can better understand the canopy ecosystem, how climate change is affecting the forest, and how to protect at-risk species.

Oldest | HUMAN FOOTPRINT

Modern humans walked Earth some 153,000 years ago, and experts have the fossilized footprint to prove it. Discovered in Garden Route National Park on South Africa's Cape South Coast, the fossil is some 30,000 years older than any previously found human tracks, proving that *Homo sapiens*—modern humans—appeared on the planet a lot earlier than previously thought. (There have been older examples from earlier species.)

How do scientists know just how old the print is? It's all thanks to a new technology that measures the amount of light emitted from energy stored in certain rock types. Also known as luminescence dating, this process can show how long grains of minerals within a rock have been exposed to sunlight—and how long it's been buried. Because this technology is rather new, scientists hope it'll help reveal even older artifacts and paint a more accurate picture of human evolution.

DONKEYS STAND OUTSIDE AN ATM IN PRAYAGRAJ (ALLAHABAD), INDIA.

URBAN JUNGLES

When the COVID-19 pandemic forced families to stay at home in an attempt to stall the spread of the virus, wild mammals roamed more freely around the world, a study has shown. By using location-tracking tags on 2,300 animals, including giant anteaters in Brazil, elephants in Asia, and brown bears in Alaska, U.S.A., scientists were able to determine that a majority of these creatures traveled farther than usual in areas with the strictest lockdowns. Without having to deal with rush hour traffic and other types of typical human interaction, the animals roamed rather freely, walking closer to roads and even prowling along empty city streets. Now, experts are using the data gathered to learn more about how humans impact wildlife—and how we can coexist in healthier ways.

A BOAR MOTHER AND PIGLETS

A RED FOX

MOUNTAIN GOATS

3D-PRINTED WOMEN IN STEM

Forget molding clay and chiseling marble: Statues of the future are 3D printed! At least that's the case with a collection of 120 life-size statues of female scientists, all 3D printed in a shiny, bright-orange material. Considered the largest collection of statues of women ever assembled in one place at one time, the exhibit features the likenesses of researchers from all areas of science, technology, engineering, and math (STEM), including wildlife warriors, space experts, coders, and cancer researchers.

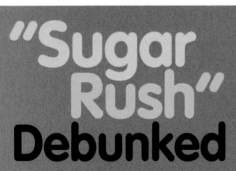

CHARITA CASTRO, A SOCIAL SCIENCE RESEARCHER, POSES WITH THE 3D-PRINTED STATUE OF HERSELF.

"Sugar Rush" Debunked

Is there such a thing as a "sugar rush"? Many experts say no. The idea that kids get a boost in energy levels after eating sweets is mostly a myth, according to recent studies. In these studies, scientists gave half the children sugary foods, while the other half got snacks made with artificial sweeteners (also known as a placebo). The result: no major differences between the two sets of kids.

So why might you feel more energetic after chomping on candy or scarfing down a few cookies? It's more about your brain than your stomach. Because sugar causes your brain to release feel-good chemicals, eating those sweets might trigger feelings of happiness—and yep, jolts of energy, too! And while sugar might make you smile, it's always smart (and healthy!) to eat sweets in moderation.

Polar Bear Takes Photos

Hoping to capture pictures of a seal coming up for air in Svalbard, Norway, photographer Audun Rikardsen left his camera and motion sensor next to a hole in the Arctic ice. But a polar bear that was also looking for a yummy seal found the equipment first!

The bear sniffed, licked, and pawed at the clicking camera. Then—swat! It smacked the contraption into the hole, where it sunk more than 450 feet (137 m) beneath the ice. The polar bear walked off, and soon Rikardsen had to leave, too.

But the camera's memory card contained 149 photos, including the amazing close-up polar bear pics. Determined to retrieve it, Rikardsen returned a year later with a remote-controlled underwater vehicle ... and found his camera at the bottom of the sea!

The camera was totally ruined. But incredibly, the memory card still contained the close-up photos. Maybe this polar bear was just camera shy.

Art Lights Up Sydney

Imagine this: You and your family are out for a nighttime walk in the city, when suddenly the buildings around you seem to burst to life. Colorful lights illuminate the facades of your favorite spaces, some seeming to dance as they move in a kaleidoscope pattern.

In Australia, it happens every year, and it's called Vivid Sydney—Australia's biggest light festival, and one of the largest in the world. Taking place in May and June, the three-week festival celebrates the creativity and innovation of artists from across the country.

After the sun goes down, with what seems like the flip of a switch, dozens of colorful displays suddenly light up the night. The installations draw people to all corners of the city, from smaller public spaces to famous landmarks like the Sydney Opera House. Starting in 2023, the festival also featured concerts and a fiery kitchen with flame-cooked foods.

15

Cool Events 2025

INTERNATIONAL MOON DAY

Celebrate the daring people who have explored Earth's moon and the amazing possibilities for future exploration.

July 20

WORLD WETLANDS DAY

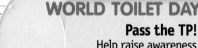

Celebrate the water-soaked ecosystems that support 40 percent of Earth's plant and animal species.

February 2

WORLD LION DAY

Let out a roar!

Show your love for these African big cats and the people working to protect them.

August 10

INTERNATIONAL DAY OF ZERO WASTE

Ditch the disposables: Help build a more sustainable future by avoiding single-use items and reusing items you already have.

March 30

WORLD TEACHERS' DAY

Give thanks—
and maybe an apple—to the people in your life who make learning fun!

October 5

INTERNATIONAL BAT APPRECIATION DAY

DON'T HANG BACK—jump in on this celebration of bats and the important roles they play in nature.

April 17

WORLD TOILET DAY

Pass the TP!

Help raise awareness for the 3.6 billion people who live without access to safe sanitation.

November 19

INTERNATIONAL TEA DAY

Raise a cup to the history, health benefits, and economic importance of this 5,000-year-old beverage.

May 21

INTERNATIONAL MOUNTAIN DAY

They really rock!
Celebrate the people and wildlife who call these treasured landscapes home.

December 11

Parrots Make Video Calls

Polly wants a ... video chat? You've probably heard about parrots that can say "hello"—but now, researchers think they like video calls, too! In a recent study, volunteers placed parrots in front of screens in separate places and started video calls. For a few days, the birds curiously looked at and around the screens. But soon, they seemed to recognize the other parrots. Then, caregivers trained the birds to ask for a video call by ringing a bell. With the tap of a beak, a parrot could select another feathered friend to chat with.

What did the social animals "chat" about? Some parrots sang or danced together, while others showed off their toys. There were even parrots that learned to make new sounds by mimicking their new friends. That's something to squawk about!

BEES SOLVE PUZZLES

A recent study by researchers in the United Kingdom discovered that buff-tailed bumblebees could learn to solve a puzzle, then show other bees in their colony how to do the same. To solve the puzzle, designed by researchers, the bees had to push a tab on a device. When a bee succeeded, a hole in the container opened and a sweet treat—sugar water— appeared inside the dish.

The results didn't just show that the insects are good problem-solvers. Researchers also found that, even though bees have incredibly tiny brains, they're smart enough to teach and learn from each other.

Graveyard SNAKES

Here's a spooky surprise! In 2021, researchers in southern Ecuador were looking for rare toads—and finding nothing. They were almost ready to go home when someone reported some strange snake sightings in a nearby graveyard. The curious researchers decided to take a look around the area, and they ultimately found three new species of snake! The sneaky snakes, which spend most of their time underground, had lost most of their native forest habitat. Looking for a safe place to live, some of them had wriggled themselves into the soil beside the graves.

GREATEST
BREAKTHROUGHS

A team lays out the fossils of *Homo naledi,* a species of early human ancestor, at the University of the Witwatersrand in South Africa.

TOP 10
BREAKTHROUGHS OF THE
21ST CENTURY

While new discoveries are made almost every day, some findings are so extraordinary that their impact lasts for centuries. They create important changes around the world and open doors to new studies, technology, and cultural shifts. Here are some of the biggest breakthroughs in recent years.

HEALTH

The Year: 2001
The Breakthrough:
Human Genome Mapping

It was an ambitious goal: Plot the chemical bases of some 25,000 genes that make up human DNA—also known as the human genome. But in the early 2000s, a team of scientists did just that. By determining the sequence of the bases in human DNA, researchers have gained a clearer understanding of what happens within the body and why, leading to new treatments for diseases and creating a flood of possibilities for advancement in medical research.

The project wrapped up in 2003, but mapping the human genome is still a work in progress. Scientists continue to update the map and fill in gaps in order to create the most complete and accurate picture of the human genome sequence. The hope? That we'll continue to learn about the human body, the origins of diseases, and how to treat them.

COMMUNICATION

The Year: 2007
The Breakthrough: Smartphones

Can you imagine life without smartphones? Up until around 2007, that was the reality for most people. It wasn't until Apple debuted the first model of its iPhone— selling some six million units—that smartphones changed our daily lives. Other tech companies soon followed with their own versions of the devices. Suddenly, instead of having to log on to a computer at home, many people had access to the internet in their pocket or bag. Soon messaging apps, video chatting, and the ability to look up anything, anywhere, all became seamless and standard, forever changing the way people around the world communicated. Today, about 86 percent of people have a smartphone.

SPACE

The Year: 2008
The Breakthrough: Water on Mars

For years, scientists searched for water on Mars. In 2008, researchers finally had solid proof, in the form of water ice. The news came a few years after an orbiter named the Mars Odyssey detected ice below the planet's surface in polar regions. When a NASA space probe touched down on Mars's surface in 2008, it set off to investigate a polar site. The probe collected a soil sample with ice and tested its makeup. The sample revealed that the ice was made of the same elements as the water found on Earth.

Scientists think much more water ice lies below Mars's surface. If it can be extracted, the ice could be a valuable resource for drinking water and making rocket fuel during any human missions to the red planet in the future.

PALEONTOLOGY

The Year: 2010
The Breakthrough: Dinosaurs' True Colors

Here's a bright fact: Dinosaurs weren't just green and brown! In 2010, scientists released the first full-body color reconstruction of a dinosaur. Using advanced imaging technology, researchers were able to see microscopic details inside the fossils, including the presence of melanin, the natural pigment that gives scales, skin, and feathers their color. *Anchiornis*, for example, likely had black, white, and gray feathers and a reddish brown crest on its head.

Scientists still have more to learn. Did dinosaurs use their coloring for camouflage, communication, or to attract mates like animals do today? By seeing dinosaurs in this new light, researchers will get a better idea of how they behaved and interacted with one another.

ANCHIORNIS

21

TECHNOLOGY

The Year: 2010
The Breakthrough: AI in Daily Life

"Alexa, what's the weather like today?" Not too long ago, people weren't able to ask a resident robot simple questions like this one. The once far-off concept of using artificial intelligence (AI) in our daily lives became reality for many starting in 2010 when Apple introduced Siri, a virtual personal assistant that uses AI to process simple tasks such as scheduling appointments, answering basic questions, and checking the forecast. In 2014, Amazon released the voice-controlled Echo device with voice assistant Alexa. It is a stand-alone device, meaning it can be used throughout the home and not just on your phone.

NATURE & ENVIRONMENT

The Year: 2019
The Breakthrough:
Climate Change Protests

It's a shocking fact: Since 2010, we've experienced the 10 warmest years on record. The 2010s were marked by melting ice sheets and glaciers, rising ocean levels, and more extreme weather events, like stronger hurricanes and increasing floods.

For decades, climate change research has offered growing evidence of the drastic impact on the environment—and, increasingly, has inspired collective action to address it. In 2018, 15-year-old Swedish activist Greta Thunberg called for action against climate change outside Sweden's parliament building. Others soon joined in, ultimately forming the world's largest climate change protest the following year.

A TRUCK DRIVES THROUGH A FLOODED STREET IN CALIFORNIA, U.S.A.

ANIMALS

The Year: 2022
The Breakthrough:
Insect Breaks Down Plastic

While tending to her beehive one day, a scientist removed a few wax worms—the larval stage of the wax moth—and placed them in a plastic bag. Later, she noticed the bag had holes in it! But the caterpillars didn't just eat their way through the bag. Their saliva had actually broken down the bag's plastic molecules. It turns out, the wax worm's spit contains enzymes that dissolve polyethylene, a type of plastic that can take years to break down in a landfill.

The wax worms demonstrated a neat bio-recycling trick that could one day help combat plastic pollution. While having millions of caterpillars feast on piles of plastic isn't the most sustainable (or speedy) solution, the potential to replicate their enzymes in a lab might be.

SCIENCE
The Year: 2022
The Breakthrough:
Fusion Ignition

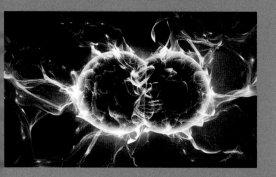

In 2022, scientists took one step closer to tapping into near-limitless supplies of energy. How? By achieving fusion ignition, a reaction that made more energy than they put in to the process. In a special lab, researchers used lasers to heat up a tiny pellet of hydrogen atoms with enough force to fuse the atoms together to create helium—and produce excess energy. The experiment took just 20 billionths of a second to complete, but its impact will last a lifetime.

It showed that fusion ignition is possible. And because the energy that's produced doesn't rely on fossil fuels or release harmful greenhouse gases, like other types of energy do, there's a chance it could someday help fight climate change. Now that's a win-win.

What was lost has been found in the thick jungles of the Amazon rainforest. In 2022, in what is now Bolivia, experts discovered ancient ruins of an urban settlement thought to have been abandoned some 600 years ago, likely by a community belonging to the Casarabe culture. Using light-based remote sensing technology called LiDAR from a helicopter, a team was able to "see" through the dense tree canopy to uncover two large sites in the southwestern Amazon. The settlement featured six-story-tall pyramids, elevated roads, and a sophisticated water system, including reservoirs and canals. While not much else is known about this civilization, it sparks hope for discoveries of more lost civilizations out there waiting to be found.

ARCHAEOLOGY
The Year: 2022
The Breakthrough:
Lost Settlement Found

In 2015, Nat Geo Explorer in Residence Lee Berger reported a shocking discovery in South Africa's Rising Star cave system: the remains of a human ancestor species new to science. But the study of *Homo naledi,* as the species was named, was just beginning. In 2023, Berger and his team announced they'd found possible evidence that *Homo naledi* carefully buried their dead inside the cave system—some 100,000 years before the first known burials by human ancestors. The team's interpretation of the graves is raising new questions about how *Homo naledi* lived, and died. Berger and his team continue to examine the fossils and the site for clues about the past. (See page 24 for more information.)

HISTORY
The Year: 2023
The Breakthrough:
Ancient Burials

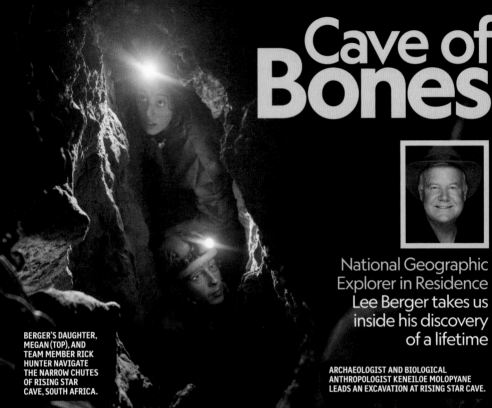

Cave of Bones

National Geographic Explorer in Residence Lee Berger takes us inside his discovery of a lifetime

BERGER'S DAUGHTER, MEGAN (TOP), AND TEAM MEMBER RICK HUNTER NAVIGATE THE NARROW CHUTES OF RISING STAR CAVE, SOUTH AFRICA.

ARCHAEOLOGIST AND BIOLOGICAL ANTHROPOLOGIST KENEILOE MOLOPYANE LEADS AN EXCAVATION AT RISING STAR CAVE.

Back in 2013, a pair of spelunkers came across what looked like human remains deep within the Rising Star cave in South Africa. The cavers had shimmied their way down a narrow chute and landed in a room some 100 feet (30 m) below ground, its dirt floor littered with fossils. They snapped photos of the bones, which ultimately wound up with Dr. Lee Berger, a paleoanthropologist who then organized an expedition into the mazelike chambers and tunnels.

BELOW THE SURFACE

Berger conducted the expedition from aboveground, at first. Because of the narrowness of the passageways—no wider than a laptop in some parts—he wasn't able to safely squeeze through. "The spaces are incredibly tight and it's extremely dangerous," he explains. "So I found smaller-size, very experienced cavers and explorers who could get in there."

At first, Berger's exploration team was able to relay significant photos, artifacts, and information to him. Their first major discovery? That the bones belonged to a never-before-known species named *Homo naledi* that lived 500,000 years ago, long before humans were known to have lived. *Homo naledi* had humanlike features, but a much smaller brain—a

characteristic often associated with lower intelligence.

But Berger had a hunch that *Homo naledi* may have been pretty advanced despite their brain size. The massive amounts of bones found in the room within the cave indicated that they may have used the spot as a burial ground—a behavior previously assumed was only acted out by humans. Was there any other evidence that would support this theory? Berger decided that he needed to see the room with his own eyes.

BERGER REACHES OUT FROM THE LAST CHUTE INSIDE RISING STAR CAVE.

A TIGHT SQUEEZE

"There's just so much you can determine by looking through the lens of someone else's camera," he said. "To fully answer our questions, I needed to see it for myself." So he spent months carefully watching what he ate and exercising to lose 55 pounds (25 kg)—losing just enough weight to squeeze into the Rising Star cave.

"I made it in, but it was an extreme journey," he says. "It's so tight that you can't put a rope next to your body. I definitely risked my life."

NEW DISCOVERIES

Berger's difficult journey was worth it in the end: Once in the room, he was blown away by what he saw—new discoveries that included evidence of the use of fire, and primitive art carved into the cave walls, possibly to mark graves. Berger spent more than four hours in the cave, narrating everything he saw, hardly believing the words

coming out of his mouth as he recorded. "To describe what I was seeing with my own eyes, in my own words, it was incredible," he said.

REWRITING HUMAN HISTORY

Once back aboveground, Berger felt confident that his discoveries debunked previous theories about human evolution. "It's an important moment for humanity," he says. "For centuries, we believed that large brains allowed us to be complex and exceptional. But it's not just about our brain. Because certain rituals were

being done thousands of years before us by another species."

BRINGING THE PAST INTO THE FUTURE

Next up, Berger hopes to carefully study all of the artifacts his team has uncovered in Rising Star cave using high-tech testing and forensics to get more clues about this mysterious species. "They're still like aliens to us," he says of *Homo naledi*. "They're complex. We hope to get more of their story as we continue to study them."

However, as *Homo naledi*'s story unfolds, one thing is for sure: Berger is staying on solid ground. "I won't be going back down there. It's too risky," he says of journeying back into Rising Star. "That was a once-in-a-lifetime opportunity."

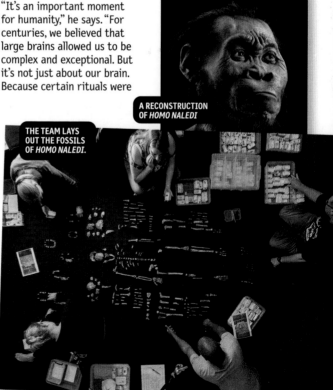

A RECONSTRUCTION OF *HOMO NALEDI*

THE TEAM LAYS OUT THE FOSSILS OF *HOMO NALEDI*.

BERGER HOLDS A SCALE NEXT TO AN ENGRAVING INSIDE THE CAVE.

How to Find a Fossil

Lee Berger and his nine-year-old son, Matthew, were searching for fossils in Johannesburg, South Africa, when Matthew stumbled over a large brown rock and spied a thin yellow bone barely sticking out of it. He'd found a fossil—and not just any fossil. This was a fossilized bone of a prehuman ancestor, which—thanks to Matthew—would soon be known to science as *Australopithecus sediba.*

Finding a fossil is hard, but if you know what to look for, you can pick one out from all the other rocks and soil around it. Here, Berger shares the clues that led him to a fossil find in South Africa's Free State Province.

Berger looks for an area of erosion that might reveal rocks that are older than those on the surface.

1 SCAN FOR THE RIGHT SPOT

2 FOCUS IN

Next, Berger narrows his search to places where fossils might be eroding out of the surrounding soil.

Berger looks for oddities or abnormalities—rocks or objects whose colors don't match the surrounding soil. In this case, he's spotted a white fleck.

▼

WHAT DOESN'T BELONG? 3

4 TAKE A CLOSER LOOK

▲ When Berger gets closer, he can see that it's part of the lower jaw, or mandible, of an ancient antelope.

EXAMINE THE DETAILS 5

Berger notices the shiny enamel of the teeth and the paler look of the bone. The mandible he's found is more than 100,000 years old.

▶

10 FAR-OUT FACTS ABOUT THE JAMES WEBB SPACE TELESCOPE

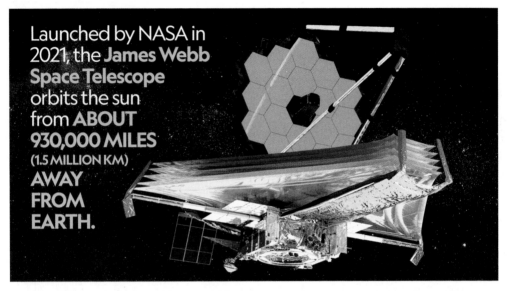

Launched by NASA in 2021, the **James Webb Space Telescope** orbits the sun from **ABOUT 930,000 MILES** (1.5 MILLION KM) **AWAY FROM EARTH.**

The largest space telescope ever launched, the Webb telescope is **TWICE AS TALL AS A GIRAFFE AND AS LONG AS A TENNIS COURT.**

TO LAUNCH THE TELESCOPE, **ENGINEERS FOLDED THE DEVICE INSIDE A ROCKET. ONCE IN SPACE, THE TELESCOPE SLOWLY UNFOLDED.**

The telescope will help scientists study the atmospheres of exoplanets, or planets outside our solar system, **AND SEARCH FOR POSSIBLE EVIDENCE THAT THEY COULD SUPPORT LIFE.**

The telescope "sees" with a honeycomb-shaped array of **18 mirrors** plated in ultrathin 24-karat gold.

The telescope is so sensitive that it could clearly see a U.S. penny from **25 miles (40 km)** away.

With its powerful ability to capture light that's traveled across space, the Webb telescope can act like a modern-day time machine, seeing light from as far back as **13.5 billion years.**

The telescope uses infrared cameras to see through dust in the universe, allowing it to get a sneak peek of newly forming stars and planets.

A sunshield protects one side of the telescope from heat, keeping it cooler, while the other side's temperature is hot—a difference of more than **600°F** (333°C).

In 2023, the telescope detected a **MASSIVE SPOUT OF WATER VAPOR** coming from Saturn's moon Enceladus. The geyser was more than **6,000 miles** (9,660 km) **long.**

29

DIY Candy DNA Model

DNA is made up of four chemical bases: **adenine (A)**, **guanine (G)**, **thymine (T)**, and **cytosine (C)**. These chemicals, when linked together like a chain, carry information that tells our bodies how to look and function. Make your own chain with this sweet science activity!

A always binds with T, and C always binds with G.

YOU'LL NEED

- 12 pieces of soft candy in four different colors (3 of each color), such as gummy bears or gumdrops
- 2 licorice twists or rope candy
- 6 toothpicks
- Paper
- Pen or marker

STEP 1

Sort your soft candies by color on a piece of paper. Label each pile with the letter of a chemical base: **A, G, T,** or **C.**

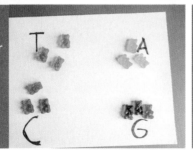

STEP 2

Pick up one **A** candy and one **T** candy, and slide them both onto a toothpick, so they're side by side. Repeat twice.

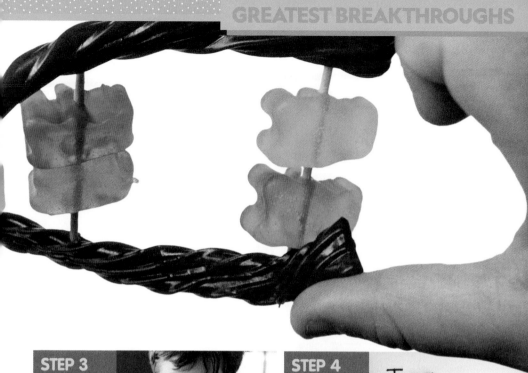

STEP 3

Pick up one **G** candy and one **C** candy, and slide them side by side onto a toothpick. Repeat twice.

STEP 4

Take all your **A**, **T** and **G**, **C** toothpicks and lay them on your piece of paper.

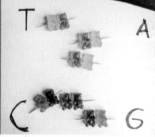

STEP 5

Mix up your A, T and G, C toothpicks and lay them side by side. On either end of the toothpicks, lay a licorice twist.

STEP 6

Carefully stick one end of each toothpick into a licorice twist, leaving about an inch (2.5 cm) of space between each toothpick.

STEP 7

Stick the other end of each toothpick into the second piece of licorice, so your toothpicks are connected on both sides.

STEP 8

Hold one end of your model flat. Carefully flip over the other end to create a twist. Your model is complete!

QUIZ WHIZ

What's your innovation IQ? Find out with this quiz!

Write your answers on a piece of paper. Then check them below.

1 **True or false?** The human body is made up of about 25,000 genes.

2 A scientist figured out that wax worms can break down the molecules of what item?
a. aluminum can
b. plastic bag
c. glass bottle
d. cardboard box

3 Launched in 2021, the _____ Space Telescope is the largest in orbit.
a. Hubble
b. Spitzer
c. Gamma Ray
d. James Webb

4 **True or false?** Paleontologists think all dinosaurs were only green and brown.

5 A species of human ancestor named *Homo naledi* was discovered where?
a. Morocco
b. Netherlands
c. Norway
d. South Africa

Not **STUMPED** yet? Check out the *NATIONAL GEOGRAPHIC KIDS QUIZ WHIZ* collection for more **GROUNDBREAKING** questions!

ANSWERS: 1. True; 2. b; 3. d; 4. False: They were many colors.; 5. d

Write a Letter That Gets Results

Knowing how to write a good letter is a useful skill. It will come in handy when you want to ask an expert for information or advice. Whether you're writing to your local park ranger or emailing a scientist in the field, a great letter will help you get your message across. Most important, a well-written letter makes a good impression.

CHECK OUT THE EXAMPLE BELOW FOR THE ELEMENTS OF A GOOD LETTER.

Your address

Date

Salutation
Always use "Dear" followed by the person's name; use Mr., Mrs., Ms., or Dr. as appropriate.

Introductory paragraph
Give the reason you're writing the letter.

Body
The longest part of the letter, which provides background and your questions. Be specific!

Closing paragraph
Explain what you will do with the answers.

Complimentary closing
Sign off with "Sincerely" or "Thank you."

Your signature

Cameron Lopez
555 Maple Street
Richmond, Virginia 23220

May 1, 2025

Dear Ranger of Richmond River Park,

I am writing to ask you for advice on how to attract local wildlife to my backyard.

Richmond River Park is my favorite place to visit. My family and I go there almost every month. Whenever I'm there, I enjoy seeing all of the different birds, frogs, chipmunks, and other animals around the park. Northern cardinals are my favorite birds!

Last time I was there, a ranger told me that many of the species I see at the park also live near my house! The ranger said that if I want northern cardinals to visit my yard, I should learn about the foods that they eat and the plants that they nest in, and ask my parents to help me add them to our yard.

I would like to know: What do cardinals like to eat? And which types of plants do they pick for building their nests? Lastly, where can my parents find the plants you recommend?

With your advice, I hope to give northern cardinals another place to find food and raise their chicks. That way, my favorite birds will have an inviting space near my house to visit whenever they want!

Thank you very much for your time.

Sincerely,

Cameron Lopez

Cameron Lopez

COMPLIMENTARY CLOSINGS

Sincerely, Thank you, Regards, Best wishes, Respectfully

AMAZING
ANIMALS

EXTRAORDINARY ANIMALS

Gecko Makes Prank Calls

GOLD DUST DAY GECKO

AN ADULT GOLD DUST DAY GECKO IS ABOUT AS LONG AS A TOILET-PAPER TUBE.

Kailua-Kona, Hawaii, U.S.A.
When veterinarian Claire Simeone received nearly a dozen mysterious, silent phone calls from Ke Kai Ola, the Marine Mammal Center's hospital for Hawaiian monk seals, she worried it might be an emergency. But back at the clinic, nobody admitted to calling her. So Simeone, who was also the hospital's director, searched through each room until she found the prank caller: a gold dust day gecko lounging on the touch screen of a telephone.

After sneaking into the hospital, the lizard was probably attracted by the bright screen. Then the cold-blooded creature stuck around to soak up the phone's warmth, reptile expert Ron Tremper says. The gecko's feet—covered in tiny hairs that help it grip leaves and branches—pressed against the touch screen like human fingertips. "Every time it moved its feet, the gecko called another person—including me," Simeone says.

Simeone eventually moved the jokester outside, where it could sit in warm spots—without ringing up expensive phone bills.

SAFETY FIRST! SNUGGLES SECOND.

Chicken "Crossing Guard"

Newstead, New Zealand
Why did the chicken cross the road? Because she "works" in the parking lot!

Decked out in a yellow safety vest, a hen named Henry patrols the lot at Newstead Country Preschool. Each morning she greets the arriving students, and her presence reminds motorists to drive slowly and carefully. That helps the kids stay safe.

The school's owner, Tracy Trigg, rescued the hen when she appeared at her friend's house, looking thin and lost. Trigg, who also teaches at the school, brought the friendly bird to the farm attached to the preschool. (Students interact with farm animals as part of their lessons.) But Henry didn't want to stay in the field. "The parking lot was where all the people were, so that's where Henry would turn up in the mornings," Trigg says. "She would rather hang out with us than the other chickens."

After a few days, Trigg let Henry take on the job permanently. Her payment? Cuddles and a bit of tasty cheese.

Bird "Snuggles" Rhino

YOUR FACE IS SO COMFY.

MalaMala Game Reserve, South Africa
Who says you can't cuddle a rhino?

Zaheer Ali was leading a safari when he noticed a white rhinoceros with a red-billed oxpecker on its horn. Ali stopped to watch as the bird plucked ticks and insects off the rhino's skin, which is a normal behavior.

But then something surprising happened: The bird leaned on the rhino's horn and seemed to rest. "I knew this moment was special," Ali says.

It's not unusual to see these two species together, rhino conservationist Brent Cook says. "Oxpeckers often feed on the parasites living on the rhino's skin," he says. "In exchange, the rhino receives complimentary pest control."

Plus, the oxpecker—which has much stronger eyesight—will make a shrill hissing sound to warn the rhino of danger from things like hyenas and poachers.

Cook thinks that the bird had just finished a tasty meal and felt at ease in a warm spot. We hope these animals stay BFFs.

BIG Question

Can a groundhog predict when spring will arrive?

Groundhogs are also known as woodchucks and whistle pigs.

A GROUNDHOG PEEKS OUT FROM ITS BURROW.

A HANDLER HOLDS PHIL IN 2021.

Groundhog Day is related to the midwinter holiday Candlemas. When the day is celebrated in Germany, a hedgehog predicts the weather.

Every February 2, people gather in Punxsutawney, Pennsylvania, U.S.A., to watch a groundhog come out of its burrow. Legend has it that if "Punxsutawney Phil" sees his shadow, the startled groundhog will go back into his burrow to wait out six more weeks of winter. If he doesn't see his shadow, an early spring is supposedly on the way. This Groundhog Day tradition goes all the way back to 1887.

Groundhogs have regular hibernation patterns, and the males always come out of their burrows in early February to claim their territory. So their annual appearance is just their natural instinct. But can that predict the weather? Data gathered between 2012 and 2021 showed that Punxsutawney Phil was correct only 40 percent of the time. Sorry, Phil—that's not much better than a wild guess.

ANIMAL MYTHS BUSTED

Some people mistakenly think adult opossums hang by their tails or that porcupines shoot their quills. What other misconceptions are out there? Here are some common animal myths.

MYTH Elephants are afraid of mice.

HOW IT MAY HAVE STARTED People used to think that mice liked to crawl into elephants' trunks, which could cause damage and terrible sneezing. So it makes sense that elephants would be afraid of the rodents.

WHY IT'S NOT TRUE An elephant's eyesight is so poor that it could barely even see a mouse. Plus, an elephant isn't afraid to live among predators such as tigers, rhinos, and crocodiles, so a mouse would be the least of its worries!

Who are you again?

MYTH Goldfish only have a three-second memory.

HOW IT MAY HAVE STARTED While an adult human's brain weighs about three pounds (1.4 kg), an average goldfish's brain weighs only a tiny fraction of that. So how could there be any room for memory in there?

WHY IT'S NOT TRUE Research has shown that goldfish are quite smart. Phil Gee of the University of Plymouth in the United Kingdom trained goldfish to push a lever that dropped food into their tank. "They remembered the time of day that the lever worked and waited until feeding time to press it," Gee says. One scientist even trained goldfish to tell the difference between classical and blues music!

MYTH Touching a frog or toad will give you warts.

HOW IT MAY HAVE STARTED Many frogs and toads have bumps on their skin that look like warts. Some people think the bumps are contagious.

WHY IT'S NOT TRUE Dermatologists say warts are caused by a human virus, not frogs or toads. But the wartlike bumps behind a toad's ears *can* be dangerous. These parotid glands contain a nasty poison that irritates the mouths of some predators and often the skin of humans. So toads may not cause warts, but they can cause other irritations. It's best not to handle these critters—warty or not!

Cute Animal
SUPERLATIVES

**Funky features. Super-
powers. Sensational size.**
No doubt, all animals are cool.
But whether they've got cool
colors, funky hair, or endless
energy, some species are extra
adorable. Here are 15 of the
cutest creatures on Earth.

BEST FUZZ

What's all the fuzz about? A snowy egret chick
is born with a cap of soft, frizzy feathers. As it
grows, the fuzz transforms into long, feathery
plumes in a bright-white hue, which gives the
large bird—native to the coastlands of North
and South America—its name.

BEST BREAKTHROUGH

Here's the *tooth* about baby
turtles: These reptiles are born
with temporary appendages called
carbuncles, or egg teeth. They're
sharp enough to crack the shells
and help the baby turtles break
free from their eggs on their own.
After the turtles hatch, they will
eventually lose the egg teeth.

MOST COLORFUL

The rainbow-hued rufous-tailed hummingbird flits
around parts of Central and South America, where it
feeds on fragrant, brightly colored flowers. It uses its
long, strawlike tongue to suck up sweet nectar.

BEST TEAMWORK

High five! Meerkat pups often bond soon after birth and spend most of their time together exploring their environment and playing. Native to Africa's Kalahari Desert, the extremely social animals are super supportive of one another, with a community working together to share the load of raising and protecting their pups.

BEST COAT

The lovely locks of the white-faced saki monkey make this primate look like it's sporting a fur coat. Its long, bushy tail is just as lush and helps the monkey balance as it leaps from tree to tree in the rainforests of South America.

BEST NAPPER

Tigers love their catnaps! In fact, the animals snooze some 18 hours a day—snagging z's whenever and wherever they can. Why so sleepy? The big cats usually rest after a big meal, which helps them conserve energy for their next hunt. Once they're up, they're recharged and ready to go.

BEST SPIKES

The spikes on porcupinefish say "don't mess with me" to predators. These fish can also puff up and balloon their bodies up to three times their normal size when threatened. A coat of spiky scales adds an extra layer of defense.

DEEPEST DIVER

How low can you go? When it comes to underwater diving, the Cuvier's beaked whale goes the lowest, swimming some 10,000 feet (3,048 m) below the ocean surface—the deepest ever observed among marine mammals.

LONGEST LEAPER

The athletic snow leopard can jump farther than 49 feet (15 m), more than the length of an average school bus! This big cat's short, sturdy forelimbs and long hind limbs help it make such big leaps.

HEAVIEST TOAD

Known for its extraordinary size, the warty, poisonous cane toad is native to South and Central America and is invasive to many places. One cane toad recently discovered in an Australian rainforest weighed nearly six pounds (2.7 kg), the largest on record.

FASTEST-GROWING FISH

So much for being a kid! Just about 18 days after it's hatched, a female African killifish grows to its full body size, lays eggs, and produces its own young, making it the fastest-maturing vertebrate in the animal kingdom.

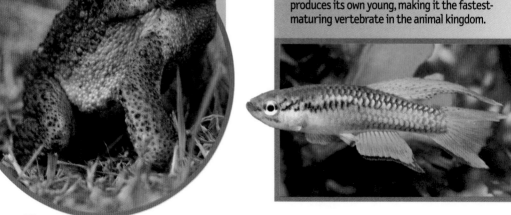

BEST NUZZLER

Rabbits have the sweetest way to say they're sorry: nuzzling noses! Researchers say that if a pair of bonded bunnies has a falling out, one will rub noses with the other to apologize and end the spat. Bunnies also touch noses to communicate with one another or to sniff out a new scent.

BEST SPOTS

Ladybugs' spots aren't just there to look cool: Their colorful exteriors double as a warning for predators like birds, frogs, wasps, spiders, and dragonflies that they taste terrible. And they actually do, thanks to an icky fluid ladybugs release from their legs when threatened.

BEST GRIP

Tree frogs just love hanging around! When the agile amphibians leap from branch to branch in their rainforest habitat, they rely on their lightning-quick reflexes, long limbs, and super-strong grip to, well, hang on. A sticky substance on their toe pads also helps the frogs get a good grasp.

FARTHEST FLYING BAT

The Nathusius' pipistrelle is an itty-bitty bat that can fly super far. One of these thumb-size bats recently set a record by flying from Russia to the French Alps, a total distance of some 1,500 miles (2,200 km).

WHAT IS Taxonomy?

Because our planet has billions and billions of living things called organisms, people need a way of classifying them. Scientists created a system called taxonomy, which helps to classify all living things into ordered groups. By putting organisms into categories, we are better able to understand how they are the same and how they are different. There are eight levels of taxonomic classification, beginning with the broadest group, called a domain, followed by kingdom, down to the most specific group, called a species.

Biologists divide life based on evolutionary history, and they place organisms into three domains depending on their genetic structure: Archaea, Bacteria, and Eukarya. (See page 195 for "The Three Domains of Life.")

SAMPLE CLASSIFICATION

FIRE SALAMANDER

Domain:	Eukarya
Kingdom:	Animalia
Phylum:	Chordata
Class:	Amphibia
Order:	Caudata
Family:	Salamandridae
Genus:	*Salamandra*
Species:	*Salamandra salamandra*

Where do animals come in?

Animals are a part of the Eukarya domain, which means they are organisms made of cells with nuclei. More than one million species of animals, including humans, have been named. Like all living things, animals can be divided into smaller groups, called phyla. Most scientists believe there are more than 30 phyla into which animals can be grouped based on certain scientific criteria, such as body type or whether or not the animal has a backbone. It can be pretty complicated, so another, less complicated system is used to group animals into two categories: vertebrates and invertebrates.

HEDGEHOG

TIP:
Here's a sentence to help you remember the classification order:
Did **K**ing **P**hillip **C**ome **O**ver **F**or **G**ood **S**oup?

BY THE NUMBERS

There are 16,900 vulnerable or endangered animal species in the world. The list includes:

- **1,340 mammals,** such as the snow leopard, the polar bear, and the fishing cat
- **1,400 birds,** including the Steller's sea eagle and the black-banded plover
- **3,551 fish,** such as the Mekong giant catfish
- **1,842 reptiles,** including the Round Island day gecko
- **2,345 insects,** such as the Macedonian grayling

- **2,606 amphibians,** such as the emperor newt
- **And more,** including 251 arachnids, 745 crustaceans, 256 sea anemones and corals, 214 bivalves, and 2,178 snails and slugs

ROUND ISLAND DAY GECKO

Vertebrates
Animals WITH Backbones

Fish are cold-blooded and live in water. They breathe with gills, lay eggs, and usually have scales.

Amphibians are cold-blooded. Their young live in water and breathe with gills. Adults live on land and breathe with lungs.

Reptiles are cold-blooded and breathe with lungs. They live both on land and in water.

Birds are warm-blooded and have feathers and wings. They lay eggs, breathe with lungs, and are usually able to fly. Some birds live on land, some in water, and some on both.

Mammals are warm-blooded and feed on their mothers' milk. They also have skin that is usually covered with hair. Mammals live both on land and in water.

BIRD: MANDARIN DUCK

AMPHIBIAN: POISON FROG

Invertebrates
Animals WITHOUT Backbones

Sponges are a very basic form of animal life. They live in water and do not move on their own.

Echinoderms have external skeletons and live in seawater.

Mollusks have soft bodies and can live either in or out of shells, on land or in water.

Arthropods are the largest group of animals. They have external skeletons, called exoskeletons, and segmented bodies with appendages. Arthropods live in water and on land.

Worms are soft-bodied animals with no true legs. Worms live in soil.

Cnidaria live in water and have mouths surrounded by tentacles.

MOLLUSK: MAGNIFICENT CHROMODORIS NUDIBRANCH

SPONGE: SEA SPONGE

ARTHROPOD: PRAYING MANTIS

Cold-Blooded
versus
Warm-Blooded

Cold-blooded animals, also called ectotherms, get their heat from outside their bodies.

Warm-blooded animals, also called endotherms, keep their body temperatures level regardless of the temperature of their environment.

Seals Solve Ocean Mysteries

DO I HAVE SOMETHING ON MY HEAD?

Antarctica

These researchers don't need beakers or lab coats—they're seals!

Scientists wanted to collect hard-to-get data that might provide clues to science mysteries, like how climate change is affecting the ocean and the animals that live there. So an international team enlisted the help of Weddell and southern elephant seals.

First, researchers harmlessly glued sensors to the seals' heads that monitored behavior, location, water temperature, and the amount of salt in the water. Then the seals swam away, diving up to 6,500 feet (1,980 m) under the sea ice for up to 90 minutes at a time while the sensors transmitted the data. (The trackers fell off later.)

"They can go where boats and scientists can't," Antarctic marine ecologist Sara Labrousse says.

The information has helped scientists learn more about how animals and their prey are affected by changes in the ocean— and even why mysterious holes in sea ice are appearing. "We don't have a lot of data beneath the sea ice, so it's very precious information," Labrousse says. We'd give these seals an A+ in science class.

A WEDDELL SEAL SPORTS A SCIENTIFIC SENSOR.

WEDDELL SEAL

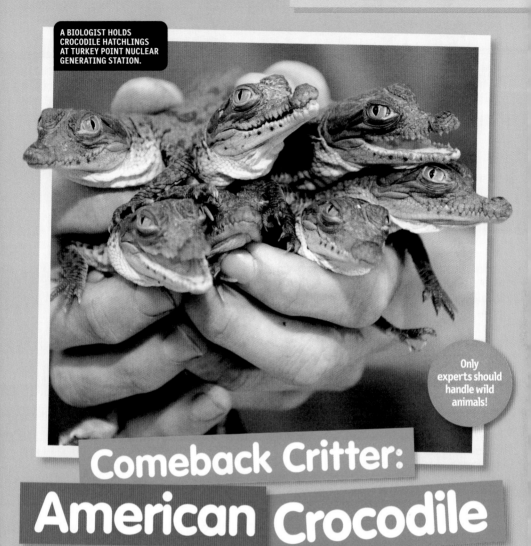

A BIOLOGIST HOLDS CROCODILE HATCHLINGS AT TURKEY POINT NUCLEAR GENERATING STATION.

Only experts should handle wild animals!

Comeback Critter:
American Crocodile

Homestead, Florida, U.S.A.
This might be the best egg hunt ever.

In 2011, scientists were excited to find a record number of American crocodile hatchlings at the Turkey Point Nuclear Generating Station: 568! That's good news because about a quarter of all crocs in the United States call this spot home.

In the 1970s, habitat loss and hunting caused the American crocodile population to dwindle to fewer than 300 animals. But in 1978, workers at the power plant found a nest along the human-made cooling canals,

which happen to be perfect croc nurseries. So conservationists decided to start studying and tracking these animals. By capturing and releasing the hatchlings in safer areas, they help protect them from predators like birds, crabs, turtles, and even other crocodiles.

Over the decades, this team has processed, tagged, and released more than 8,000 hatchlings. "Crocodiles are big, toothy creatures, so they have a bad reputation," says wildlife biologist Mike Lloret, who works at the plant. "It's important to respect them, but we can learn to live alongside them without fear."

PORCUPINE RESCUE

How kind humans nursed this prickly creature back to health

A North American porcupine huddled in the stairwell of a parking garage in Winchester, Virginia, U.S.A. The youngster was sick, exhausted, and missing a patch of quills on his back. Far from his forest home, the confused porcupine must have crawled into the building in search of shelter. Eventually, a surprised maintenance worker stumbled on the critter and quickly called the local police.

The scientific name for porcupine means "quill pig."

CAR CHASE

"I thought for sure the worker had seen a raccoon because I'd never heard of a porcupine in our area," police officer Felicia Marshall says. These animals were once considered pests and had been wiped out in Virginia more than a hundred years ago. Conservationists have been glad to see them slowly moving back to their historical range over the past 30 years. But a parking garage is no place for a porcupine.

Using a long pole with a loop around the end, Marshall chased the 10-pound (5-kg) male as he scurried around and under parked cars for about 15 minutes. "Whenever I was able to get close enough to put the catch pole around him, he would use his paws and break free," she says. "And all the while he made these huffing sounds, like he was annoyed that I was chasing him."

PRICKLY PATIENT

Eventually, Marshall captured the animal and drove him to the Blue Ridge Wildlife Center. There, the veterinary team gave the porcupine a full checkup: While a worker held the prickly animal with leather gloves, head veterinarian Jen Riley carefully felt around for injuries. From the missing quills, they guessed that the year-old porcupine had been in a tussle with another animal.

They also saw that he was breathing heavily and had ticks on his face. "When animals feel sick, they're less likely to groom themselves and get those ticks off," Riley says. After plucking off the bloodsuckers, the team took x-rays of the patient. "With porcupines, it's important to

THIS IS A WEIRD DREAM.

VET JEN RILEY LISTENS TO THE PORCUPINE'S LUNGS WITH A STETHOSCOPE.

48

THE HEALTHY PORCUPINE IS RELEASED IN A WOODED AREA OF FREDERICK COUNTY, VIRGINIA, U.S.A.

A porcupine has about 30,000 quills.

During the day, baby porcupines stay hidden on the ground while Mom sleeps in the trees.

AFTER FILLING UP ON TWIGS, THE PORCUPINE IS TOO STUFFED FOR LETTUCE.

use the x-ray because it's hard to feel everything around those quills."

From those scans, Riley saw that the animal had a lung infection—without care, this little porcupine would not survive.

BEDDING AND BREAKFAST

The team placed the porcupine in his own room at the wildlife center: Porcupines are nocturnal, so they didn't want to disturb his rest during the day. His cage was filled with soft towels, comfy blankets, and lots of twigs and leaves. Each day, the workers mixed a little cherry-flavored medicine into a few teaspoons of baby food made of pumpkin, apples, or squash. (The medicine was meant for kids, but the veterinarian approved it for the porcupine, too.)

At first, the porcupine sat hunched in the corner, and he wanted to eat only the supersweet baby food. But as the medicine started to work, he began eating normal porcupine chow: leaves, twigs, and branches that the rescue workers clipped from oak and maple trees behind the center. "Each

evening we'd fill his whole cage with twigs and branches—you could barely see him!" Riley says. "Then the next morning, it'd all be picked apart and we'd have to go out and do it again."

After 10 days, the caretakers could see that the porcupine was breathing easier and moving around his cage. His eyes were bright and alert. It was time to release him back into the wild.

The team carried the porcupine in a pet carrier to a patch of woods. As soon as they opened the door, the animal scurried straight up a tree.

"They feel safe up in the trees—they can get a good look around," Riley says. "It's like he went up there to check out his new home."

So. Many. Penguins!

A recently discovered **giant colony**

helps scientists understand why **Adélies** rule the roost.

ADÉLIE PENGUINS LIVE IN ANTARCTICA, THE DRIEST, COLDEST, AND WINDIEST CONTINENT ON EARTH.

Just two penguin species live only in Antarctica: Adélies and emperor penguins.

Squawk! Gurgle! Honk!

Along the bustling "highways" crisscrossing Antarctica's Danger Islands, more than a million Adélie penguins waddle to and from the ocean. It's a lot of traffic and noise—but until recently scientists didn't even know this metropolis existed.

That is, until penguin poo helped them find it.

Few people have ever explored the Danger Islands. Researchers could never get close enough because of heavy sea ice that could trap their boats. So no one really knew how much wildlife was there.

Then satellite imagery from space spotted guano, or poo, stains on the islands, hinting that a large number of penguins might be present.

"Penguin guano is a pinkish red color and looks like practically nothing else in the Antarctic," ecologist Heather Lynch says. "Once we viewed the images, we figured there had to be penguins on the Danger Islands."

Then Lynch's team got another surprise: The Danger Islands are home to more than 1.5 million Adélie penguins.

Before the discovery, scientists had been concerned that Adélies were disappearing, possibly because of climate change. But now that they've uncovered this super colony, the known Adélie population in Antarctica is not only thriving but super busy, too.

PENGUIN LIFE

Throughout the year, Adélies log more than 8,000 miles (12,875 km) on the "road," commuting back and forth from their nests to the ocean to hunt for krill, squid, lanternfish, or jellyfish for dinner. With so many residents on the move, traffic can be tricky.

"The Adélies have fairly distinct highways," seabird ecologist Barbara Wienecke says. "The paths get incredibly congested, so like humans, the birds sometimes have to take detours to avoid getting stuck in traffic."

And like a bustling city, the noise never stops. Adélie chicks and parents identify each other mostly by sound—not by sight. So they squawk on their commute to let their family know they're coming back from fishing for the day. And if they've been away on a long hunting trip, each bird sings a unique hum to make sure they've found the correct partner.

The chatter isn't all sweet, though.

"If a neighbor gets too close, an Adélie can sound a nest alarm by making loud, sharp calls, which basically mean 'This is my nest! Go away!'" Wienecke says.

And don't forget the splat sounds they make while pooing. Adélies go often, and even all over each other! They're not trying to hit each other, though—the wind tends to blow the guano toward other nests.

NOSY NEIGHBORS

All that noise can be distracting, but Adélies have to stay focused to prevent a big-city theft of their valuables—that is, their pebbles.

Penguins use the small rocks to build nests for their chicks. Because pebbles can be scarce on the island, one Adélie might swipe a few stones from another. In rare cases, if the parents and chicks are away from the nest, a nonbreeding neighbor might try to steal the entire nest and connect it to their own nest to build an even bigger home. The birds fight back against these intruders by biting them

ADÉLIES DIVE FOR FOOD TO FEED THEMSELVES AND THEIR CHICKS.

or slapping them with their wings to scare them off.

Despite squabbles, neighbors can be helpful. "When the nests are all built within pecking distance of each other, it makes it harder for predatory seabirds like south polar skuas and giant petrels to target the colony," Wienecke says. "If they did, they'd have a lot of Adélies banding together against them."

Scientists have gotten involved to protect Adélies, too. "Since our expedition, a proposed marine protected area was expanded to include the Danger Islands," Lynch says. "And in the meantime, the area's dangerous sea ice will likely keep out most of the people curious about the Adélie penguins."

That way, penguin cities can keep hustling, bustling, and making noise for years to come.

Emperors reach nearly four feet (1.2 m) tall and can weigh up to 50 pounds (23 kg); Adélies only stand up to two feet (0.6 m) tall and weigh about 10 pounds (5 kg).

MORE THAN 1.5 MILLION ADÉLIE PENGUINS LIVE IN THIS CROWDED COLONY ON THE DANGER ISLANDS.

awes8me

An octopus's arms can think independently from its brain.

1 SNEAKY SMARTS

Octopuses are curious creatures. They can open the lids of jars, and some have even found escape routes from their aquarium enclosures. They can also wriggle their boneless bodies through passages as small as a quarter! Octopuses learn quickly and can recognize individual human faces.

CLEVER CREATURES

THESE ANIMALS ARE AT THE TOP OF THEIR CLASS IN SMARTS.

NO BIRDBRAIN

African gray parrots are known for being chatterboxes. They're excellent at mimicking humans and can form simple sentences. They're also one of a few animals capable of reasoning, or coming up with an answer based on information they already have. They can figure out puzzles and work together to solve problems.

SMART LITTLE PIGGY

They might like to wallow in mud, but **domestic pigs** clean up in the intelligence department. Pigs can learn tasks, like operating levers to get food, and they are one of a few animal species that understand how mirrors work.

5

ALL FOR ONE
Talk about teamwork! These **army ants** are joining together to build a living ant tower so some individuals can climb to this plant stem and retrieve food for the community. Researchers discovered that no single ant calls the shots in the tower-building; they make decisions as a colony.

4

THIRST FOR KNOWLEDGE
Chimpanzees, one of the closest relatives to humans, use things in nature such as leaves and mosslike sponges to soak up water for drinking. They pass on this trick to other family members, which is a type of social learning only the smartest of animals achieve.

6

NUTS FOR LEARNING
When it comes to finding nuts, **gray squirrels** are the experts. In one study, researchers hid several hazelnuts to discover how squirrels solve a puzzle. The squirrels were quick learners, and they even changed tactics to get their nut reward more quickly.

7

CRAFTY CROW
If a **New Caledonian crow** can't find a tool for the job, it just makes one! The South Pacific bird can bend twigs into hooks to retrieve insects hidden in logs.

8

CATCH ME IF YOU CAN!
Being playful is considered a sign of intelligence—which puts **dolphins** near the top of the list of smartest animals. Several species of dolphins ride the waves created by boats, and some dolphins play tag by nudging each other and then swimming away for a high-speed chase!

UNICORNS

OF THE SEA

SCIENTISTS TRY TO **SOLVE THE MYSTERY** OF THE NARWHAL'S **GIANT TUSK.**

C hilly water laps against an iceberg in the Arctic Ocean. Suddenly, a pod of narwhals—a species of whale that sports a unicorn-like horn on its head—emerges from the sea near the iceberg's edge.

Narwhals live in the Arctic Ocean. Like most whales, they're jumbo-size—up to 3,500 pounds (1,588 kg)—and surface to breathe. And like some whale species such as orcas, they live in pods. (Narwhals usually have 15 to 20 in a group.) But a narwhal has one thing that no other whale does: a giant tusk growing out of its noggin.

For centuries people have been trying to figure out what this tusk—actually an enlarged tooth—is used for. Scientists have come up with a couple theories that may help solve this gnawing puzzle.

TUSK, TUSK

A narwhal's swordlike tusk first pokes from its jaw through the animal's upper lip when it's about three months old. This is the only tooth the whale develops. Over time, the tusk can grow to be half the length of the whale's body. New research shows that narwhals may use these long appendages to snag prey like arctic cod, using quick jabs to stun the fish before they eat them.

TOOTH SLEUTHS

Another theory is that a male narwhal uses the tooth to attract a female. Similar to a peacock's flashy feathers, the tusk makes the male stand out to potential mates. The animals have been observed scraping their tusks together, as though they are in a fencing match. This may be a way for male members of a pod to identify one another.

There's still plenty that scientists don't know about narwhals, and they will continue to look for answers. In the meantime, it appears that these mysterious whales still have a few secrets up their tusks.

SURFACING ABOVE WATER, A GROUP OF NARWHALS TAKES A BREATH OF AIR.

THIS POD OF MALES SWIMS THROUGH ARCTIC WATERS.

A NARWHAL MOM TRAVELS WITH HER BABY.

GIANTS OF THE DEEP

Some of the world's largest animals live in the ocean.
But just how big can these animals get? Scientists aren't always sure because some creatures are rare or in hard-to-reach parts of the ocean. Here are measurements for a few of the largest marine species ever discovered (plus a human for comparison).

ADULT HUMAN
6
FEET (1.8 M)

JAPANESE SPIDER CRAB
12.1
FEET (3.7 M)
LEG SPAN

SPERM WHALE
78.7 FEET (24 M) TOTAL LENGTH

GIANT OCEAN MANTA RAY
23
FEET (7 M)
DISK WIDTH

LEATHERBACK SEA TURTLE
7
FEET (2.1 M)
SHELL LENGTH

GIANT SQUID
39.4 FEET (12 M) TOTAL LENGTH

BLUE WHALE
108.3 FEET (33 M) TOTAL LENGTH

GIANT PACIFIC OCTOPUS
32.2
FEET (9.8 M)
RADIAL SPREAD

GIANT TUBE WORM
9.8
FEET (3 M)
TUBE LENGTH

CARIBBEAN GIANT BARREL SPONGE
8.2
FEET (2.5 M)
BASE DIAMETER

SOUTHERN ELEPHANT SEAL
22.5
FEET (6.9 M)
TOTAL LENGTH

WHALE SHARK
61.7 FEET (18.8 M) TOTAL LENGTH

SharkFest

Dive in to join the party with these 5 surprising sharks.

Not all sharks are gigantic, toothy eating machines. Among the 500 species, there are a few surprising sharks. Some have teeth so small that they can't take a bite out of anything. Others are practically vegetarian! Discover five species of sharks with mind-blowing traits.

A group of sharks is called a shiver.

1 Fishy Friends: Lemon Sharks

Love hanging out with your BFF? So do lemon sharks! Young lemon sharks often stick together for protection from larger sharks and other predators. Scientists say this species hangs out with the same friends for years. And when scientists studied the pups in a predator-free environment, these sharks still chose to swim together rather than alone. Maybe these fish need matching friendship bracelets.

TWO LEMON SHARKS HANG OUT NEAR THE BAHAMA ISLANDS.

2 Green Glowers: Chain Catsharks

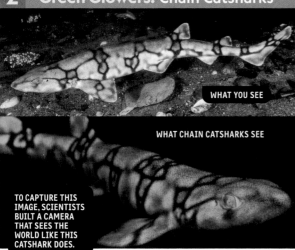

WHAT YOU SEE

WHAT CHAIN CATSHARKS SEE

TO CAPTURE THIS IMAGE, SCIENTISTS BUILT A CAMERA THAT SEES THE WORLD LIKE THIS CATSHARK DOES.

Through your eyes, the chain catshark seems to have brownish yellow skin with black chain-shaped markings. But to another chain catshark swimming 1,600 to 2,000 feet (488 to 610 m) below the surface, the fish glows in the dark! Pigments in the sharks' skin absorb the blue light in the ocean and reflect it as green. These sharks have special cells in their eyes—called receptors—to see it. Because the glow patterns are different for males and females, scientists think these shy sharks use this ability to attract mates.

3 | Salad Snackers: Bonnethead Sharks

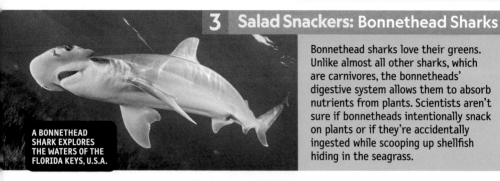

A BONNETHEAD SHARK EXPLORES THE WATERS OF THE FLORIDA KEYS, U.S.A.

Bonnethead sharks love their greens. Unlike almost all other sharks, which are carnivores, the bonnetheads' digestive system allows them to absorb nutrients from plants. Scientists aren't sure if bonnetheads intentionally snack on plants or if they're accidentally ingested while scooping up shellfish hiding in the seagrass.

4 | Ocean Oldies: Greenland Sharks

A Greenland shark swimming through deep, freezing Arctic water today might have been born when George Washington became the first president of the United States! This shark species can live for nearly 300 years—and possibly as many as 500 years. That's the longest of any vertebrate (an animal with a backbone). Experts think their icy cold habitat and slow lifestyle (a Greenland shark's heart beats only once every 12 seconds; yours beats about once a second) might be their secret to growing seriously old.

A GREENLAND SHARK SWIMS BELOW THE ARCTIC OCEAN ICE, OFF THE COAST OF CANADA.

Sharks have been on Earth longer than trees.

5 | Gentle Giants: Whale Sharks

Sharks are relatives of manta rays.

A WHALE SHARK WITH ITS MOUTH OPEN SWIMS AMONG REMORA FISH.

A whale shark's mouth is so wide that a 10-year-old kid could fit inside. But don't worry: These easygoing sharks stick to a diet of tiny shrimplike plankton about as small as a few grains of sand. The largest fish in the world, whale sharks can be longer than a school bus and weigh 50,000 pounds (22,680 kg). They feed by swimming slowly with their mouths open, filtering plants and animals from the water.

PINK POWER

Flamingos
are some of the toughest birds on Earth!

Think flamingos are pushovers? Think again: They might be the most extreme birds in the animal kingdom!

"Their pink color and wobbly-looking legs can cause people to assume they're kind of dainty," says Felicity Arengo, a flamingo researcher at the American Museum of Natural History. "But flamingos are actually much tougher than they look." Check out these five adaptations to decide.

They Have a Leg Up

Lake Natron in Tanzania, a country in East Africa, is loaded with corrosive chemicals that could burn off human skin. It's a watery graveyard for many of the other birds that land there. (Animals that perish in the lake are gradually mummified.)

But flamingos can wade in the water all day. Their fragile-looking, stilt-like legs are covered in armor—hundreds of hard, flexible scales atop their thick, leathery skin. This thick covering protects the birds when they're in toxic waterways all over the world.

Their Beaks Have Impressive Bites

Like the ocean's largest whales, flamingos are filter feeders. But instead of swimming for their dinners, they just kick the mud where food—like brine shrimp, algae, and fly larvae—lives, dip their heads, and slurp up their meals.

Unlike humans, both their lower and upper jaws move, allowing the birds to open and shut their mouths rapidly—as fast as 20 times a second—which pumps food-filled water inside their beaks. A short, comb-like structure running along the edge of their beaks keeps large

The black feathers under a flamingo's wings can be seen only when the bird is flying.

AN AMERICAN FLAMINGO PREPARES TO FEED ITS THREE-DAY-OLD CHICK.

A group of flamingos is called a flamboyance or a stand.

THREE AMERICAN FLAMINGOS WALK THROUGH A BREEDING COLONY NEAR THE GULF OF MEXICO.

particles out, while another strainer around their tongues captures the tasty tidbits. Yum!

They Can Drink Anything

Flamingos can be found on every continent except Australia and Antarctica. Most of the birds live in supersalty lakes, marshes, and lagoons. And some of those water habitats are fed by near-boiling hot springs. So what do flamingos drink? Salt water—minus the salt.

Located in their heads, tiny organs called salt glands filter out the salt from the water they sip, then the salt discharges through their nostrils. Even species that live in deserts, like the Chilean flamingo, have this adaptation to drink from pools in salt flats.

When it comes to fresh water, flamingos can safely guzzle from hot springs, which reach temperatures up to 140°F (60°C). How? Experts think it has something to do with extra-tough linings all flamingos have in their mouths and

throats. Scientists have also discovered blood vessels in the birds' heads that might help them regulate their body temperature by shedding the heat they swallow, sort of like how a car's radiator helps get rid of excess heat from the engine.

They Don't Get Cold Feet

If humans doze off in freezing water, they will suffer frostbite—or worse. Not flamingos. The birds simply break their feet free from the ice, then bury their beaks in the icy water to snack. In fact, some flamingos only leave for warmer areas when the ice gets too thick to feed. Experts think the same armor that protects the flamingos in corrosive water likely helps them handle icy conditions as well—as does their ability to regulate their body temperature.

Their Nests Are Like Little Castles

Flamingos make domelike mud nests in the middle of corrosive waters. This helps keep their single eggs—and later, their chicks—safe from predators. The mounds also keep everything mostly dry when rain raises the water level.

After chicks hatch, they're watched over by babysitters in flamingo nurseries so the parents can feed. Away from the nests, juvenile and adult flamingos stick together in large flocks, which confuses predators trying to pick a target among the wall of pink. This proves that these birds aren't just tough—they're smart, too.

A COLONY OF AMERICAN FLAMINGOS NESTS IN THE YUCATÁN PENINSULA IN MEXICO.

59

INCREDIBLE
ANIMAL FRIENDS

MONKEY DOTES ON IGUANA

Krefeld, Germany

This white-faced saki rarely scaled back her affection for her green iguana bestie. The saki, a type of monkey, loved petting and snuggling her reptile pal as they lounged together on tree branches at the Krefeld Zoo.

The saki and iguana met after they were placed in the zoo's Rainforest House, a tree-filled enclosure that's home to 40 different types of animals from tropical areas. "Both green iguanas and white-faced sakis spend most of their time in treetops," zoo spokesperson Petra Schwinn says. "One day these two crossed paths." The curious saki examined the reptile, patting its skin with her long fingers.

The pals continued to have hangout sessions, eating together at the enclosure's feeding station. But most of their "playdates" were in the trees and involved the saki petting the iguana and tickling its chin. The reptile, meanwhile, seemed to soak up the attention.

The animals have since moved to separate zoos. But keepers and visitors haven't forgotten about their friendship. "They made a good team," Schwinn says.

WHITE-FACED SAKI

RANGE South America

WEIGHT Around 4 pounds (2 kg)

FACE-OFF Only the male white-faced saki has white fur covering its face. The fur on a female's face is mostly brown.

SWEET TREATS Sakis eat fruit, honey, leaves, and flowers.

GREEN IGUANA

RANGE Central and South America

WEIGHT Up to 17 pounds (8 kg)

TALL TAIL If it's caught by a predator, the green iguana can detach its tail and grow another.

FUNNY NAME These animals are sometimes referred to as "bamboo chickens."

HOW ABOUT A NECK RUB?

MONKEY

IGUANA

BIRD HANGS OUT WITH BUNNY

YOU'RE MY BFF: BIRD FRIEND FOREVER.

Kildare, Ireland

Bunny the European rabbit and Pidg the common pigeon didn't let anything come between their friendship—even a wall!

After being found weak and alone, the animals were brought separately to what was then the Kildare Animal Foundation Wildlife Unit. Both needed warmth to survive, but volunteer Aideen Magee had only one incubator. So she put the rabbit and the bird inside together, setting a cardboard wall between them so that they'd each have their own space. When McGee went to check on the duo a little later, she saw that Bunny had knocked down the barrier and was cuddling with Pidg!

McGee took the cardboard wall away so that the animals could snuggle 24/7. Soon after, Bunny became sick, and Pidg refused to leave the rabbit's side.

"The bird comforted Bunny and kept him going," says animal manager Dan Donoher. Once Bunny recovered, the friends spent their time eating together, grooming each other, and curling up at nap time.

After about six months, Pidg and Bunny were released back into the wild. They're no longer side by side, but when they needed it most, these critters had each other's backs.

COMMON PIGEON

WEIGHT About 13 ounces (369 g)

DIET Seeds, grains, and fruit

EGG ALERT It takes about 17 days for their eggs to hatch.

ROCK ON They're sometimes called rock doves.

EUROPEAN RABBIT

WEIGHT Up to 5 pounds (2.2 kg)

DIET Grass, bark, buds, and roots

ALL GROWN UP Bunnies become independent after about a month.

DISTRESS SIGNAL They thump their feet when threatened.

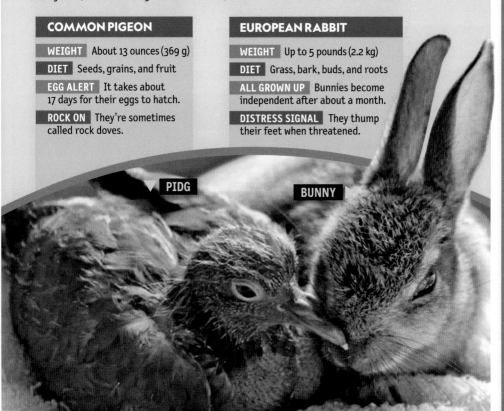

PIDG

BUNNY

10 WILD FACTS ABOUT PLANET PROTECTORS

Thanks in part to their cuteness, **GIANT PANDAS** have a habitat in China that's being protected and restored—**and that protects dozens of lesser-known species around them, too.**

Striped hyenas chow down on already dead animals, keeping their habitat clean and even **helping stop the spread of diseases.**

The **GRAY WOLVES** in Yellowstone National Park **keep their ecosystem in balance by hunting elk,** which protects the trees that the elk eat, making more habitat for birds and beavers.

When **black-tailed prairie dogs** dig their burrows, they mix up **dead plant matter and animal waste,** making the land more fertile for growing grass.

Black-and-white ruffed lemurs chow down on fruits in Madagascar, seeds and all, THEN POO THEM OUT. New plants will grow where the poo lands.

Some farmers build **NEST BOXES** to welcome **BARN OWLS,** which can consume thousands of crop-eating rodents each year.

CORAL REEFS act like **UNDERWATER BARRIERS** to slow incoming waves, keeping coastal communities safer from floods and storms.

Reindeer help SLOW CLIMATE CHANGE BY MUNCHING ON dark-colored plants in the Arctic tundra, exposing lighter-colored plants below that better reflect heat.

As a GRAY HAIRSTREAK BUTTERFLY travels from one cotton flower to another, it carries sticky pollen with it, helping the plants reproduce.

The phytoplankton in a **SPERM WHALE'S POO** suck up carbon dioxide from the ocean and release oxygen, helping to cool the planet.

JAVAN SLOW LORIS

DEADLY CUTIES

Nine species of slow loris live throughout Southeast Asia.

This adorable animal has some seriously KILLER traits.

Don't be fooled by the crazy-cute slow loris. The snuggly looking creature is the only venomous primate on the planet—and its bite packs enough toxin to kill prey in just a few seconds. The toxin is also powerful enough to kill or severely harm humans, but it's very rare for the slow loris to bite people without first being provoked.

And venom isn't the only killer move the slow loris has. Check out three ways the adorable slow loris is actually downright dangerous.

KILLER LOOKS

A slow loris's sweet face markings might say "Oh, he-ey!" to you, but they say "Danger!" to other animals. To a potential predator like a large snake or hawk eagle, the markings are like flashing red lights near the loris's mouth, warning that the loris could fight back with its deadly venom.

HIDDEN HUNTER

Huge eyes make slow lorises look harmlessly huggable. But these peepers also make them effective hunters. A special layer behind the retina called a tapetum lucidum (pronounced tuh-PEE-tum loo-SUH-dum) reflects light back through the retina and gives a loris better nighttime vision for nocturnal hunting.

TWICE AS TOXIC

Unlike other venomous animals that produce venom in one place, slow lorises produce toxins in two places: in their saliva and in glands in their underarms. When lorises lick these glands and mix its oils with their saliva, they cook up an even more toxic mixture they can inject with a single bite.

A JAVAN SLOW LORIS HANGS OUT IN THE TREE CANOPY OF JAVA, AN ISLAND IN INDONESIA.

Bet You Didn't Know!

7 bee facts to buzz about

HONEYBEE

1 Bees have special **stomachs** for carrying nectar.

2 Some bees may **sleep** on flowers.

3 A bee beats its **wings** up to 12,000 times each minute.

4 Male bees can't **sting.**

5 In summer, a single **hive** can house up to **80,000** honeybees.

6 The alkali bee can visit up to **6,000** flowers a day.

7 Sweat bees like the **taste** of human perspiration.

Bizarre BUGS

Butterflies are beautiful, and fireflies are fantastic. But zoom in on the insect world, and you'll find zombie-makers, explosive tushies, and more.

ZOMBIE-MAKER

In some scary movies, scientists accidentally create zombies. But female **jewel wasps** turn bugs into brainless beings on purpose. When she's ready to lay an egg, the wasp stings a **cockroach** to paralyze it. Then she sticks her stinger into the roach's brain, probing around for just the right spot to inject mind-altering chemicals.

After the first sting wears off and the roach can move again, the wasp leads the insect zombie by its antenna to a burrow and lays her egg on the roach's leg. A healthy cockroach would fight back or run away. But this roach sits still while the wasp seals up the burrow with small pebbles—and the roach inside. Three days later, the wasp larva hatches and eventually feasts on the cockroach.

BUTT BLASTER

Beware this bottom! **Bombardier beetles** take precise aim and blast stinky, boiling-hot acid from their butts to fend off predators. Why doesn't the liquid hurt the beetles while it's inside them? These insects have a series of chambers in their bodies that keep two chemicals separated. But when a beetle is in danger, it opens the valves and combines the chemicals. Then ... boom!

The beetles can even use the gassy defense after they've been swallowed: Scientists have watched unlucky frogs puke up bombardier beetles.

COSTUME DESIGNER

With their long, slender bodies and soft abdomens, **caddisfly** larvae look like lunch to every fish in the stream. So after hatching, they quickly construct a dashing disguise. First the youngsters find pebbles, sticks, shells, or pieces of leaves. Then using special silk produced in glands around their mouths, they paste their collection together.

The silk acts like double-sided tape to build the one-inch (2.5-cm)-long portable shelters that the larvae will use for up to two years. As adults, caddisflies only survive a few weeks. But soon new caddisfly youngsters will get dressed up all over again.

GROSS!

HEAT GENERATOR A group of **northern giant hornets**—the world's largest hornet—are unstoppable when attacking a bee or wasp hive. The nearly two-inch (5-cm)-long invaders bite off their prey's heads, chomping all the adults in the colony. Then they take over the hive, feeding the bee or wasp larvae to their own young.

But **Japanese honeybees** have outsmarted these warriors. When a hornet comes to scope out the hive, up to 500 honeybees surround the scout, wiggling and buzzing for an hour. Their body heat raises the temperature at the center of the ball to 117°F (47°C), killing the hornet. (The bees can survive up to 122°F [50°C].) The dead hornet scout can't tell its buddies about the hive, and the bees stay safe.

ROYAL FIGHTERS A few hours after the reigning queen in a colony of **Indian jumping ants** dies, an epic battle begins. For about a month, female worker ants jab each other with their antennae and nip each other with their superlong jaws, which they normally use for hunting. Exhausted, the losers give up and get back to work hunting other insects and tending to the young.

But a few of the toughest females become sort of like princesses. Worker ants can never be true queens, but these royal ladies can help keep the colony alive for years and years. As they prepare to produce eggs, their brains shrink up to 25 percent, which might give them more energy for this regal duty. Good thing they don't have to wear crowns.

BIG CATS

Not all wild cats are big cats, so what are big cats? To wildlife experts, this group includes tigers, lions, leopards, snow leopards, jaguars, cougars, and cheetahs. As carnivores, they survive solely on the flesh of other animals. Big cats are excellent hunters thanks to powerful jaws; long, sharp claws; and daggerlike teeth.

A TIGER MOM AND HER TWO CUBS

WHO'S WHO?

BIG CATS IN THE *PANTHERA* GENUS MAY HAVE a lot of features in common, but if you know what to look for, you'll be able to tell who's who in no time.

FUR

SNOW LEOPARD

A snow leopard's thick, spotted fur helps the cat hide in its mountain habitat, no matter the season. In winter its fur is off-white to blend in with the snow, and in summer it's yellowish gray to blend in with plants and the mountains.

A jaguar's coat pattern looks similar to that of a leopard, as both have dark spots called rosettes. The difference? The rosettes on a jaguar's torso have irregularly shaped borders and at least one black dot in the center.

JAGUAR

Most tigers are orange-colored with vertical black stripes on their bodies. This coloring helps the cats blend in with tall grasses as they sneak up on prey. These markings are like fingerprints: No two stripe patterns are alike.

TIGER

Lions have light brown, or tawny, coats and a tuft of black hair at the end of their tails. When they reach their prime, most male lions have shaggy manes that help them look larger and more intimidating.

LION

LEOPARD

A leopard's yellowy coat has dark spots called rosettes on its back and sides. In leopards, the rosettes' edges are smooth and circular. This color combo and pattern help leopards blend into their surroundings.

JAGUAR
Up to 348 pounds
(158 KG)
5 to 6 feet long
(1.5 TO 1.8 M)

BENGAL TIGER
Up to 716 pounds
(325 KG)
5 to 6 feet long
(1.5 TO 1.8 M)

LEOPARD
Up to 198 pounds
(90 KG)
4.25 to 6.25 feet long
(1.3 TO 1.9 M)

SNOW LEOPARD
Up to 121 pounds (55 KG)
4 to 5 feet long (1.2 TO 1.5 M)

AFRICAN LION
Up to 575 pounds
(261 KG)
4.5 to 6.5 feet long
(1.4 TO 2 M)

Weirdest. Cat. Ever.

THE SERVAL MIGHT LOOK STRANGE, BUT THAT'S A GOOD THING WHEN IT COMES TO HUNTING.

SERVALS CAN CATCH UP TO 30 FROGS IN THREE HOURS WHILE HUNTING IN WATER.

SERVAL KITTENS STAY WITH MOM UP TO TWO YEARS BEFORE LIVING ON THEIR OWN.

Servals can chirp, purr, hiss, snarl, and growl.

ALL EARS

The serval's big ears are key to the animal's hunting success. Servals rely on sound more than any other sense when they're on the prowl. Thanks to their jumbo ears—the biggest of any wild cat's relative to body size—servals can hear just about any peep on the savanna. (If a person had ears like a serval's, they'd be as big as dinner plates!) To make the most of their super hearing, servals avoid creating noise while hunting. So instead of stalking prey like some cats do, servals squat in clearings and sit still—sometimes for several hours—as they listen for food.

A serval sits patiently in a grassy field, swiveling its head back and forth like a watchful owl. The predator is scanning the savanna for a meal not with its eyes, but with its oversize ears.

An unseen rodent stirs under the thick brush, and the wild cat tenses. It crouches on its legs and feet before launching up and over the tall grass. Guided only by sound, the serval lands directly on the once invisible rat.

Thanks to its extra-long legs, stretched-out neck, and huge ears, the serval is sometimes called the "cat of spare parts." This wild cat might look weird to some people. "But put together, their bizarre-looking body parts make them really successful hunters," says Christine Thiel-Bender, a biologist who studies servals in their African home.

In fact, servals catch prey in more than half their attempts, making them one of the best hunters in the wild cat kingdom. That's about 20 percent better than lions hunting together in a pride.

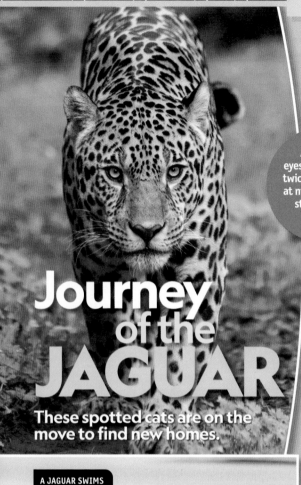

Journey
of the
JAGUAR

These spotted cats are on the move to find new homes.

A jaguar's eyesight is nearly twice as powerful at night to help it stalk prey in the dark.

The jaguar once prowled through more than seven million square miles (18 million sq km) stretching through North and South America. But in the past century, things like cattle ranching and the growth of cities have cut this territory in half. Few jaguars have been seen in the United States, and their southern range now barely extends into Argentina. The separation of these pockets of jaguars means fewer mates will meet—and fewer cubs will be born each year.

SAFE PASSAGE

Over the past decade or so, special corridors of land have been set aside to allow jaguars to get from one habitat to another. But as humans have cleared trees, shrubs, and grass along these corridors, they've become more dangerous for the jaguars, as they have nowhere to hide. As a result, wildlife ecologist Alan Rabinowitz launched the Jaguar Corridor Initiative (JCI) to protect the "superhighway" of land that the jaguars were using—and therefore their entire range.

HOME OF THE RANCH

Another key to keeping the jaguars safe? Educating farmers who live along the corridors. In the past, when jaguars traveled past a pasture of cattle, they may have tried to eat the easy prey, which would make the cats targets for ranchers protecting their herds. But thanks to new guidelines on keeping farm animals fenced in at night, both the cats and the livestock are safer.

A JAGUAR SWIMS ACROSS THE PARAGUAY RIVER IN BRAZIL.

Jaguar moms typically give birth to two to four cubs at a time.

A JAGUAR STALKS PREY IN BRAZIL'S CUIABÁ RIVER.

CHEETAH RESCUE

AFTER BEING RESCUED FROM WILDLIFE TRAFFICKERS, FIVE SIX-WEEK-OLD CHEETAHS KEEP WARM IN FRONT OF A HEATER.

How conservationists are saving these cats from smugglers

In the back seat of an SUV, a cheetah cub bared his teeth and hissed. Around his neck was a rope, which not too long ago had been used to tie him to the base of a tree. His eyes darted in every direction, taking in his surroundings.

The people who peered into the vehicle meant only one thing to the alarmed cheetah: danger. Stolen from his mother to be someone's pet, the wild cat probably hadn't had many good interactions with humans.

What the cheetah, called Astur, didn't know was that the faces outside were friendly— these people came to rescue him.

ASTUR THE CHEETAH CUB PEEKS OUT OF A CRATE AT HIS RESCUERS.

Cheetah brothers often stay together for life. A female is usually solitary until she has cubs.

Tracking Astur

The people are part of a team of wildlife conservationists who work to stop smugglers from selling cheetahs in Somaliland, an independent region in the East African country of Somalia. The rescuers heard about Astur from informants who keep a lookout for animals that are being trafficked, or illegally traded, in the area. The conservationists learned that Astur had been stolen from the wild and might be sold to a wildlife trafficker. Then that trafficker would sell the cheetah as a pet.

Many people in Somaliland don't know that taking cubs from the wild is against the law. People there who attempt to sell the cats are often trying to make extra money for their families and protect their goat herds from the predators. The rescuers hoped they could convince the man trying to sell Astur to give the cat to them instead of a pet smuggler.

"Sometimes sellers do the right thing and give up the animals when asked," says National Geographic Explorer Timothy Spalla, who is working to end the cheetah trade in Africa and the Middle East.

But before the team could talk to the seller, he drove away. He *did* know that having a cub was illegal and was afraid of being arrested. But the police quickly caught up to the vehicle and handed Astur over to the rescuers.

Check-Up Time

Veterinarian Asma Bile Hersi tried to treat the cub as soon as he was picked up by the team. She checked him as best she could for obvious injuries like open wounds and broken bones. At about seven months old, Astur was older than most cheetah cubs Hersi had treated—and *much* fiercer.

"The people who were keeping him didn't feed him very well," Hersi says. "He was hungry, so that's why he was fighting everyone."

Hersi and the others wanted to get Astur to Hargeysa, Somaliland's capital, so the anxious cub could get a full medical examination. After two days of driving, the team arrived at a rescue center run by the Cheetah Conservation Fund, an organization that cares for cheetahs that were removed from the wild at a young age. There, veterinarian Anna Ciezarek took over examining a distressed Astur. Ciezarek sedated Astur before examining him carefully.

"Ultimately, Astur didn't need treatment," Ciezarek says. "Other cubs aren't so lucky—many of them arrive in very poor condition."

A New Home

To help Astur adjust to the rescue center and feel safe, caregivers put him in a comfortable enclosure. They also focused on having short, friendly interactions with the cat so he'd begin to trust his human caretakers. According to Joe Bottiglieri, the center's cheetah care manager when Astur arrived, just being near the cub without looking scary can be helpful. "Gaining their trust takes time and patience," Bottiglieri says.

Now that he's older, Astur has become more settled at the rescue center. He lives with four other male cheetahs named Bagheer, Cizi, Darth, and Shamsi. His caregivers say Astur still doesn't like people very much, but he's learned to respond to commands like "come here" and "down." When Astur cooperates, he gets treats like antelope, a favorite cheetah snack.

Protecting Cheetahs

Because he was taken from the wild so young, Astur doesn't know how to survive on his own; he'll spend the rest of his life at the rescue center. Still, he'll hang out with fellow cheetahs, play on plenty of climbing structures, chase around lots of toys, and be cared for by experts who know how to keep him healthy.

Meanwhile, the fight against cheetah smuggling in this region continues. "These animals belong to the wild, not in a sanctuary," says Shukri Haji Ismail Mohamoud, Somaliland's environment minister. "We'll keep fighting for cheetahs like Astur to be safe."

THIS SIX-WEEK-OLD ORPHAN BOTTLE-FEEDS EVERY FEW HOURS TO GET THE NUTRIENTS IT WOULD'VE RECEIVED FROM MOM.

Cheetah cubs chirp to communicate.

Most big cats hunt at night, but cheetahs hunt during the day.

ASTUR THE CHEETAH IS EXAMINED FOR INJURIES. TISSUES IN HIS EARS AND AN EYE MASK HELP KEEP HIM CALM.

Naughty
PETS

POCKETS
ARE
PURR-FECT
FOR
CATNAPS.

WHOA,
HOW'D ALL
THIS FIT INTO
THAT LITTLE
POUCH?

NAME Snickers

FAVORITE ACTIVITY
Back-to-school
clothes shopping

FAVORITE TOY Belt
made of yarn

PET PEEVE School
uniforms

NAME Chewy

FAVORITE ACTIVITY
Exploring the insides
of pillows

FAVORITE TOY
Stuffed teddy bear

PET PEEVE Zippers

I'M SOOO
LIVING MY
BEST
DOG LIFE.

GOOD
THING I
COATED THE
SINK WITH
TOOTHPASTE.

NAME Queso

FAVORITE ACTIVITY
Turning on the faucet while the
cat is sleeping in the sink

FAVORITE TOY Soap bubbles

PET PEEVE Cat beds

NAME Sabacca

FAVORITE ACTIVITY
Watching humans perform
tricks in the pool

FAVORITE TOY Pool raft

PET PEEVE
Not being allowed to drink
the pool water

DOLPHIN

REAL ANIMAL HEROES

DOLPHINS PROTECT SWIMMER

A BOTTLENOSE DOLPHIN COASTS ALONGSIDE ADAM WALKER AS HE SWIMS TOWARD THE NEW ZEALAND SHORE.

Cook Strait, New Zealand

Long-distance swimmer Adam Walker had been swimming for three hours when he found himself surrounded by a pod of 12 bottlenose dolphins. Then he saw something swimming beneath him that was a different size and shape from the others: a great white shark.

The swimmer didn't know how long the shark had been trailing him, but he thinks the dolphins were trying to shield him from the shark. "They swam with me until the shark left," Walker says. "One dolphin rolled on its side and swam facing me, as if to say, 'We've got your back.'"

Scientist Rochelle Constantine, who studies marine mammals, can't say for sure that the animals were protecting Walker. "But dolphins are known for helping helpless things," she says. "And a pod of dolphins can do some damage to a solo shark, so the shark likely backed off because they were there."

Whatever the dolphins were up to, Walker is thankful for their presence.

TALK ABOUT POD SQUAD GOALS.

DOG RESCUES KITTY

Billings, Montana, U.S.A.

Chloe the pug rarely barks. She only acts excited when she wants a carrot snack. Then she spins like a top and points toward the refrigerator. But one freezing cold morning this normally quiet pup went berserk.

Owner Amanda Bjelland was dressing for work when Chloe asked to go out. But as soon as Bjelland closed the door, Chloe barked to come in. Yapping loudly, she followed her owner from room to room. Bjelland was frustrated. "What do you want?" she asked, and let the dog out again.

This time, Chloe ran straight to their backyard pond. She spun around and sat. "Now I know something is wrong," Bjelland said. She raced to the pond herself.

Her Siamese cat, Willow, had fallen through the ice! Bjelland rescued the half-frozen kitty and wrapped her in blankets. For two days, the pug stayed by Willow's side. "It's amazing," she says. "I never would have known if it hadn't been for Chloe."

75

Prehistoric TIMELINE

HUMANS HAVE WALKED on Earth for some 300,000 years, a mere blip in the planet's 4.5-billion-year history. A lot has happened during that time. Earth formed, and oxygen levels rose in the millions of years of the Precambrian time. The productive Paleozoic era gave rise to hard-shell organisms, vertebrates, amphibians, and reptiles.

Dinosaurs ruled Earth in the mighty Mesozoic. And 66 million years after dinosaurs became extinct, modern humans emerged in the Cenozoic era. From the first tiny mollusks to the dinosaur giants of the Jurassic and beyond, Earth has seen a lot of transformation.

THE PRECAMBRIAN TIME

4.5 billion to 539 million years ago

- Earth (and other planets) formed from gas and dust left over from a giant cloud that collapsed to form the sun. The giant cloud's collapse was triggered when nearby stars exploded.
- Low levels of oxygen made Earth a suffocating place.
- Early life-forms appeared.

THE PALEOZOIC ERA

539 million to 252 million years ago

- The first insects and other animals appeared on land.
- 450 million years ago (mya), the ancestors of sharks began to swim in the oceans.
- 430 mya, plants began to take root on land.
- More than 360 mya, amphibians emerged from the water.
- Slowly, the major landmasses began to come together, creating Pangaea, a single supercontinent.
- By 300 mya, reptiles had begun to dominate the land.

What Killed the Dinosaurs?

It's a mystery that's boggled the minds of scientists for centuries: What happened to the dinosaurs? Although various theories have bounced around, a recent study confirms that the most likely culprit is an asteroid or comet that created a giant crater. Researchers say that the impact set off a series of natural disasters like tsunamis, earthquakes, and temperature swings that plagued the dinosaurs' ecosystems and disrupted their food chains. This, paired with intense volcanic eruptions that caused drastic climate changes, is thought to be why half of the world's species—including the dinosaurs—died in a mass extinction.

DINO TIMES

THE MESOZOIC ERA

252 million to 66 million years ago

The Mesozoic era, or the age of the reptiles, consisted of three consecutive time periods (shown below). This is when the first dinosaurs began to appear. They would reign supreme for more than 150 million years.

TRIASSIC PERIOD

252 million to 201 million years ago

- The first mammals appeared. They were rodent-size.
- The first dinosaurs appeared.
- Ferns were the dominant plants on land.
- The giant supercontinent of Pangaea began breaking up toward the end of the Triassic.

JURASSIC PERIOD

201 million to 145 million years ago

- Giant dinosaurs dominated the land.
- Pangaea continued its breakup, and oceans formed in the spaces between the drifting landmasses, allowing sea life, including sharks and marine crocodiles, to thrive.
- Conifer trees spread across the land.

CRETACEOUS PERIOD

145 million to 66 million years ago

- The modern continents developed.
- The largest dinosaurs developed.
- Flowering plants spread across the landscape.
- Mammals flourished, and giant pterosaurs ruled the skies over small birds.
- Temperatures grew more extreme. Dinosaurs lived in deserts, swamps, and forests from the Antarctic to the Arctic.

THE CENOZOIC ERA—PALEOGENE AND NEOGENE PERIODS

66 million to 2.6 million years ago

- Following the dinosaur extinction, mammals rose as the dominant species.
- Birds continued to flourish.
- Volcanic activity was widespread.
- Temperatures began to cool, eventually ending in an ice age.
- The period ended with land bridges forming, which allowed plants and animals to spread to new areas.

FIELD NOTES
FROM A
PALEONTOLOGIST

Meet paleontologist
Rodolfo M. Salas-Gismondi

Salas-Gismondi has made it his mission to uncover everything there is to know about prehistoric animals in Amazonia.
As one of the first Peruvian vertebrate paleontologists, he's unearthed fossils for creatures like the giant penguin, ground sloths, saber-toothed cats, and crocodilian species that lived long ago. Here, Salas-Gismondi shares what it's like to study fossils for a living.

Q: How did you get into paleontology?

A: As a kid, even as young as five years old, I was fascinated with dinosaurs. I drew them and read everything I could about them. I eventually started going out on my own to look for fossils and got into studying prehistoric marine animals, specifically those that lived in South America.

Q: How do you go about finding fossils?

A: We talk to local people who know the area well and have seen fossils. They'll take us to a site, and then we start to explore the area, and then it can take several days for us to find fossils. We've found fossils in caves and in rocks near rivers. You look everywhere.

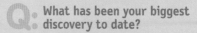

Q: What, exactly, do you look for?

A: Skulls and teeth are important for diagnostics, or to determine when these species lived. One big discovery we had lately was a complete skull of a dolphin from the early Miocene epoch in the Napo riverbank, a tributary of the Amazon River. The river was low in the dry season, exposing 20-million-year-old rock where the skull was partially embedded.

Q: What has been your biggest discovery to date?

A: Finding of the skull of *Gnatusuchus*, a 13-million-year-old species of crocodile. It's one of the three different species of crocodiles that hunted clams and snails in the swampy waters of proto-Amazonia, in what is now northwestern Peru. That was part of a discovery of the largest number of crocodile species—seven different species!—coexisting in one place at any time in Earth's history.

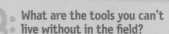

Q: What are the tools you can't live without in the field?

A: We travel by boat to most sites, so we have to pack pretty light. I pack all of my tools: picks, chisels, brushes, and plaster to stabilize the fossils. We also have to bring a tent because we camp out most of the places we go.

DINO Classification

Classifying dinosaurs and all other living things can be a complicated matter, so scientists have devised a system to help with the process. Dinosaurs are put into groups based on a very large range of characteristics.

Scientists put dinosaurs into two major groups: the bird-hipped ornithischians and the lizard-hipped saurischians.

Ornithischian

ILIUM
PUBIS
ISCHIUM

"Bird-hipped"
(pubis bone in hips points backward)

Ornithischians have the same-shaped pubis as birds of today, but today's birds are actually more closely related to the saurischians.

Example: *Styracosaurus*

Saurischian

ILIUM
PUBIS
ISCHIUM

"Lizard-hipped"
(pubis bone in hips points forward)

Saurischians are further divided into two groups: the meat-eating Theropoda and the plant-eating Sauropodomorpha.

Example:
Tyrannosaurus rex

Within these two main divisions, dinosaurs are then separated into orders and then families, such as Stegosauridae. Like other members of the Stegosauria, *Stegosaurus* had spines and plates along its back, neck, and tail.

AQUILOPS AMERICANUS HAD A FACE THAT RESEMBLED AN EAGLE.

THE STATE FOSSIL OF UTAH, U.S.A., IS THE *ALLOSAURUS*.

RESEARCHERS HAVE USED 3D PRINTERS TO REPLICATE DINOSAUR FOSSILS.

ARGENTINOSAURUS WAS THE LENGTH OF THREE SCHOOL BUSES.

4 NEWLY DISCOVERED DINOS

Humans have been searching for—and discovering—dinosaur remains for hundreds of years. In that time, at least 1,000 species of dinos have been found all over the world, and thousands more may still be out there waiting to be unearthed. Recent finds include *Daspletosaurus wilsoni*, a frightful tyrannosaur with horns around its piercing eyes.

1 ### *Ambopteryx longibrachium* (Saurischian)

Name Meaning: *Ambopteryx* is Latin for "both wings," reflecting the bat-like wings that helped it glide from tree to tree.

Length: 13 inches (32 cm)

Time Range: Late Jurassic period

Where: China

2 ### *Daspletosaurus wilsoni* (Saurischian)

Name Meaning: Dubbed "Wilson's frightful reptile," the dino is named after John "Jack" P. Wilson, who made the discovery.

Length: 30 feet (9 m)

Time Range: Late Cretaceous period

Where: Montana, U.S.A.

3 ### *Guemesia ochoai* (Saurischian)

Name Meaning: *Guemesia* is a nod to General Martín Miguel de Güemes, who fought in the Argentine War of Independence, while *ochoai* honors Javier Ochoa, who discovered the fossil.

Length: 16 feet (5 m)

Time Range: Late Cretaceous period

Where: Argentina

4 ### *Ledumahadi mafube* (Saurischian)

Name Meaning: This name means "a giant thunderclap at dawn" in Sesotho, an Indigenous language spoken in South Africa, where the fossil was found.

Length: 33 feet (10 m)

Time Range: Early Jurassic period

Where: South Africa

DINO SECRETS REVEALED

Cool technology shows surprising discoveries about dinosaurs.

It's been 66 million years since the dinosaurs went extinct. And we're *still* learning new things about them, thanks to cutting-edge technology like lasers, 3D models, x-rays, and even robotics. For instance, experts are able to run fossilized bones through a computer program to reconstruct missing bits and better understand how these animals actually functioned. Want to find out more? Check out three surprising dino discoveries that modern technology has helped scientists unearth.

SPINOSAURUS HUNT
PREHISTORIC SAWFISH.

River Beast

The Sahara seems like a strange place for a river-dwelling dinosaur. But more than 95 million years ago in what is now Morocco, a country in northern Africa, today's giant desert was actually lush with waterways deep enough for car-size fish to swim in. That's where *Spinosaurus*—a predator longer than *T. rex*—made its home.

At first, scientists believed that the sail-backed creature had some kind of watery lifestyle, perhaps hunting fish like a bear would. But after finding a partial skeleton in 2014, experts assessed that the dinosaur probably spent a lot of time in water.

And the paleontologists didn't stop there. Returning to the site in 2018, they dug up a 17-foot (5-m) *Spinosaurus* tail—one vertebra at a time. (These are the same bones that make up your spine.) Using high-speed cameras and robots, they created an eight-inch (20-cm)-long mechanical tail, which they watched paddle in an enclosed waterway. They discovered that the beast swam through rivers like a crocodile and could propel itself with eight times more power than related land dinosaurs. In fact, *Spinosaurus* is the first large dino found that had a tail designed for swimming.

A YOUNG *MUSSAURUS* CHECKS OUT TWO RHYNCHOSAURS (PRONOUNCED REEN-KOH-SOARS) AS AN ADULT LOOKS ON.

Baby Steps

Dinosaurs lumbered on all fours like a *Stegosaurus* or scrambled around on two legs like a *Tyrannosaurus.* But not all dinosaurs moved the same way as they grew up.

Paleontologist Alejandro Otero found that out by using a high-tech machine called a CT scanner to take x-rays of *Mussaurus* bones (pronounced moo-SOAR-us). He turned the x-rays into 3D models using a computer program and then simulated how the dinosaur stood at different ages.

What did the simulations show? It turns out that, like human babies, *Mussaurus* hatchlings walked on all fours—but started walking on their two hind limbs as they grew older.

A NEWLY HATCHED *DEINONYCHUS* CHICK IS WATCHED OVER BY DAD.

Cracking the Case

A fossilized dinosaur egg looks kind of like a rock. So scientists were surprised to discover that the eggs of *Deinonychus* (pronounced die-NAHN-uh-kus) were probably blue!

When exposed to heat and pressure, microscopic dino remains can transform into stuff that can last for millions of years. This lets scientists take a closer look. When paleobiologist Jasmina Wiemann struck the *Deinonychus* eggs with a laser, the light reflecting back revealed compounds that give modern eggs bright colors and speckling.

This helped her figure out the blue color, but it also suggested something else: Like modern birds with similarly colorful eggs, *Deinonychus* likely sat on open-air nests to hatch its eggs.

83

QUIZ WHIZ

Explore just how much you know about animals with this quiz!

Write your answers on a piece of paper. Then check them below.

1 Which clever creature uses leaves and moss to soak up water for drinking?
a. domestic pig
b. gray squirrel
c. chimpanzee
d. dolphin

2 **True or false?** Groundhogs are also known as whistle pigs.

3 Caddisfly larvae produce _____ to construct shelters that protect their soft bodies.
a. silk
b. milk
c. venom
d. paste

4 Striped hyenas _____ to keep their habitat clean, which helps stop the spread of disease.
a. carry seeds
b. build dams
c. munch on plants
d. eat dead animals

5 **True or false?** *Ambopteryx* is Latin for "both wings."

Not **STUMPED** yet?
Check out the *NATIONAL GEOGRAPHIC KIDS QUIZ WHIZ* collection for more fun **ANIMAL** questions!

ANSWERS: 1. c; 2. True; 3. a; 4. d; 5. True

HOMEWORK HELP

Wildly Good Animal Reports

Seahorse

Your teacher wants a written report on the seahorse. Not to worry. Use these organizational tools so you can stay afloat while writing a report.

STEPS TO SUCCESS: Your report will follow the format of a descriptive or expository essay (see page 127 for "How to Write a Perfect Essay") and should consist of a main idea, followed by supporting details and a conclusion. Use this basic structure for each paragraph, as well as the whole report, and you'll be on the right track.

1. Introduction
State your **main idea.**
Seahorses are fascinating fish with many unique characteristics.

2. Body
Provide **supporting points** for your main idea.
Seahorses are very small fish.
Seahorses are named for their head shape.
Seahorses display behavior that is rare among almost all other animals on Earth.

Then **expand** on those points with further description, explanation, or discussion.
Seahorses are very small fish.
Seahorses are about the size of an M&M at birth, and most adult seahorses would fit in a teacup.
Seahorses are named for their head shape.
With long, tubelike snouts, seahorses are named for their resemblance to horses.
A group of seahorses is called a herd.
Seahorses display behavior that is rare among almost all other animals on Earth.
Unlike most other fish, seahorses stay with one mate their entire lives. They are also among the only species in which dads, not moms, give birth to the babies.

3. Conclusion
Wrap it up with a **summary** of your whole paper.
Because of their unique shape and unusual behavior, seahorses are among the most fascinating and easily distinguishable animals in the ocean.

KEY INFORMATION

Here are some things you should consider including in your report:
> What does your animal look like?
> **To what other species is it related?**
> How does it move?
> **Where does it live?**
> What does it eat?
> **What are its predators?**
> How long does it live?
> **Is it endangered?**
> Why do you find it interesting?

SEPARATE FACT FROM FICTION: Your animal may have been featured in a movie or in myths and legends. Compare and contrast how the animal has been portrayed with how it behaves in reality. For example, penguins can't dance the way they do in the movie *Happy Feet.*

PROOFREAD AND REVISE: As you would do with any essay, when you're finished, check for misspellings, grammatical mistakes, and punctuation errors. It often helps to have someone else proofread your work, too, as that person may catch things you have missed. Also, look for ways to make your sentences and paragraphs even better. Add more descriptive language, choosing just the right verbs, adverbs, and adjectives to make your writing come alive.

BE CREATIVE: Use visual aids to make your report come to life. Include an animal photo file with interesting images found in magazines or printed from websites. Or draw your own! You can also build a miniature animal habitat diorama. Use creativity to help communicate your passion for the subject.

THE FINAL RESULT: Put it all together in one final, polished draft. Make it neat and clean, and remember to cite your references.

An abstract image of outer space shows
a nebula with a black hole. Parts of the
scene are composed from NASA data.

SPACE and EARTH

Bet You Didn't Know!

7 hot facts about the sun

1 Giant **energy storms** on the **sun** can cause electrical **blackouts** on Earth.

2 Every second, the sun converts about **four million tons** (3.6 million t) of matter to energy.

3 The sun's **core temperature** can be hotter than **27 million** degrees Fahrenheit (15,000,000°C).

4 More than a **million Earths** could fit inside the sun.

5 Scientists created a **spacecraft** that could **fly into the sun's atmosphere** without burning up.

6 Experts think that the sun **once had rings,** like those around Saturn.

7 The sun is more than **4.6 billion** years old.

Bet You Didn't Know!

7 magnificent facts about moons

1 Moonquakes occur on Earth's moon.

2 There are more than 200 moons in our solar system.

3 NASA scientists hope to send astronauts back to the moon in 2025 to explore its surface.

4 Scientists think that gravity might one day break apart Mars's two moons and form Saturn-like rings around the planet.

5 Neither Venus nor Mercury has any moons.

6 The solar system's largest moon, Jupiter's Ganymede, is one and a half times larger than Earth's moon.

7 One of Saturn's moons, Enceladus, has two large geysers that spew water vapor and ice.

PLANETS

CERES

MARS

EARTH

VENUS

MERCURY

JUPITER

SUN

MERCURY

Average distance from the sun:
35,983,125 miles (57,909,227 km)
Position from the sun in orbit: 1st
Equatorial diameter: 3,032 miles
(4,879 km)
Length of day: 59 Earth days
Length of year: 88 Earth days
Known moons: 0

VENUS

Average distance from the sun:
67,238,251 miles (108,209,475 km)
Position from the sun in orbit: 2nd
Equatorial diameter: 7,520 miles
(12,103 km)
Length of day: 243 Earth days
Length of year: 225 Earth days
Known moons: 0

EARTH

Average distance from the sun:
92,956,050 miles (149,598,262 km)
Position from the sun in orbit: 3rd
Equatorial diameter: 7,900 miles
(12,750 km)
Length of day: 24 hours
Length of year: 365.25 days
Known moons: 1

MARS

Average distance from the sun:
141,637,725 miles (227,943,824 km)
Position from the sun in orbit: 4th
Equatorial diameter: 4,220 miles
(6,792 km)
Length of day: 24.6 Earth hours
Length of year: 1.88 Earth years
Known moons: 2

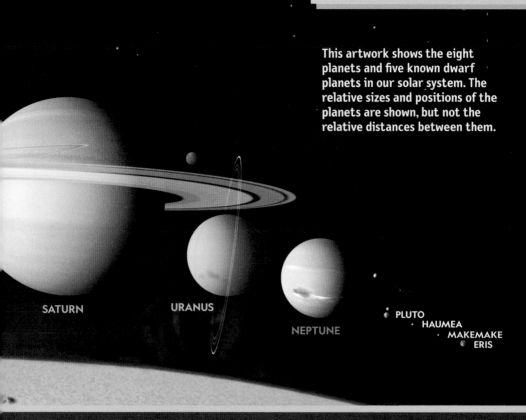

This artwork shows the eight planets and five known dwarf planets in our solar system. The relative sizes and positions of the planets are shown, but not the relative distances between them.

SATURN

URANUS

NEPTUNE

PLUTO
· HAUMEA
· MAKEMAKE
ERIS

JUPITER

Average distance from the sun:
483,638,564 miles (778,340,821 km)

Position from the sun in orbit: 6th

Equatorial diameter: 86,880 miles
(139,820 km)

Length of day: 9.9 Earth hours

Length of year: 11.9 Earth years

Known moons: At least 95*

SATURN

Average distance from the sun:
886,489,415 miles (1,426,666,422 km)

Position from the sun in orbit: 7th

Equatorial diameter: 72,367 miles
(116,464 km)

Length of day: 10.7 Earth hours

Length of year: 30 Earth years

Known moons: 146*

URANUS

Average distance from the sun:
1,783,744,300 miles (2,870,658,186 km)

Position from the sun in orbit: 8th

Equatorial diameter: 31,518 miles
(50,724 km)

Length of day: 17.2 Earth hours

Length of year: 84 Earth years

Known moons: 27

NEPTUNE

Average distance from the sun:
2,795,173,960 miles (4,498,396,441 km)

Position from the sun in orbit: 9th

Equatorial diameter: 30,599 miles
(49,244 km)

Length of day: 16.1 Earth hours

Length of year: 164.8 Earth years

Known moons: 14

*Includes provisional moons, which await confirmation and naming from the International Astronomical Union.

For information about dwarf planets, see page 92.

DWARF PLANETS

Haumea

Eris

Pluto

Thanks to advanced technology, astronomers have been spotting many never-before-seen celestial bodies with their telescopes. One recent discovery? A population of icy objects orbiting the sun beyond Pluto. The largest, like Pluto itself, are classified as dwarf planets. Smaller than the moon but still massive enough to pull themselves into a ball, dwarf planets nevertheless lack the gravitational "oomph" to clear their neighborhood of other sizable objects. So, although larger, more massive planets pretty much have their orbits to themselves, dwarf planets orbit the sun in swarms that include other dwarf planets, as well as smaller chunks of rock or ice.

So far, astronomers have identified five dwarf planets in our solar system: Ceres, Pluto, Haumea, Makemake, and Eris. There are many more newly discovered dwarf planets that will need additional study before they are named. Astronomers are observing hundreds of newly found objects in the frigid outer solar system. As time and technology advance, the family of known dwarf planets will surely continue to grow.

CERES
Position from the sun in orbit: 5th
Length of day: 9 Earth hours
Length of year: 4.39 Earth years
Known moons: 0

PLUTO
Position from the sun in orbit: 10th
Length of day: 6.39 Earth days
Length of year: 248 Earth years
Known moons: 5

HAUMEA
Position from the sun in orbit: 11th
Length of day: 3.9 Earth hours
Length of year: 285 Earth years
Known moons: 2

MAKEMAKE
Position from the sun in orbit: 12th
Length of day: 22.5 Earth hours
Length of year: 305.34 Earth years
Known moons: 1*

ERIS
Position from the sun in orbit: 13th
Length of day: 1.1 Earth days
Length of year: 558 Earth years
Known moons: 1

*Includes provisional moons, which await confirmation and naming from the International Astronomical Union.

BLACK HOLES

BLACK HOLE →

A black hole really seems like a hole in space. Most black holes form when the core of a massive star collapses, falling into oblivion. A black hole has a stronger gravitational pull than anything else in the known universe. It's like a bottomless pit, swallowing anything that gets close enough to it to be pulled in. It's black because it pulls in light. Black holes come in different sizes. The smallest known black hole has a mass about three times that of the sun. The biggest one scientists have found so far has a mass about 66 billion times greater than the sun's. Really big black holes at the center of galaxies probably form by swallowing enormous amounts of gas over time. In 2019, scientists released the first image of a black hole's silhouette (left). The image, previously thought impossible to record, was captured using a network of telescopes.

What if aliens came to Earth?

Humans haven't explored our own solar system (or the universe beyond) well enough to rule out the presence of extraterrestrials. How cool would it be if we found out aliens do exist? Aliens that could pay us a visit from outside our solar system would possess amazing technology light-years ahead of our own. After all, these travelers figured out how to cross vast distances between stars. But not everyone is ready to welcome aliens to Earth. Physicist Stephen Hawking believed in extraterrestrials and feared that any alien visitors would likely use their technology to ransack our planet for its resources. He thought Earthlings might be enslaved or wiped out. But who knows for sure? For now, those extraterrestrials are staying extra hidden.

UFO-HAUL

10 STELLAR FACTS ABOUT STARS

It takes about **50 million years** for a star the size of our sun to form.

SM0313, one of the **OLDEST KNOWN STARS** in the universe, was "born" **13.6 billion** years ago.

POLLUX

POLLUX, A STAR LOCATED IN THE GEMINI CONSTELLATION, HAS A RADIUS THAT'S NEARLY NINE TIMES BIGGER THAN THE SUN'S.

Stars sparkle in shades of blue, red, orange, yellow, and white.

Between **100 and 400 billion** stars are in the Milky Way galaxy—but only about 9,000 are visible to the naked eye from Earth.

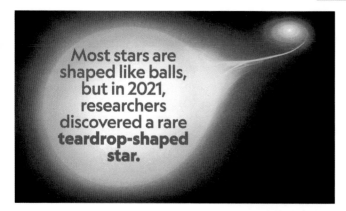

Most stars are shaped like balls, but in 2021, researchers discovered a rare **teardrop-shaped star.**

Heavy metal elements like **PLATINUM** and **GOLD** are created **when neutron stars collide.**

NASA's Hubble Space Telescope recently detected a star that's so far away, its light takes

12.9 billion years to reach Earth.

TAURUS CONSTELLATION

Humans' fascination with the night sky goes way back! A roughly 17,000-year-old painting found in a cave in France is believed to be a map of a constellation.

THE SUN accounts for more than **99 percent** of the solar system's total mass.

DESTINATION VENUS

Move over, Mars! Three upcoming missions could solve some of Venus's biggest mysteries.

HERE ARE FOUR MYSTERIES SCIENTISTS HOPE TO SOLVE ABOUT THIS PUZZLING PLANET.

1 What does Venus's surface look like?

Detailed maps of Earth's moon and Mars exist, but scientists want a sharper view of Venus as well. The planet's dense clouds make getting images of the ground difficult. And the planet's hostile environment means rovers like Mars's Perseverance can't visit.

Scientists think huge volcanoes and large lava channels cover Venus, as they do on neighboring planets. NASA's mission, called VERITAS, will launch around 2031 to find out.

2 Was Venus once more Earthlike?

Some astronomers call Venus "Earth's evil twin." It's nearly the same size as Earth, a similar distance from the sun, and probably made of iron and molten rock (like Earth is). Scientists suspect that billions of years ago, Venus had a mild, sunny climate, much like Earth's today. But nowadays, it's a raging, hostile planet.

To discover why, NASA's DAVINCI mission, set to launch around 2029, will drop a probe through Venus's clouds toward its surface. As it falls, the probe will monitor the atmosphere for gases such as helium and krypton. Measuring the gases might reveal how Venus's environment has changed over time.

3 Did Venus have oceans?

Research shows that Venus's hydrogen levels suggest the planet used to have a lot more water. So DAVINCI will also test how the planet's hydrogen levels have changed over time, giving scientists clues about how much water covered Venus billions of years ago.

4 What's going on underground?

Radar imagery suggests to scientists that Venus's surface is covered by as many as 85,000 volcanoes—and some might still be active.

VOLCANOES ON VENUS MIGHT LOOK LIKE THIS.

On Earth, volcanic eruptions are the result of tectonic plate activity below Earth's surface. Tectonic plates are giant slabs of rock that form Earth's crust; when they shift, they cause earthquakes and force molten rock aboveground. But scientists don't think Venus has multiple tectonic plates; its crust is likely one solid piece. How can scientists better understand these volcanic eruptions?

The European Space Agency's EnVision mission—launching in the early 2030s—will use radar to map the activity beneath Venus's surface. Scientists will study that data to learn what's fueling the planet's many eruptions.

OCEANS ON VENUS MIGHT HAVE LOOKED LIKE THIS.

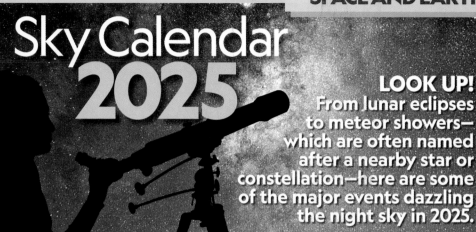

Sky Calendar 2025

LOOK UP!
From lunar eclipses to meteor showers—which are often named after a nearby star or constellation—here are some of the major events dazzling the night sky in 2025.

- **JANUARY 3–4**
QUADRANTID METEOR SHOWER PEAK. Featuring up to 40 meteors an hour, it is the first meteor shower of every new year.

- **MARCH 14**
TOTAL LUNAR ECLIPSE. Look for the moon to darken and then take on a deep red color as it passes completely through Earth's umbra—or dark shadow. It will be visible in North America, Central America, and South America.

- **MARCH 29**
PARTIAL SOLAR ECLIPSE. The moon will cover only part of the sun, creating a shape that looks like a cookie with a bite taken from it. It will be visible throughout Canada, Greenland, northern Europe, and northern Russia.

- **MAY 6–7**
ETA AQUARID METEOR SHOWER PEAK. View about 30 to 60 meteors an hour.

- **AUGUST 12–13**
PERSEID METEOR SHOWER PEAK. One of the best—see up to 60 meteors an hour! Best viewing is in the direction of the constellation Perseus.

- **SEPTEMBER 7**
TOTAL LUNAR ECLIPSE. The second total lunar eclipse of 2025 will be visible from Asia, Australia, and central and eastern Europe and Africa.

- **SEPTEMBER 21**
SATURN AT OPPOSITION. This is your best chance to view the ringed planet in 2025.

- **SEPTEMBER 23**
NEPTUNE AT OPPOSITION. Check out the giant blue planet, which will be visible through a telescope throughout the night as a tiny blue dot.

- **OCTOBER 7**
SUPERMOON, FULL MOON. The moon will be full and at a close approach to Earth, likely appearing bigger and brighter than usual. Look for two more supermoons on November 5 and December 4.

- **DECEMBER 7**
MERCURY AT GREATEST WESTERN ELONGATION. Look for the planet low in the eastern sky just before sunrise, as it will be in the highest point above the horizon.

- **DECEMBER 13–14**
GEMINID METEOR SHOWER PEAK. A spectacular show—see up to 120 multicolored meteors in an hour!

- **DECEMBER 21–22**
URSID METEOR SHOWER PEAK. Check out meteors shooting across the sky—most visible after midnight. Meteors appear around the constellation Ursa Minor.

- **2025–VARIOUS DATES**
VIEW THE INTERNATIONAL SPACE STATION (ISS). Parents and teachers: You can visit spotthestation.nasa.gov to find out when the ISS will be flying over your neighborhood.

Note: Dates may vary slightly depending on your location. Check with a local planetarium for the best viewing times in your area.

A LOOK INSIDE

The distance from Earth's surface to its center is about 3,950 miles (6,435 km) at the Equator. There are four layers: a thin, rigid crust; the rocky mantle; the outer core, which is a layer of molten iron and nickel; and finally the inner core, which is believed to be mostly solid iron and nickel.

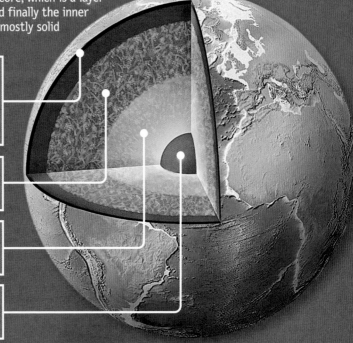

The **CRUST** includes tectonic plates, landmasses, and the ocean. Its average thickness varies from 5 to 25 miles (8 to 40 km).

The **MANTLE** is about 1,800 miles (2,900 km) of hot, thick, solid rock.

The **OUTER CORE** is liquid molten rock made mostly of iron and nickel.

The **INNER CORE** is a solid center made mostly of iron and nickel.

What if you could dig to the other side of Earth?

Got a magma-proof suit and a magical drill that can cut through any surface? Then you're ready to dig some 7,900 miles (12,714 km) to Earth's other side. First you'd need to drill up to 25 miles (40 km) through the planet's ultra-tough crust to its mantle. The heat and pressure at the mantle are intense enough to turn carbon into diamonds—and to, um, crush you. If you were able to survive, you'd still have to bore 1,800 more miles (2,897 km) to hit Earth's Mars-size core that can reach 11,000°F (6093°C). Now just keep drilling through the core and then the mantle and crust on the opposite side until you resurface on the planet's other side. But exit your tunnel fast. A hole dug through Earth would close quickly as surrounding rock filled in the empty space. The closing of the tunnel might cause small earthquakes, and your path home would definitely be blocked. Happy digging!

ROCK STARS

Rocks and minerals are everywhere on Earth! And it can be a challenge to tell one from the other. So what's the difference between a rock and a mineral? A rock is a naturally occurring solid object made mostly from minerals. Minerals are solid, nonliving substances that occur in nature—and the basic components of most rocks. Rocks can be made of just one mineral or, like granite, of many minerals. But not all rocks are made of minerals: Coal comes from plant material, while amber is formed from ancient tree resin.

Igneous

Named for the Greek word meaning "from fire," igneous rocks form when hot, molten liquid called magma cools. Pools of magma form deep underground and slowly work their way to Earth's surface. If they make it all the way, the liquid rock erupts and is called lava. As the layers of lava build up, they form a mountain called a volcano. Typical igneous rocks include obsidian, basalt, and pumice, which is so chock-full of gas bubbles that it actually floats in water.

ANDESITE

GRANITE PORPHYRY

Metamorphic

Metamorphic rocks are the masters of change! These rocks were once igneous or sedimentary, but thanks to intense heat and pressure deep within Earth, they have undergone a total transformation from their original form. These rocks never truly melt; instead, the heat twists and bends them until their shapes substantially change. Metamorphic rocks include slate as well as marble, which is used for buildings, monuments, and sculptures.

MICA SCHIST

BANDED GNEISS

Sedimentary

When wind, water, and ice constantly wear away and weather rocks, smaller pieces called sediment are left behind. These are sedimentary rocks, also known as gravel, sand, silt, and clay. As water flows downhill, it carries the sedimentary grains into lakes and oceans, where they are deposited. As the loose sediment piles up, the grains eventually get compacted or cemented back together again. The result is new sedimentary rock. Sandstone, gypsum, limestone, and shale are sedimentary rocks that are formed this way.

LIMESTONE

HALITE

Identifying Minerals

With so many different minerals in the world, how do we know what makes each one unique? Fortunately, each mineral has physical characteristics that geologists and amateur rock collectors use to tell them apart. Check out the physical characteristics below: color, luster, streak, cleavage, fracture, and hardness.

Color

When you look at a mineral, the first thing you see is its color. In some minerals, this is a key factor because their colors are almost always the same. For example, azurite (below) is always blue. But in other cases, impurities can change the natural color of a mineral. For instance, fluorite (above) can be green, red, violet, and other colors as well. This makes it a challenge to identify by color alone.

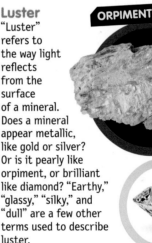

FLUORITE

AZURITE

Luster

"Luster" refers to the way light reflects from the surface of a mineral. Does a mineral appear metallic, like gold or silver? Or is it pearly like orpiment, or brilliant like diamond? "Earthy," "glassy," "silky," and "dull" are a few other terms used to describe luster.

ORPIMENT

DIAMOND

Streak

The streak is the color of a mineral's powder. When minerals are ground into powder, they often have a different color from when they are in crystal form. For example, the mineral pyrite usually looks gold, but when it is rubbed against a ceramic tile called a streak plate, the mark it leaves is black.

PYRITE

Cleavage

"Cleavage" describes the way a mineral breaks. Because the structure of a specific mineral is always the same, it tends to break in the same pattern. Not all minerals have cleavage, but the minerals that do, like this microcline, break evenly in one or more directions. These minerals are usually described as having "perfect cleavage." But if the break isn't smooth and clean, cleavage can be considered "good" or "poor."

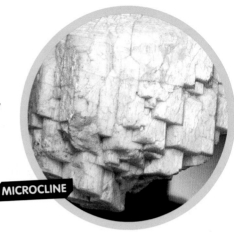

MICROCLINE

GOLD

Fracture

Some minerals, such as gold, do not break with cleavage. Instead, geologists say that they "fracture." There are different types of fractures, and, depending on the mineral, the fracture may be described as jagged, splintery, even, or uneven.

Hardness

The level of ease or difficulty with which a mineral can be scratched refers to its hardness. Hardness is measured using a special chart called the Mohs Hardness Scale. The Mohs scale goes from 1 to 10. Softer minerals, which appear on the lower end of the scale, can be scratched by the harder minerals on the upper end of the scale.

RATING	MINERAL NAME	EXAMPLES
1	TALC	BAR OF SOAP
2	GYPSUM	FINGERNAIL
3	CALCITE	COPPER PENNY
4	FLUORITE	SOFT IRON NAIL
5	APATITE	STEEL POCKETKNIFE BLADE
6	ORTHOCLASE	WINDOW GLASS
7	QUARTZ	HARDENED STEEL FILE
8	TOPAZ	TOPAZ
9	CORUNDUM	RUBY, SAPPHIRE
10	DIAMOND	DIAMOND

MOHS HARDNESS SCALE

A HOT TOPIC

WHAT GOES ON
INSIDE A STEAMING, BREWING VOLCANO?

If you could look inside a volcano, you'd see something that looks like a long pipe, called a conduit. This leads from inside the magma chamber under the crust up to a vent, or opening, at the top of the mountain. Some conduits have branches that shoot off to the side, called fissures.

When pressure builds from gases inside the volcano, the gases must find an escape, and they head up toward the surface! An eruption occurs when lava, gases, ash, and rocks explode out of the vent.

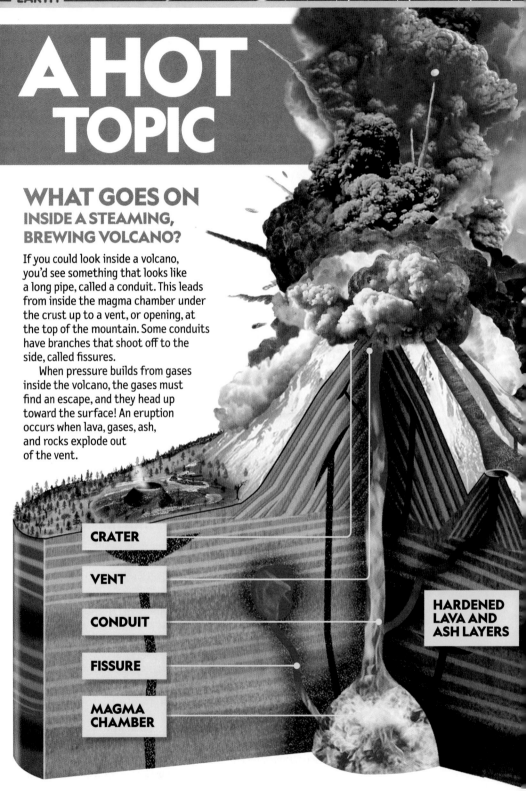

CRATER

VENT

CONDUIT

FISSURE

MAGMA CHAMBER

HARDENED LAVA AND ASH LAYERS

TYPES OF VOLCANOES

CINDER CONE VOLCANO
Eve Cone, Canada

Cinder cone volcanoes look like an upside-down bowl. They spew cinder and hot ash. Some of these volcanoes smoke and erupt for years at a time.

COMPOSITE VOLCANO
Licancábur, Chile

Composite volcanoes, or stratovolcanoes, form as lava, ash, and cinder from previous eruptions harden and build up over time. These volcanoes spit out pyroclastic flows, or thick explosions of hot ash and gas that travel at hundreds of miles an hour.

SHIELD VOLCANO
Mauna Loa, Hawaii, U.S.A.

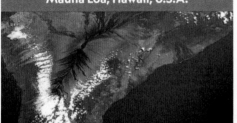

The gentle, broad slopes of a shield volcano look like an ancient warrior's shield. Its eruptions are often slower. Lava splatters and bubbles rather than shooting forcefully into the air.

LAVA DOME VOLCANO
Mount St. Helens, Washington, U.S.A.

Dome volcanoes have steep sides. Hardened lava often plugs the vent at the top of a dome volcano. Pressure builds beneath the surface until the top blows.

RING OF FIRE

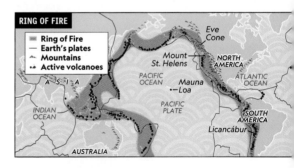

RING OF FIRE
- Ring of Fire
- Earth's plates
- Mountains
- Active volcanoes

Eve Cone

Mount St. Helens

NORTH AMERICA

A S I A

PACIFIC OCEAN

Mauna Loa

PACIFIC PLATE

ATLANTIC OCEAN

INDIAN OCEAN

SOUTH AMERICA

Licancábur

AUSTRALIA

Although volcanoes are found on every continent, most are located along an arc known as the Ring of Fire. This area, which forms a horseshoe shape in the Pacific Ocean, stretches some 24,900 miles (40,000 km). Several of the large, rigid plates that make up Earth's surface are found here, and they are prone to shifting toward each other and colliding. The result? Volcanic eruptions and earthquakes—and plenty of them. In fact, the Ring of Fire hosts 90 percent of the world's recorded earthquakes and about 75 percent of its active volcanoes.

SUPER-VOLCANOES

MAUNA LOA, IN HAWAII, IS THE LARGEST ACTIVE VOLCANO ON EARTH.

THE BIGGEST

How do you determine the size of a volcano? One way is to measure its height. In this category, Mauna Kea in Hawaii, U.S.A., is the clear winner. Its summit is 13,797 feet (4,205 m) above sea level. But if you measure it from where it actually begins, under the Pacific Ocean, it's almost three times as tall: 33,500 feet (10,211 m)! It's not only the world's tallest volcano, but the world's tallest mountain, too—taller even than Mount Everest in Nepal's Himalaya mountains, which is 29,032 feet (8,849 m) from bottom to top. Mauna Kea is still considered active, even though its last eruption

was about 4,500 years ago. That's because there's still magma beneath it, which means it likely won't stay asleep forever.

In terms of how much space it takes up on land—also known as the footprint—the world's biggest volcano is Tamu Massif, located about 1,000 miles (1,609 km) off the coast of Japan. This extinct, bowl-shaped shield volcano covers an area of more than 100,000 square miles (258,999 sq km), which is bigger than the entire state of New Mexico, U.S.A. That's roughly 50 times the size of the world's largest active volcano: Hawaii's Mauna Loa, which covers an area of just 2,000 square miles (5,180 sq km).

CASTLE GEYSER AT YELLOWSTONE NATIONAL PARK

ANAK KRAKATAU, "CHILD OF KRAKATAU," VOLCANO, INDONESIA

Scientists didn't discover Tamu Massif until 1993, and, at first, they mistakenly thought it was three separate volcanoes. That's because, believe it or not, Tamu Massif is not easy to see: It sits 6,500 feet (1,981 m) under the Pacific Ocean!

THE MOST POWERFUL

Yellowstone National Park—located in Wyoming, Montana, and Idaho—is the oldest national park in the United States. But it's also home to a supervolcano, a kind of volcano that's thousands of times more powerful than a regular volcano. Supervolcanoes aren't shaped like mountains—instead, they usually look like giant depressions in the ground. These depressions, called calderas, have huge magma chambers under Earth's crust. They form after an eruption, when the ground above the now semi-empty magma chamber collapses, creating a giant depression. Yellowstone is actually made up of three calderas, which were created after massive eruptions 2.1 million years ago, 1.3 million years ago, and 640,000 years ago. Thankfully, there's no evidence that magma is building up beneath Yellowstone's calderas, and scientists don't predict any eruptions in the near future.

Unfortunately, scientists in 1600 couldn't predict that a small Peruvian volcano called Huaynaputina would be responsible for the largest volcanic eruption in South America, and one of the largest eruptions on Earth. Before it blew, Huaynaputina caused four days of serious earthquakes. Once it erupted, it sent an ash plume almost 22 miles (35.5 km) into the sky. The eruption set off deafening thunder and 40 hours of darkness. By the time it was over, it had sent hot mud pouring into the ocean 75 miles (121 km) away.

More than 200 years later, on the island of Krakatau, in Indonesia, another huge eruption took place. In 1883, the Krakatau volcano produced a fast-moving, superhot surge of gas and rock that traveled across water to an island some 24 miles (38.6 km) away. The volcano's explosion could be heard almost 3,000 miles (4,828 km) away. Ash spewed from the volcano and traveled almost 3,800 miles (6,116 km). The eruption was so powerful that, within a year of the explosion, it caused temperatures to drop, and they didn't climb back to normal for another four years. Even now, Krakatau is experiencing small eruptions, getting ready for another big bang, but no one knows when it might erupt again.

1938 POSTER FOR YELLOWSTONE NATIONAL PARK

QUIZ WHIZ

Are your space and Earth smarts out of this world? Take this quiz!

Write your answers on a piece of paper. Then check them below.

1

True or false? Limestone is an example of igneous rock.

2 What is the name of the NASA mission that will explore whether Venus had oceans?

a. DAVINCI
b. EnVision
c. Mariner
d. VERITAS

3 How far would you have to dig through Earth to get to the other side?

a. 3,950 miles (6,357 km)
b. 7,900 miles (12,714 km)
c. 11,850 miles (19,071 km)
d. 15,800 miles (25,428 km)

4 Yellowstone National Park contains _____ calderas, which were created after massive volcanic eruptions.

a. one
b. two
c. three
d. four

5 Which term do scientists use to describe the color of a mineral's powder?

a. luster
b. streak
c. cleavage
d. fracture

Not **STUMPED** yet? Check out the
NATIONAL GEOGRAPHIC KIDS QUIZ WHIZ book collection
for more fun **SPACE AND EARTH** questions!

ANSWERS: 1. False: It is a sedimentary rock.; **2.** a; **3.** b; **4.** c; **5.** b

HOMEWORK HELP

ACE YOUR SCIENCE FAIR

You can learn a lot about science from books, but to really experience it firsthand, you need to get into the lab and "do" some science. Whether you're entering a science fair or just want to learn more on your own, there are many scientific projects you can do. So put on your goggles and lab coat, and start experimenting.

Most likely, the topic of the project will be up to you. So remember to choose something that is interesting to you.

THE BASIS OF ALL SCIENTIFIC INVESTIGATION AND DISCOVERY IS THE SCIENTIFIC METHOD. CONDUCT YOUR EXPERIMENT USING THESE STEPS:

Observation/Research—Ask a question or identify a problem.

Hypothesis—Once you've asked a question, do some thinking and come up with some possible answers.

Experimentation—How can you determine if your hypothesis is correct? You test it. You perform an experiment. Make sure the experiment you design will produce an answer to your question.

Analysis—Gather your results, and use a consistent process to carefully measure the results.

Conclusion—Do the results support your hypothesis?

Report Your Findings— Communicate your results in the form of a paper that summarizes your entire experiment.

Bonus!

Take your project one step further. Your school may have an annual science fair, but there are also local, state, regional, and national science fair competitions. Compete with other students for awards, prizes, and scholarships!

EXPERIMENT DESIGN
There are three types of experiments you can do.

MODEL KIT—a display, such as an erupting volcano model. Simple and to the point.

DEMONSTRATION—shows the scientific principles in action, such as a tornado in a wind tunnel.

INVESTIGATION—the home run of science projects, and just the type of project for science fairs. This kind demonstrates proper scientific experimentation and uses the scientific method to reveal answers to questions.

AWESOME
EXPLORATION

A wheelchair athlete leads a group of mountain bikers on a trail in Washington State, U.S.A.

Our Earth needs extra love, and here's how you can help! *National Geographic Kids* editor Allyson Shaw shares 10 tips for making an impact.

10 WAYS TO PROTECT THE PLANET

EAT MORE PLANTS.

"Cattle ranching is the top reason people cut down trees in the Amazon rainforest. By reducing the amount of meat we eat and swapping in other protein sources, we can potentially limit the demand and avoid losing so many trees."

SWITCH YOUR TP!

"Ask your parents to buy toilet paper made of sustainable bamboo, recycled content, or wheat straw. Why? Twenty-eight pounds (12.7 kg) per person gets flushed each year, and much of that comes from old-growth forests. You'll save trees by going sustainable."

WATCH WHAT YOU FLUSH.

"On the topic of flushing, make sure you're only putting human waste and toilet paper in the toilet. Things like medicine and pet waste don't get processed by wastewater treatments and go right back into our oceans. This can make sea animals sick."

ORGANIZE A FUNDRAISER.

"Find an eco-friendly cause close to your heart. Then, with your parents' permission, whip up something sweet to sell to your neighbors, with all proceeds going to a related organization."

VISIT YOUR LOCAL RECYCLING CENTER.

"By getting to see how it all works, you'll understand how to become a better recycler. You'll learn things that you'll remember forever about carefully recycling."

PLAN A NEIGHBORHOOD CLEANUP.

"Grab some gloves and a trash bag and pick up trash in your neighborhood. Not only does it make your surroundings cleaner, but you can prevent trash from winding up in the ocean—or worse, in a marine animal's mouth—if it lands in a sewer or a nearby waterway."

BUY LESS STUFF.

"Overconsumption is a huge global problem. It takes natural resources like oil to make new things, not to mention that people's junk winds up clogging landfills. Heading to a birthday party? Gift your friend with a membership to an accredited zoo or aquarium instead of buying a toy."

SAY NO TO EXPLOITING WILD ANIMALS.

"Wild animals living in roadside attractions or in people's homes are in distress. So discourage your parents and relatives from supporting people who keep these animals as pets, whether it's on social media or in a facility. These animals deserve to be in the wild or appropriate animal shelter."

LEAVE SHELLS ON THE BEACH.

"Scientists are discovering that shells are disappearing from shores around the world. They're important for beach ecosystems, as they become houses for hermit crabs, places for fish and octopuses to hide in the water, and attachment systems for seagrass and algae. Fragments of shells on the shoreline can also prevent erosion. If you find a pretty shell, take a picture and leave it."

VISIT LOCAL ZOOS AND AQUARIUMS.

"Just be sure they are accredited by the Association of Zoos and Aquariums, which gives money back to important causes that support animals. The Smithsonian's National Zoo in Washington, D.C., for example, was able to save golden lion tamarins from extinction through this type of funding. A list of accredited zoos can be found on aza.org."

SCIENCE BLOOPERS

EVEN NAT GEO EXPLORERS MAKE MISTAKES—AND LAUGH ABOUT THEM LATER.

JAIN MEASURES A YOUNG CANTOR'S GIANT SOFTSHELL TURTLE.

ABOVE, RACHUENE POINTS TO THE NEST OF AN AFRICAN GRASS OWL LIKE THE ONE AT RIGHT.

BEST NEST

THE SCIENTIST	Tselane Rebotile Rachuene
COOL JOB	Ecologist and conservationist
THE LOCATION	Highveld grasslands of South Africa

"I research and protect African grass owls—but they're tough to find because they nest on the ground. One time I was working in the field alone, walking in a zigzag pattern through the waist-high grass for hours. I clapped my hands and shouted so the mama owls would fly up and show me where their nests are. After a long and exhausting search of the area, I found nothing.

"A few weeks later, I returned with an assistant. This time we passed a rope through the grass, which safely and gently startles the birds. There—an owl! We found a nest just three feet (0.9 m) from where I'd searched before. (I keep careful records of where I've been.)

"Sometimes I go six months without finding a bird, which can feel like a failure. But it's always worth it to keep searching: These shy and rare birds deserve it."

RACHUENE KEEPS A YOUNG OWL CALM IN A BAG WHILE HE INSPECTS THE TAGS ON ITS LEGS.

WILD RIDE

THE SCIENTIST	Ayushi Jain
COOL JOB	Conservationist and Nat Geo Photo Ark EDGE Fellow
THE LOCATION	Chandragiri River, India

"Local people call me when they find a Cantor's giant softshell turtle in trouble. One time when I arrived, they'd placed the animal in a large water tank. I gently tipped the tank over so I could examine the turtle. But it immediately ran toward the river. (Unlike other turtles, softshell turtles—which can grow three feet [0.9 m] wide and weigh 220 pounds [100 kg]—can move *fast*.)

"I grabbed it, but the strong turtle just dragged me along behind it. Acting quickly, my colleague ran ahead and threw a piece of cloth over its head. Suddenly, the turtle stopped—and everyone burst out laughing.

"We examined the turtle, then released it into the river. I learned to have multiple assistants around to help control the animal so I don't have another wild turtle-back ride."

THIS THREE-FOOT (0.9-M) GRABBER HOLDS A BOTTLE TO HELP WALDMAN COLLECT SAMPLES.

SINKING FEELING

THE SCIENTIST Ariel Waldman
COOL JOB Microscopic wildlife filmmaker
THE LOCATION San Francisco Bay Area, California, U.S.A.

"I was gathering samples from salt ponds to look at the micro-algae and other extremophiles—organisms that live in this superharsh environment. But I'd lost my three-foot (0.9-m)-long grabber tool I use to scoop up water into a bottle without getting too close to the edge.

"I didn't want to go back, so I grabbed the bottle with my hand and stepped near the pond's edge and—*crunch.* My foot broke through a layer of solid-looking salty crust into a pool of goopy mud that clung to my leg like quicksand. I panicked, but luckily my partner was able to pull me out. Now I have an even longer grabber—one that's five feet (1.5 m) long—and I learned to never forget it again."

JEWELRY JUMBLE

THE SCIENTIST Nora Shawki
COOL JOB Archaeologist
THE LOCATION Tombos, Sudan

"I was digging down toward an ancient tomb, when we came upon the skeleton of a woman who was wearing a necklace. The jewelry was made of my favorite stone, lapis lazuli. I thought, This is incredible!

"I forgot all my training and excitedly reached down to pick up the necklace. But of course, over the past 3,000 years, the thread had disappeared. So all the tiny beads scattered into the shifting sand under my feet. I froze, then painstakingly picked up every last bead—all 43 of them—and placed them in a bag. I learned to be more patient and control my excitement: I need to check that everything is stable before handling artifacts."

BEAD

SHARK SPIN

THE SCIENTIST Aviad Scheinin
COOL JOB Marine conservationist
THE LOCATION Mediterranean Sea, Israel

"Once, my team caught a 10-foot (3-m)-long female dusky shark that we hoped to tag and study. But first we had to secure it to the side of the boat.

"You need one strong researcher to hold the dorsal fin, or back fin, while another ties special ropes around the tail and the pectoral fins on the sides. But the two workers weren't communicating well—and the shark could tell. While no one was holding the dorsal fin, the shark quickly rolled, which released the side fins' rope. We were left with just the tail rope.

"I knew we might hurt the shark if we kept it in this position. So I cut it free without taking samples or attaching a tag. This mistake was a reminder of how strong and agile these sharks are and how important it is to follow the rules: They keep everyone safe!"

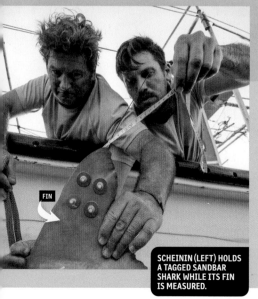

FIN

SCHEININ (LEFT) HOLDS A TAGGED SANDBAR SHARK WHILE ITS FIN IS MEASURED.

Critter Close-Ups

Nat Geo Explorer and photographer Joel Sartore travels to zoos, aquariums, and rescue centers around the world to snap pics of all 25,000 animal species living in captivity for his project: National Geographic Photo Ark. He works with the animals' keepers to make sure they're comfortable and safe—but things can get a little wild sometimes. Here are a few of Sartore's memorable moments.

Sartore uses plain black or white backgrounds in his pictures because he wants the focus to be on the animals and nothing else in his quest to save them from extinction.

NATIONAL GEOGRAPHIC
PHOTO ARK
JOEL SARTORE

Moment of CHILL
KEEL-BILLED TOUCAN

• Native to southern Mexico, Central America, and northern Colombia and Venezuela
• Tracy Aviary in Salt Lake City, Utah, U.S.A.

All toucans are cool. They're big birds—over a foot and a half (46 cm) long—so they don't have a lot to fear from other animals in the forest. And that meant they were also very mellow in my photo tent. With other species of animals, I often work with keepers and handlers to choose the right individual that would feel comfortable doing a photo shoot. But with toucans, I know it'll always be a good shoot. They just don't get rattled.

Flocks of keel-billed toucans roost together in tree trunks.

Moment of YUM
COQUEREL'S SIFAKA

• Native to Madagascar
• Houston Zoo in Houston, Texas, U.S.A.

These sifakas can leap 20 feet (6 m) in a single bound.

For this shoot, we set up a shelf for the sifaka—a type of lemur—high on a wall. They're arboreal animals [meaning they live mostly in trees], so we thought he'd feel more comfortable there.

"We spread peanut butter all over the wall to entice him to the spot. Of course, he jumped right up and rubbed the peanut butter on his hands and started licking it off.

"Once he was done, he sat and stared at me—I bet he was wondering if I had any more peanut butter.

How You Can Help

Moment of **SQUEE**
MALAYAN TAPIR

- *Native to Malaysia and Sumatra*
- *Minnesota Zoo in Apple Valley, Minnesota, U.S.A.*

" I came to this zoo to photograph another animal, but the staff insisted I also take a photo of their Malayan tapir calf.

"So they led the mom and six-day-old baby into my photo space. The baby stood calmly while the mom ate some leaves, just like they behave in the wild. Their coloring mimics the shadowy pattern of sunlight on the forest floor so they can hide in plain sight and eat without much fear. I'm so glad I got this shot. "

Servals use their big ears to help them hunt.

Moment of **OOPS**
SERVAL

- *Native to parts of northwest Africa and sub-Saharan Africa*
- *Lincoln Children's Zoo in Lincoln, Nebraska, U.S.A.*

" When I came to snap pics of Johnny the serval, I used a bright orange clip to hold the black backdrop in place against a metal bar. Johnny was really focused on that clip, not on me. Eventually, he just hopped up on top of the bar—bringing the whole thing crashing down, including the light stands I'd carefully set up. Johnny was fine, but it made a big mess. We set everything back up—without the orange clip—and got a great photo. "

SERVAL

Threatened by: Hunting and habitat loss

How you can help: Some people want a pet savannah cat—a cross between a serval and a domestic cat. But breeding servals takes them out of the wild, and their offspring don't make good pets.

MALAYAN TAPIR

Threatened by: Habitat destruction and hunting

How you can help: The tapir's habitat is cut down to create products made of wood. Cut back on your paper waste and recycle what you use to help preserve trees.

COQUEREL'S SIFAKA

Threatened by: Habitat loss and hunting

How you can help: Sifakas are losing their forest homes in Madagascar because the wood is sometimes used to make products. Ask your parents not to buy products made of rosewood and instead look for items that come from sustainably managed forests.

KEEL-BILLED TOUCAN

Threatened by: Climate change and disease

How you can help: Wild animals suffer when they're kept as pets. Never purchase an animal that should be in the wild, and ask your family not to like photos of them as pets or attractions on social media.

DARE TO EXPLORE

How three Nat Geo Explorers uncovered brand-new species.

THE **RAINFOREST TREKKER**

Pedro Peloso is a biologist who studies amphibians and reptiles. He describes taking a leap to discover a new frog species.

"I was in a canoe, paddling through the Pau-Rosa National Forest in Brazil at nighttime. I heard a familiar frog call and cruised to the riverbank to find the animal. It was high up in a tree hanging over the river, so I stepped on a tree branch and jumped up—*gotcha!*

"The branch broke, and I fell into the water. But I still had the frog in my hand. When I got a closer look, I realized this was not the species I expected to catch based on the call. Could it be something new? We knew we had to investigate.

"We compared its coloring, body shape, call, and even its DNA to other frogs. It took us seven years to figure it out. Finally, we officially named this new frog the mapinguari (mah-PIN-goo-ah-ree) clown tree frog after a mythical rainforest beast."

"Discovery comes to those who search for it. So start by going outside and seeing what's there."

WANT TO BE A RAINFOREST TREKKER?	
STUDY	Biology
WATCH	Nature and wildlife documentaries
READ	Any field guide about the animals near you

NEW LIZARD! *AGAMA WACHIRAI*

WACHIRA VIEWS A CROWNED EAGLE CHICK IN A FOREST IN NAIROBI, KENYA.

"When you're a scientist, you get excited about *everything*. Let it carry you away!"

THE **CURIOUS DISCOVERER**

Ecologist **Washington Wachira** is an expert on the birds of Kenya. He talks about finding an unknown species of lizard.

"I was in the desert helping to study larks. As I watched one of the birds through my binoculars, I spotted a basking lizard nearby. It had a pattern of spots I'd never seen before. I stopped to take some pictures, and soon I found more lizards with the same spots.

"A few days later, I emailed the photos to friends who specialize in reptiles, and together we studied it more. Once we knew for sure it was a new species, my teammates suggested naming it after me, *Agama wachirai*. It was the greatest honor of my career."

WANT TO BE A CURIOUS DISCOVERER?	
STUDY	Geography and biology
WATCH	WildEarth channel
READ	National Geographic's *Animal Encyclopedia*

NEW SPECIES! MAPINGUARI CLOWN TREE FROG

PELOSO (FRONT) AND TWO OTHER BIOLOGISTS CRUISE DOWN THE JAÚ RIVER IN BRAZIL.

These new species were also recently identified.

The **rose-veiled fairy wrasse** was discovered in the ocean waters near the Maldives and Sri Lanka.

Found in the mountains of western Mexico, this new species of spiny lizard is called *Sceloporus huichol.*

Uvariopsis dicaprio was named for actor Leonardo DiCaprio, who helped stop logging in the Ebo forest in Cameroon, where this tree was discovered.

Identified by a skull fossil in Argentina, this "new" dinosaur, *Guemesia ochoai,* lived more than 70 million years ago.

THE MUSEUM DETECTIVE

Silvia Pavan is a mammalogist who investigates how mammals are related. She explains how she found a new species hiding in a museum.

"I wanted to understand the family tree of short-tailed opossums—nobody had studied and organized their whole evolution before. So I gathered a lot of museum specimens and took small samples of the animals' skin, muscles, or hair to study their DNA. Then I carefully examined things like fur color and skull characteristics.

"**This work is all about solving mysteries, so never lose your curiosity.**"

"One day, I found an opossum with red fur on its head. It looked nothing like the other species of opossums from the part of Brazil where it had been found. I had a hunch it was an undescribed species—and the DNA confirmed it! We named the species after the saci (sah-SEE), a gnome from Brazilian folklore that wears a red cap and protects the forest. I also found three other new opossums!"

PAVAN STUDIES A SACI OPOSSUM SPECIMEN IN A LAB.

WANT TO BE A MUSEUM DETECTIVE?

STUDY	Mammalogy and biology
WATCH	*The Life of Mammals*
READ	*Ultimate Explorer Field Guide: Mammals* by Nat Geo Kids

PHOTO SECRETS REVEALED

HOW FOUR SNEAKY PHOTOGRAPHERS GOT THE SHOT

Wildlife photographers often use some tricky tactics to get amazing shots. Check out four incredible pictures—and hear straight from the photographers about how they used their own sneaky methods to get the pics.

SPOTTING JAGUARS

PHOTOGRAPHER: Steve Winter
ANIMAL: Jaguar
LOCATION: Brazil's Pantanal region

"Jaguars are big cats. But they're extremely good at hiding. I needed to set a trap—a camera trap—to get a photo of this juvenile.

"Camera traps take pictures when an animal steps into an invisible beam of light. The tricky part is figuring out where to put one. For help, I got advice from scientists who monitored jaguar movements with GPS collars.

"I set my camera trap on a large tree limb. Just three weeks later, this 10-month-old jaguar tripped the beam ... and even looked into the camera!"

BIRD HERD

PHOTOGRAPHER: Jay Fleming
ANIMAL: Great egret chicks
LOCATION: Chesapeake Bay, Maryland, U.S.A.

"Wading birds like egrets raise their chicks on small islands. I had to paddle about five miles (8 km) in a kayak and search very carefully for these birds' nest because the chicks' green skin helps them blend in with the grasses.

"These two-week-old chicks were only about a foot (30 cm) tall, so to photograph them at their level, I was lying all the way back in my kayak. I had to plant my foot in the mud to keep the kayak steady and set up my camera to take multiple shots with just one click."

SPLASHDOWN

PHOTOGRAPHER: Paul Nicklen
ANIMAL: Emperor penguins
LOCATION: Ross Sea, Antarctica

"Emperor penguins are not known for their climbing ability. They basically have to rocket out of the ocean to get back onto the sea ice. To do this, they dive deep and then swim upward at a sharp angle to accelerate. I really wanted to get a shot of a penguin launching out of the water.

"I spent six weeks with some penguins to figure out their favorite landing spots. Knowing that penguins can zoom up to six feet (1.8 m) in the air and land beyond the edge of the ice, I spread myself out on the ice where I had seen these birds appear and waited for an explosion of penguins, making sure not to block their path from the water. But I didn't get the picture I wanted. Finally, I figured out that I was too close to the water. I moved back and waited behind a block of ice. My new placement allowed me to capture this one as it landed, while another penguin catapulted into the air behind him."

FISH FACE

PHOTOGRAPHER: Birgitte Wilms
ANIMAL: Clownfish
LOCATION: Off the coast of Papua New Guinea

"Clownfish are quick. They constantly dart back and forth across their home, which is actually another animal called an anemone. In return for a safe place to live, clownfish defend the anemone from predatory fish by biting or aggressively swimming toward any intruders ... including photographers like me.

"All the clownfish I tried to photograph before this one were too fast. My pictures were a split second too late, catching only a tail or no fish at all. So I had to use some tricks. I quietly steadied myself on the bottom so the ocean current wouldn't push me away, and patiently waited—clownfish get defensive if you approach their home. Then I focused my camera on where I thought the fish would appear and waited for it to come out in search of food. Getting a shot with eye contact was a moment of joy!"

WILD VET ADVENTURE
WITH ONE WILDLIFE DOCTOR

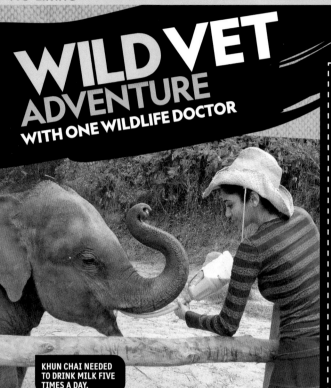

KHUN CHAI NEEDED TO DRINK MILK FIVE TIMES A DAY.

Animals can't tell their doctors when they aren't feeling well. So that makes the job of a wildlife veterinarian a little ... well, wild. Meet Gabby Wild, who travels the world to provide medical care for animals in zoos, shelters, national parks, and rescue centers. Here, the wildlife vet tells you how she treated one animal in need of a little medicine—and a lot of care.

ELEPHANT CALF GETS SOME TLC

"In Thailand, a country in Southeast Asia, people sometimes use elephants as work animals to help on their farms. One farmer illegally stole an elephant calf from the forest, which he thought would be cheaper than buying an adult elephant. But soon the calf was close to dying. The farmer realized the young elephant needed medical help.

"He brought the youngster to a wildlife hospital where I was working, and we named the calf Khun Chai, which means 'prince' in Thai. We observed that he didn't want to play with the other elephants and refused to drink the milk we offered him.

"I had studied some elephant behavior, and I thought that maybe he just didn't want to be bothered. So when I went into his enclosure, I sat quietly on the ground and only looked at him out of the corner of my eye. About a half hour later, I could feel a light tap on my shoulder—Khun Chai was patting me with his trunk!

"From that moment on, Khun Chai followed me all around the rescue center. I fed him milk five times a day, walked him three times a day, and bathed him a few times a week. As he ate and gained weight, he became a healthy elephant.

"We decided that because people had raised Khun Chai, it would be dangerous to release him back into the forest. So eventually we moved him to a local conservation center where he could live with other elephants. I'm glad I could help him grow up to be healthy and happy."

A male Asian elephant usually lives with its mother for about five years.

Bet You Didn't Know!

7 weird facts about jobs

1 Some people work as professional **roller-coaster testers.**

2 Human **dog-food tasters** are paid to **sample** and evaluate pet food products.

3 In the mid-1800s, England's Queen Victoria employed **a royal rat catcher.**

4 **Snake milkers** collect **venom** for making **medicine** and snakebite antidotes.

5 It takes about **45 minutes** for an astronaut to put on a **space suit.**

6 **A dog** named Brynn was elected the **mayor** of Rabbit Hash, Kentucky, U.S.A.

7 Former U.S. president **Barack Obama's** first job was **scooping ice cream.**

121

CREW MEMBERS AND THEIR SLED DOGS STAND ON PACK ICE THAT TRAPPED THE *ENDURANCE* IN THE WEDDELL SEA.

TRAPPED IN ICE!

HOW EXPLORERS FOUND THIS MISSING SHIP 100 YEARS AFTER IT SANK

The sailors couldn't stop shivering. It was November 21, 1915, and they were stranded on sea ice off the coast of Antarctica. In the distance, they could see their abandoned ship, named *Endurance*, stuck in the ice and flooding with seawater.

Suddenly, the crew heard the ship's wood groan and crack. The ice forced itself against the vessel, then quickly retreated. The ship "then gave one quick dive and the ice closed over her forever," wrote the expedition leader, Ernest Shackleton. For the next 106 years, *Endurance* would remain lost 10,000 feet (3,048 m) beneath the sea.

ADVENTURE GONE WRONG

Shackleton and 27 crew members set out in 1914 to try to cross Antarctica by land—but they had to sail there first. The 144-foot (44-m)-long ship was specially built for the chilly polar waters, with extra-thick wood planks to keep the dangerous pack ice floating in the ocean from damaging the ship.

But just three months after setting sail from Buenos Aires, Argentina, the boat became stuck in pack ice too thick to sail through. The worthy vessel held up for nine months as the ice pushed it north. But in October, the pressure from the ice buckled the planks, and water slowly

ERNEST SHACKLETON

ICE FORCED *ENDURANCE* ONTO ITS SIDE.

UNDERWATER CAMERAS TOOK THESE IMAGES OF THE SUNKEN SHIP.

THE SHIP'S NAME

poured in. On October 27, Shackleton ordered his crew to gather their equipment and supplies and abandon the ship, pitching tents on the ice about a mile and a half (2.4 km) away. A few weeks later, they watched *Endurance* sink beneath the Weddell Sea.

LONG JOURNEY HOME

At first, the crew tried to drag their lifeboats over the ice, but the snowy and icy terrain was too difficult to cross on foot. So the group camped out on the pack ice as it drifted north. The crew survived the next five months by living off penguins, seals, and seaweed.

Finally, the ice broke up enough to allow the crew to sail in the lifeboats. For seven days, they sailed more than a hundred miles (161 km) till they arrived at the uninhabited Elephant Island. But the crew couldn't survive there for long. So with five crew members, Shackleton made a dangerous attempt to get help: They sailed 800 miles (1,287 km) over 16 days across freezing, stormy seas to South Georgia Island. Once they arrived, the six men hiked for 36 hours across the island to reach a whaling station. They were dirty, cold, and exhausted—but alive.

With a new ship, Shackleton returned to the uninhabited island to rescue the rest of his crew. All 28 people survived the ordeal. But the *Endurance* remained lost under the sea.

LOST SHIP FOUND

Ocean archaeologist Mensun Bound grew up on the Falkland Islands, not far from the Weddell Sea. Inspired by the adventurers, he was determined to find the lost ship.

In 2019, Bound and his team tried unsuccessfully to find the ship. They set out again in February 2022 and—just like the *Endurance*—got stuck in pack ice. Luckily, the tide rose a few hours later, and the explorers could sail on.

Bound carefully reviewed the original sailors' records to choose the search area. The team scanned 107 square miles (277 sq km) of the seafloor with remote-controlled underwater cameras for more than three weeks. With only three days before the ship had to be back in port, drifting sea ice forced Bound to search elsewhere.

On March 5, 2022, the cameras revealed exciting images: broken masts, ropes, a crewman's boot, and the ship's bell. The next day, nearly two miles (3.2 km) below the surface, the explorers saw the ship's name in brass letters on the stern, or back. They had found the lost *Endurance*. "You see that, and your eyes pop out," Bound says. "It felt like I was tumbling back in time. I could feel the breath of Shackleton on my neck."

The *Endurance* is now a protected historic site, which means that people need a permit to study or film it; even then, explorers can't touch it. A team of experts is working on a conservation plan to protect the ship from looters as well as the effects of a warming ocean due to climate change. For now, the *Endurance* remains safe beneath the sea.

ME-OLOGY
THE STUDY OF ME!

Lee Berger, Ph.D., D.Sc., is a National Geographic Explorer in Residence, a Senior Carnegie Science Fellow, and director of the Centre for the Exploration of the Deep Human Journey at the University of the Witwatersrand in Johannesburg, South Africa. He is an award-winning paleoanthropologist whose explorations into human origins in Africa over the past 25 years have resulted in the discovery of more hominin fossil remains than any other person in the field.

What is a paleoanthropologist?

A paleoanthropologist is a scientist who studies the history of life on Earth through fossils. Specifically, we examine human remains to find out more about the origins of the human species.

When did you decide this is what you wanted to be, and how did you go about it?

Growing up in rural Georgia, U.S.A., I didn't really know I could make paleoanthropology a career. I took classes in geology and archaeology in college and later found paleoanthropology by working with a famous scientist on a research project in Africa. There, I found my first hominid fragment—a tiny fragment of a limb bone—and was hooked.

What are some of the challenges of your work either in the field or in the lab?

We have to search far and wide for early human fossils, and some of the spaces are very hard to reach. In particular, the chambers leading to Rising Star cave in South Africa— where I made my biggest discovery to date—are incredibly tight and extremely dangerous to access. At first, I found smaller-size, very experienced cavers and explorers who could get in there, and I had to conduct the expedition from above ground. Eventually, I lost weight and was able to access the cave myself, but it was an extreme journey. I risked my life.

Can you tell us about one of your favorite or most rewarding experiences?

Despite the scary aspect of my journey into Rising Star cave, once I was there, I was blown away by what I saw: evidence of the use of fire and primitive art carved into the cave walls that told us more about this early human species. I spent over four hours in the cave, documenting it all. It was incredible.

Are there essential tools that you need while exploring in the field?

Most paleoanthropologists have a similar field kit. It includes chisels (to extract fossils from stone), a rock hammer (to break off pieces of rocks for testing or while searching for fossils), brushes (to help brush away debris and dust and reveal), and maybe some other tools like a screwdriver. We also use cameras and voice recorders to document what we see in the caves that can't be removed.

Why is it important to learn about early humans?

Early humans are still like aliens to us. They're so complex, and they may have evolved so much earlier than we previously thought. By taking what we've found in Rising Star cave and using high-tech testing and forensics on the fossils, we can add more pieces to the puzzle of the origins of our human species.

THIS YEAR'S CHALLENGE

It's amazing what we can learn about people from the objects they use in daily life and the ways that they interact with their surroundings. Carvings on cave walls, evidence of the use of fire, and indications of burial helped Dr. Berger learn more about early hominins. Turn to page 24 for more details on his groundbreaking discoveries.

Imagine that a thousand years from now a scientist discovers your house. Gather five items that you think will help the scientist learn about YOU. Think about your favorite toys, books, or games; hobbies or sports; foods or clothing; household items you use every day; or anything that tells your story.

Ask a parent or guardian to take a photo of your collection and email it, along with the completed entry form, to: almanac2025@natgeo.com

Get details and the official rules at **natgeokids.com/almanac.**

LAST YEAR'S CHALLENGE

In our *Elephant-stagram Challenge,* we asked you to think about the power of social media as a communication tool and a way to raise awareness about things people believe are important. The catch was that you had to write a profile and posts from the perspective of an elephant to help bring attention to their endangered status. You totally trumpeted your response!

• Your entries came from 27 states and Washington, D.C., with the most from California, Florida, and Texas. We even received entries from four Canadian provinces.

• Most of you created profile pages for African elephants (62 percent) and Asian elephants (17 percent), but 21 percent of you didn't name a species.

This year's **Grand Prize Winner Bianca Morelli Grandi** (age 11) even included information and posts from an extinct elephant "cousin," the mammoth. Her entry featured four threats facing elephants and included other facts about their lives.

Congratulations to Bianca and to everyone who entered. Thanks for your creativity and for caring about elephants!

See more entries online at **natgeokids.com/almanac.**

QUIZ WHIZ

Discover just how much you know about exploration with this quiz!

Write your answers on a piece of paper. Then check them below.

1 How does Nat Geo Explorer Joel Sartore work to save species from extinction?

a. studying animals' habitats
b. planting trees in forests
c. photographing animals in zoos
d. teaching conservation classes

2 **True or false?** Switching to toilet paper made from bamboo can help protect old-growth forests.

3 How long does it take an astronaut to put on a space suit?

a. 45 seconds
b. 4.5 minutes
c. 45 minutes
d. 4.5 hours

4 The rose-veiled fairy wrasse was recently discovered near which country?

a. the Bahamas
b. Maldives
c. Madagascar
d. New Zealand

5 What's the name of the now sunken ship once sailed by Ernest Shackleton and his crew?

a. *Endurance*
b. *Fortitude*
c. *Perseverance*
d. *Stamina*

Not **STUMPED** yet? Check out the *NATIONAL GEOGRAPHIC KIDS QUIZ WHIZ* collection for more fun **EXPLORATION** questions!

ANSWERS: 1. c; 2. True; 3. c; 4. b; 5. a

HOMEWORK HELP

How to Write a Perfect Essay

Need to write an essay? Does the assignment feel as big as climbing Mount Everest? Fear not. You're up to the challenge! The following step-by-step tips will help you with this monumental task.

1 **BRAINSTORM.** Sometimes the subject matter of your essay is assigned to you; sometimes it's not. Either way, you have to decide what you want to say. Start by brainstorming some ideas, writing down any thoughts you have about the subject. Then read over everything you've come up with and consider which idea you think is the strongest. Ask yourself what you want to write about the most. Keep in mind the goal of your essay. Can you achieve the goal of the assignment with this topic? If so, you're good to go.

2 **WRITE A TOPIC SENTENCE.** This is the main idea of your essay, a statement of your thoughts on the subject. Again, consider the goal of your essay. Think of the topic sentence as an introduction that tells your readers what the rest of your essay will be about.

3 **OUTLINE YOUR IDEAS.** Once you have a good topic sentence, you then need to support that main idea with more detailed information, facts, thoughts, and examples. These supporting points answer one question about your topic sentence—"Why?" This is where research and perhaps more brainstorming come in. Then organize these points in the way you think makes the most sense, probably in order of importance. Now you have an outline for your essay.

4 **ON YOUR MARK, GET SET, WRITE!** Follow your outline, using each of your supporting points as the topic sentence of its own paragraph. Use descriptive words to get your ideas across to readers. Go into detail, using specific information to tell your story or make your point. Stay on track, making sure that everything you include is somehow related to the main idea of your essay. Use transitions to make your writing flow.

5 **WRAP IT UP.** Finish your essay with a conclusion that summarizes your entire essay and restates your main idea.

6 **PROOFREAD AND REVISE.** Check for errors in spelling, capitalization, punctuation, and grammar. Look for ways to make your writing clear, understandable, and interesting. Use descriptive verbs, adjectives, and adverbs when possible. It also helps to have someone else read your work to point out things you might have missed. Then make the necessary corrections and changes in a second draft. Repeat this revision process once more to make your final draft as good as you can.

FUN and GAMES

An excited Labrador retriever pup plays fetch with a tennis ball in a backyard.

SHIVERING SHAPES

A winter wind has given these photos of cold-weather animals a frosty twist. Look at each photo and the clues. On a separate sheet of paper, unscramble the letters to identify what's in each picture.

ANSWERS ON PAGE 354

1

HWAANLRS

CLUE: If the mythical unicorn lived in the sea, it might look a little like these mammals swimming through northern waters.

2

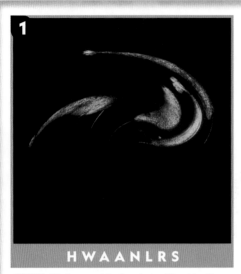

TACNLITA FUPFNI

CLUE: Its beak may look a little clownish, but this North Atlantic bird is all business when it comes to raising its chicks on sea cliffs.

3

LYORA INEUNGP

CLUE: Emperors and kings live nearby, but this flightless bird from Antarctica wears the yellow-feathered crown.

4

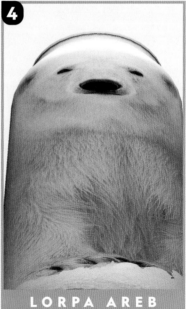

LORPA AREB

CLUE: This Arctic marine mammal chills out on the ice and snow as it waits to seal the dinner deal.

CRITTER CHAT

If animals used social media, what would they say? Follow this striped skunk's night as it updates its feed.

WHO TOOTED?

STRIPED SKUNK

LIVES IN: Most of North America
SCREEN NAME: Stinker
FRIENDS: ⌵

SPOTTED SALAMANDER
SoftSpot

STAR-NOSED MOLE
FingerFace

GREAT HORNED OWL
ImAHoot

START

6:00 p.m.

Stinker: Tonight I'm teaching my kits how to be skunks. First lesson: Finding grasshoppers. #SkunkSchool

ImAHoot: My chicks are about to leave the nest. Those 10 weeks *flew* by!

SoftSpot: I remember when I laid my own 200 eggs in the pond where I hatched. Hmm ... I haven't seen 'em since.

FingerFace: I sniffed one on a swim! It's a larva now, with gills and a tail.

ImAHoot: How did you smell it *underwater*?

FingerFace: I just blew out bubbles, held them with my nose-fingers, then inhaled the smelly bubbles again. (What, like it's hard?)

8:00 p.m.

Stinker: Yikes—is that rustling a red fox? Or a badger? You better stay back. My stinky spray will make you sick!

FingerFace: Uh-oh, I'm going to cover my nostrils now—and hide underground!

SoftSpot: Smart move, @Stinker. I'll release the killer milky toxin from my tail and back just in case. #IAmNotFood

ImAHoot: Let's not overreact—I don't see any foxes here! (Plus, I haven't eaten today, and you all look so yummy.)

5:30 a.m.

Stinker: Time to tuck the kits into the ole hollowed log.

SoftSpot: I'm glad I'm too old to be told when to go to bed. I'm almost 30!

ImAHoot: And I'm 28. But it's still my bedtime. Good night—er, day.

FingerFace: It might be daytime, but y'all can still wish upon a star!

Stinker: If you're talking about your nose again ...

WHAT IN THE WORLD?

SPOTTED IN NATURE

These photographs show close-up views of things with spots. On a separate sheet of paper, unscramble the letters to identify what's in each picture.

ANSWERS ON PAGE 354

FHSI

IDBR GSEG

ETHHEAC

EDRE

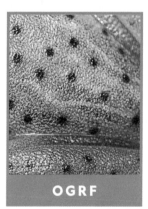
OGRF

HOMRSMOU

TELEBE

IYLL

QDSIU

FUNNY FILL-IN

DINING WITH DINOSAURS

Ask a friend to give you words to fill in the blanks in this story and write them on a separate sheet of paper. Then read the story out loud and fill in the words for a laugh.

Having dinner with dinosaurs is a really *big* deal. _____ and I were invited to eat at
(friend's name)

the home of a(n) _____ named _____ with her two dinosaur friends.
(type of dinosaur) (female celebrity)

She's much bigger than a(n) _____ and a better cook, too. Dinner was a heaping
(mythical creature)

portion of barbecued _____ with a side of steamed _____ .
(something gross, plural) (type of seafood, plural)

We sat atop the chef's pet, a(n) _____ . I started to take a bite of my meal, but a(n)
(animal)

_____ _____ suddenly _____ across the table! Surprised,
(color) (same type of seafood) (past-tense verb)

I jumped back from the food, _____ _____ everywhere. " _____ !"
(verb ending in -ing) (liquid) (silly expression)

roared the chef as she dropped the _____ she was holding. Barbecue sauce splashed
(noun)

everywhere—including on the pet. I think I'll skip dessert.

133

FIND THE HIDDEN ANIMALS

Animals often blend in with their environment to hide. Find each animal listed below in one of the pictures. On a separate sheet of paper, write the letter of the correct picture and the animal's name.

ANSWERS ON PAGE 354

1. spider crab
2. monkey grasshopper
3. Indian grass mantis
4. echo parakeets
5. yellow-footed tortoise

A

B

C

D

E

CRITTER CHAT

TAIL ME ABOUT IT!

If animals used social media, what would they say? Follow this silky anteater's day as it updates its feed.

SILKY ANTEATER

LIVES IN: Forests from southern Mexico to South America
SCREEN NAME: AntsBeware
FRIENDS: ⌄

HARPY EAGLE	**OCELOT**	**GREEN ANACONDA**
FeatherCrown	TreeCat	BigSnake

START

7:00 p.m.

AntsBeware
> #WhoWoreItBetter: Me or the fluffy seed pods of the kapok tree?

> You know I'm bad at this game—it's why I can't ever find you!

FeatherCrown

> Great camo, @AntsBeware—gotta stay hidden from @FeatherCrown. #ThatBirdIsTooBig #6FootWingspan

TreeCat

> Good thing I don't only *look* for prey—I also smell and feel their body heat.

BigSnake

AntsBeware
> I know **@BigSnake** spends most of his time in the water ... I wish he'd stay there forever.

10:00 p.m.

AntsBeware
> Cute alert! My mate just picked up our baby from its tree-hole nest.

TreeCat

> Non-cute alert: Pretty soon you'll puke up some half-digested insects for its dinner.

BigSnake

> You *both* raise your baby? Mama anacondas sometimes eat the dads.

> Scary! My partner and I are bonded for life. We even "kiss" by rubbing our bills.
FeatherCrown

> Mates are overrated. I raised my kitten just fine on my own.
TreeCat

6:00 a.m.

AntsBeware
> I'll give a prize to whoever guesses how many ants I slurped up last night.

> One really big ant? I only swallow one meal a month: a caiman, tapir, or ocelot.

BigSnake

> Don't forget I'm a predator, too. @AntsBeware, I'll guess "a few." That's how many critters I eat a night.

TreeCat

AntsBeware
> You're both way off—try 8,000!

> My raised head feathers = I'm shocked! But what was the prize?

FeatherCrown

AntsBeware
> What else? Ants!

FROM THE PAGES OF *QUIZ WHIZ:*

STUMP
YOUR PARENTS

Answer the questions on a separate sheet of paper. If your parents can't answer these questions, maybe they should go to school instead of you!

ANSWERS ON PAGE 354

1 How long is the Ultra-Trail du Mont-Blanc race through France, Switzerland, and Italy in the Alps mountain range?

THE ALPS IN ITALY

A. 20 miles (32 km)
C. 106 miles (170 km)
B. 55 miles (89 km)
D. 176 miles (283 km)

2 Bigger than a 12-story building, the world's tallest snowperson was constructed where?

A. Winnipeg, Canada
B. Santiago, Chile
C. Bethel, Maine, U.S.A.
D. Antarctica

3 What natural element inspired a Swiss engineer to invent Velcro?

A. wasp exoskeletons
B. spiky seed pods
C. loopy moss
D. pineapple skins

4 What did many ankylosaurs have at the end of their tails?

A. a barb   C. feathers
B. a club   D. wings

5 What does the word "dachshund" mean in German, the language spoken in this dog breed's native country?

A. badger dog
B. sea dog
C. shrimpy
D. hot dog

6 At birth, a koala is about the size of an adult _____ .

A. bee   C. rat
B. tarantula   D. sloth

7 Found in southern African deserts, green blob-like formations known as living stones are actually _____ .

A. plants
B. snails
C. mushrooms
D. zebra poo

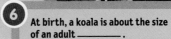

8 According to the lunar calendar used by many Asian cultures, the year 2025 is the year of which animal?

A. tiger   C. dragon
B. rabbit   D. snake

9 Which artist painted views of the water lilies in the gardens of Giverny, France?

A. Pablo Picasso
B. Jackson Pollock
C. Claude Monet
D. Georgia O'Keeffe

10 What does a walrus do to survive in icy Arctic waters?

A. It swims faster.
B. It wraps itself in seaweed.
C. It slows its heartbeat.
D. It wears a sweater.

SIGNS OF THE TIMES

Seeing isn't always believing. Two of these funny signs are not real. Can you spot which two are fake?

ANSWERS ON PAGE 354

NEXT BIG THING 1000 m

1

Lost

2

THIS WAY OTHER WAY THAT WAY

3

MULE PARKING ONLY NO MOTORIZED VEHICLES ALLOWED

4

WHEN NOTHING GOES RIGHT GO LEFT

5

LOW FLYING UFO

6

7

WHAT IN THE WORLD?

HEART-TO-HEART

These photographs show close-up and faraway views of heart-shaped things. On a separate sheet of paper, unscramble the letters to identify what's in each picture. **ANSWERS ON PAGE 354**

LUODC

OPER

FALE

LFWEOR

SDILNAS

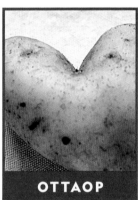

OTTAOP

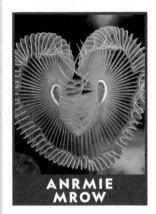

ANRMIE MROW

VIOALRI

OROD AHLEDN

FUNNY FILL-IN

WILD RIDE

Ask a friend to give you words to fill in the blanks in this story and write them on a separate sheet of paper. Then read the story out loud and fill in the words for a laugh.

My friends and I were waiting to ride the _____ at the amusement park. But when we got
(noun, plural)

to the front of the line, a park employee asked us if we would like to test a(n) _____ new
(adjective)

ride instead. As we climbed into a(n) _____-shaped car, another park employee said, "Welcome
(noun)

to the _____ _____ , the world's _____ roller coaster!"
(verb ending in –ing) _(noun)_ _(adjective ending in –est)_

Our car suddenly _____ . Then the car shot up _____ feet—we were so high,
(past-tense verb) _(large number)_

I thought I could touch the _____ . The people below looked like _____ .
(something in the sky, plural) _(animal, plural)_

Next we did a barrel roll over the _____ teacups and flew over the _____
(verb ending in –ing) _(mythical creature)_

waterslide. Finally, our car _____ _____ backward as fast as a(n) _____
(adverb ending in –ly) _(past-tense verb)_ _(noun)_

before coming to a stop where we started. What a hair-_____ experience!
(verb ending in –ing)

My _____ felt a little _____ , but I still went on the ride again—twice.
(body part) _(adjective)_

THE SWOOPING SPACESHIP

139

KEEP IT COOL.

CRITTER CHAT

If animals used social media, what would they say? Follow this wolverine's day as it updates its feed.

WOLVERINE

LIVES IN: Northern North America and Eurasia
SCREEN NAME: WolfyWeasel
FRIENDS: ⌄

GYRFALCON	CARIBOU	ARCTIC GROUND SQUIRREL
FierceFlier	BouWho	ColdRodent

START

8:00 a.m.

 WolfyWeasel
A grizzly bear 🐻 just took down a moose. Should I try to steal a piece of the meal? #DareMe

 FierceFlier
You're only, like, 30 pounds (13 kg). Take my advice and chase small mammals. 🐭

 BouWho
I'd stay away from grizzlies if I were you. That's what I tell my calf. #BewareTheBear

 ColdRodent
If it'll keep you from sniffing me out in my burrow, go for it. ✖

8:30 a.m.

 WolfyWeasel
I bit the bear on the butt, distracting it long enough to swipe a chunk. #WhatAThrill

---

  BouWho
You're wild. My biggest excitement? A dip in the river.

 ColdRodent
Pipe down—I'm trying to get my seven months of sleep, and I'm grumpy when I haven't eaten. #SleepsInsteadOfEats

 FierceFlier
Yeah @ColdRodent, aren't you supposed to be sleeping *right now*?

 ColdRodent
Yes! I sleep super deeply all winter by cooling my body temp. I shiver to warm up a bit every few weeks, but you woke me! #SnoozySelfie

4:00 p.m.

 WolfyWeasel
I'm on top of the world! #MountainClimber #NeverSitStill

GOING UP! ICE WALL

 FierceFlier
Whoa, how'd you get up there? I build my nest on sheer cliffs, but I can fly.

 BouWho
It's those long claws! My herd walks hundreds of miles each year, but our hooves can't get up that icy wall.

 ColdRodent
You aren't full and sleepy after that moose? 😴

  WolfyWeasel
My territory's more than 500 square miles (808 square km)—I've got places to be!

140

WHAT IN THE WORLD?

SCHOOL DAZE

These photographs show close-up views of things at school. On a separate sheet of paper, unscramble the letters to identify what's in each picture. **ANSWERS ON PAGE 354**

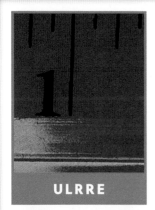

ULRRE

RAETW NIFONTUA

RSREAE

NLALOPBIT EPN

LOHCSO USB

NTAOBNMIIOC CLKO

IRSCSOSS

CCPAAKKB

NLEPCI NPSHEERRA

STUMP
YOUR PARENTS

Answer the questions on a separate sheet of paper. If your parents can't answer these questions, maybe they should go to school instead of you!

ANSWERS ON PAGE 354

DO I HAVE SOMETHING IN MY TEETH?

GIANT PANDAS CAN EAT MORE THAN 80 POUNDS (36 KG) OF BAMBOO A DAY.

1 What's the name of the nearly 25,000-mile (40,234-km) horseshoe-shaped belt of volcanoes in an area of the Pacific Ocean?
A. Ring of Fire
B. Pacific Flames
C. Rim of the Inferno
D. Blaze Belt

2 More than 1,400 types of _____ live in people's belly buttons.
A. bacteria
B. fungus
C. microscopic bugs
D. dust bunnies

3 Shish kebab, a type of barbecue whose name means "roast meat on a skewer," comes from which country?
A. China
B. India
C. Türkiye (Turkey)
D. Germany

4 The term "pachyderm" can refer to elephants. What does it mean?
A. large ears
B. thick skin
C. padded feet
D. four-legged

5 Which country lies on the Equator?
A. Australia
B. Brazil
C. Japan
D. Spain

6 How do giant pandas scare off their enemies?
A. They bare their teeth.
B. They roar, huff, and snort.
C. They wave their paws.
D. all of the above

7 Which of the following animals is the wombat's closest relative?
A. flying squirrel
B. koala
C. honey badger
D. lemur

8 How many days does it take for the moon to complete its orbit around Earth?
A. 7.5
B. 27.3
C. 62.7
D. 365.2

9 Which famous person was Yoda from the *Star Wars* movies designed to look like?
A. Richard Nixon
B. Babe Ruth
C. Albert Einstein
D. a mix of all four Beatles

10 Which country presented the Statue of Liberty to the United States?
A. Cuba
B. Belize
C. Ireland
D. France

FUNNY FILL-IN

ALIEN INVASION

Ask a friend to give you words to fill in the blanks in this story and write them on a separate sheet of paper. Then read the story out loud and fill in the words for a laugh.

Halloween was finally here. I dressed as a(n) _____ hero with a(n) _____ _____ .
                                              adjective   adjective   article of clothing

_____ went as _____ , Queen of the _____ . We met up with our two
friend's name   famous female   body of water

friends, who were dressed as _____ . They had _____ on their heads and had
                              mythical creature, plural   noun, plural

_____ their bodies _____ . Plus, both of them had _____ _____ and had
past-tense verb   color   large number   body part, plural

constructed a(n) _____-looking _____ . " _____ ," the pair said—they had even
                 adjective   type of transportation   nonsense word

made up a new language to go with their _____ ! Then they gave us a tour of their _____ .
                                        noun, plural   noun

But when we _____ the vehicle, we were shocked to see our friends down the street.
            past-tense verb

They were dressed as _____ , only with much simpler costumes. " _____ !"
                     same mythical creature, plural   exclamation

we said. If these were our friends, who gave us the tour? We _____ looked behind us,
                                                            adverb ending in –ly

but the creatures were gone. Suddenly something _____ above us. Guess you could say
                                                past-tense verb

Halloween was out of this world.

FIND THE HIDDEN ANIMALS

Animals often blend in with their environment to hide. Find each animal listed below in one of the pictures. On a separate sheet of paper, write the letter of the correct picture and the number of the animal's name.

ANSWERS ON PAGE 354

1. tassled scorpionfish
2. yellow-bellied marmot
3. kakapo
4. Asian giant moss mantis
5. yellow-footed rock wallabies

WHAT IN THE WORLD?

THE WHOLE THING

These photographs show close-up views of things with holes. On a separate sheet of paper, unscramble the letters to identify what's in each picture. **ANSWERS ON PAGE 354**

GUTONDHU

TRGAIU

SISWS ESHECE

IBRATB LEOH

NERNI EUTB

YEKEOHL

RALCEE

NEMOCBOHY

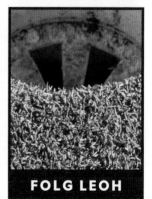

FOLG LEOH

8

9

10 THEY'LL *NEVER* FIND ME HERE! I MIGHT AS WELL TAKE A *NAP.*

11 LATER ...

STILL *NO SIGN* OF LULU! OH WELL—LET'S WATCH A *MOVIE.*

SHE'LL SHOW UP *EVENTUALLY.*

YEAH, NO NEED TO *PAW*-SE FOR HER.

12 *YIKES!* I HOPE LULU WASN'T *CAUGHT* BY *THAT CREATURE!*

DON'T BE *SILLY!* IT'S JUST A *STORY.*

13 HA! THEY HAVE *NO IDEA* WHERE I AM.

THIS IS MY CHANCE TO *STEAL* THE *SHOW...*

14 AAAAAARGH!!

AAAAAAK!!

15 I DIDN'T SEE *THAT* COMING!

16 I GUESS YOU REALLY *ARE* THE BEST AT HIDING, *PRINCESS TALLULAH!*

IT'S *JUST* LULU! BUT I *AM* THE QUEEN OF HIDE-AND-SEEK.

NOW THAT THE CAT'S OUT OF THE BAG, WHAT ELSE WILL THE PETS GET INTO? FIND OUT IN THE NEXT *UNLEASHED!*

LAUGH OUT LOUD

Where do parrots make movies?
Pollywood!

Two cockatoos, a type of parrot native to some southern Pacific countries, face each other.

JUST JOKING
MUSIC WORLD

Q What song did one octopus sing to the other?

A "I Want to Hold Your Hand, Hand, Hand, Hand, Hand, Hand, Hand, Hand."

Q What do composers take when they have a **sore throat?**

A Tchai-cough-sky drops.

Q Why did the musician decide to become an opera singer?

A Because the opera-tunity came up.

Q What do you do if you **can't find** someone to **sing with?**

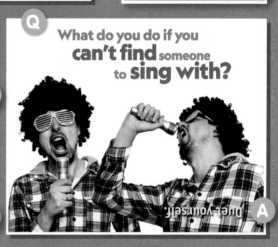

A Duet-yourself.

Q What **instrument** does a **fisherman** play?

A The bass guitar.

Q What is a trombone's favorite playground equipment?

A The slide.

FARMER 1: I taught my horse to play the violin.

FARMER 2: Is she good at it?

FARMER 1: She sure is— she's going to be in a musical!

FARMER 2: Which one?

FARMER 1: *Fiddler on the Hoof.*

150

Animal BLOOPERS

Animals make mistakes, too!

I, UH, TOTALLY MEANT TO DO THE SPLITS.

HEY, WHO TURNED OUT THE LIGHTS?

ANIMAL
Brown bear

RANGE
Northern North America, Europe, and Asia

SLIPUP SPOT
Katmai National Park and Preserve, Alaska, U.S.A.

PHOTO FAIL
If this brown bear doesn't get better at catching its food, it's never going to chomp up to 40 salmon a day to bulk up for its big winter sleep.

ANIMAL
Great egret

RANGE
Global (except polar regions)

SLIPUP SPOT
Champagne, France

PHOTO FAIL
This bird probably was hoping for a more graceful arrival when it tried to land on this frozen lake.

ANIMAL
Bengal tiger

RANGE
India, Bangladesh, Nepal, Bhutan, and China

SLIPUP SPOT
Bandhavgarh National Park, India

PHOTO FAIL
Like all tigers, this youngster is probably an excellent swimmer and a fierce predator afraid of nothing—except maybe this spooky leaf in the water.

EEK!

SPOOKY LEAF

151

Say What?

NAME Longfellow

FAVORITE ACTIVITY Leisurely Sunday drives

FAVORITE TOY GPS

PET PEEVE Speeding tickets

Sloths live in tropical climates in Central and South America.

This vacation is going to be sloth-some!

I have a fear of speed bumps, but I'm slowly getting over it.

I JUST FEEL LIKE HANGING OUT TODAY.

KNOCK, KNOCK.
Who's there?
Kenya.
Kenya who?
Kenya hurry up? We're late for our flight!

I love traveling slow much!

We're going on a three-week vacation. We're going to walk to the other side of this forest.

RIDDLE ME THIS

If an **electric train** is traveling **east,** but there is a strong wind from the **west,** which way will the **smoke** from the train blow?

Electric trains don't produce smoke.

A baseball team won 5-0, but not a single player ran around the bases. How is that possible?

All the players were married.

Which animal **wears a coat** in winter and **pants** in summer?

A dog.

If a **cat** can **jump** five feet high, why **can't** it **jump through** a window that is only **three feet high?**

The window is closed.

I'm **alive** without **air.** I'm always **drinking** but **never thirsty.** What am I?

A fish.

It comes in only one **color,** but many different **sizes.** It lives where there's **light,** but will **die** in the **rain.** What is it?

Your shadow.

What **grows up** while growing **down?**

A goose.

What has **four fingers** and a **thumb,** gives you a **hand** in the lab, but **can't pick up** anything?

A rubber glove.

153

ANIMAL PRANKSTERS

TRICKY FOXES

Can a two-pound (0.9-kg) ball of fluff play a practical joke?

Fennec fox keepers at the Endangered Wolf Center in Eureka, Missouri, U.S.A., think so. They've been tricked multiple times by fennec fox pair Fezz and Daisy.

The duo watches closely when staff enter their enclosure to clean it. The keepers wear treat pouches on the back of their belts so they can give the animals snacks at the end of the day. But the foxes don't like waiting. "Daisy distracts us by doing this play bow: Her front legs go down, her butt goes in the air, and she wags her tail superfast," says Regina Mossotti, former director of animal care and conservation. While the keepers are distracted by Daisy, Fezz swoops in and swipes a pouch. "They've fooled us a few times," Mossotti says. "Once Fezz gets away, he always turns around and looks like he's grinning, as if to say '*Ha!* We got you!'"

WATER GAMES

Can great apes be funny?

"Definitely," says Rob Shumaker, president of the Indianapolis Zoo in Indianapolis, Indiana, U.S.A. At a zoo where he used to work, Shumaker was hosing down the orangutan enclosure on a hot day. Junior, an adult male orangutan, began begging for a drink. The ape was sitting on a platform higher than Shumaker's hose could reach, so the scientist flicked some drops toward the ape. Delighted, Junior laughed out loud. A long, playful water fight followed.

When Shumaker ended the game, Junior appeared to settle down. But he was actually just waiting. A huge puddle of water had collected on his platform. When Shumaker came to say goodbye to Junior, the laughing ape made one sweep of his arm, drenching the scientist. "He totally got me!" Shumaker says.

FUNNY BITES

"HE CAN ONLY FIND SEVEN
OF HIS SHOES."

"WHERE DO YOU KEEP
YOUR AIR FRESHENERS?"

"JOEY AND TEDDY LOVE
MY NEW HOODIE."

"PULL OVER, SPEEDY."

"WHOA! IF YOU TURN
YOUR HEAD THIS WAY,
EVERYTHING LOOKS
UPSIDE DOWN!"

RIDDLE ME THIS

A **horse** is tied to a **10-foot** (3-m)-long **rope**, and there is a bale of hay **20 feet** (6 m) away from him, but the horse can still eat from it. **How is that possible?**

The other end of the rope isn't tied to anything.

At **night, they** come without being called. In the **morning,** they are **lost** without being **stolen. What are they?**

Stars.

What travels **around** the **world,** but **never leaves** its **corner?**

A stamp.

They **run fast,** but can't stand. You **ride them** like **horses,** but they don't eat grass. You can **find them** all over the world. **What are they?**

Bicycles.

What **sits** when it **stands, and jumps** when it walks?

A kangaroo.

If a **rooster** laid a **brown egg** and a **white egg,** what color **chicks** would hatch?

Neither, roosters don't lay eggs.

What part of a **bird** isn't in the **sky** and can **swim without getting wet?**

The bird's shadow.

Which is heavier, a **pound of chicken feathers** or a **pound of bricks?**

Neither, they both weigh a pound.

TONGUE TWISTERS
SAY THESE FAST THREE TIMES

Burke broke Brook's beaker.

Sherman shook soldiers' shoulders.

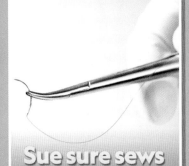

Sue sure sews swell sutures.

Boo drew blue blueberries.

Tricky twisters trick Sissy's tongue.

Bits of butter better better the batter.

The duke drank a drop of dewdrop brew.

Space-age spaceships shimmer and shine.

157

Say What?

NAME Globe Trotter

FAVORITE ACTIVITY
Horsing around

FAVORITE SPORT
Stable tennis

PET PEEVE
Bad weather ...
especially when it reins

I have an unbridled enthusiasm for travel.

My last trip was mag-neigh-ficent!

QUIT STALLING; IT'S TIME TO LEAVE!

We don't want to miss the mane event.

Traffic was a night-mare!

KNOCK, KNOCK.
Who's there?
Neigh.
Neigh who?
I just met your neighbors.

Horses sleep standing up.
They "lock" their legs
to stop themselves from
collapsing while asleep.

158

FUNNY BITES

JUST JOKING
FUNNY BONES

Q SHHHH! Why shouldn't you **tell secrets in a cornfield?**

A Because it's all ears.

Q What happened when the man lost all his hair?

A He bawled.

Q Why did the zombie rip off his tuxedo and kick off his feet?

A He wanted to be footloose and fancy-free.

TEACHER: Molly, why are you standing during the test?

MOLLY: Because you told us we need to be able to think on our feet.

Q How do **clowns** come up with their **material?**

A They use their funny bones.

Q Why did the boy bring a ladder to class?

A He wanted to be head and shoulders above the rest of the students.

It's a LONG story ...

TINA AND LOUISE WERE HIKING ON A SAVANNA WHEN TINA YELLED, "WOW! DID YOU SEE THAT OSTRICH RUN BY?"

"Uh ... no, I didn't," Louise said sheepishly.

"What?" Tina said. "It was huge—I can't believe you missed it!"

They hiked on, and a few minutes later, Tina exclaimed, "Wow! That was amazing! Did you see that elephant? It just crossed our path on the trail ahead."

Embarrassed, Louise replied, "Oh ... no, I didn't see it."

"I can't believe you missed it," Tina said.

Thirty seconds later, Tina looked back at Louise and yelled, "Whoa! Did you see that?"

Louise was annoyed at this point. "Yes, I did!" she lied.

Tina replied, "Then why did you step in it?"

JUST JOKING

GIGGLES ON THE GO

Q What's big, sticky, and flies?

A A jelly-copter.

Q What did the **submarine** say to the one **next to it?**

A "Hey, we're in sink!"

Q Where does Cinderella sit when she flies in an airplane?

A In coach.

Q Why did the boy drag his television into the middle of the street?

A Because his dad told him to get the show on the road.

Q Why did the man stack all his goods on a bike?

A He wanted to pedal his wares.

I'M STARTING TO FEEL DIZZY NOW ...

JUNE: Did you hear about the girl who blew a giant bubble so she could travel around the world in it?

ELIJAH: No, did it work?

JUNE: Yes, it totally abs-orb-ed her.

TONGUE TWISTERS
SAY THESE FAST THREE TIMES

Frilled lizards lounge lazily.

Sharp shirts, sharper sharks.

Vik views a rare whale well.

One mumbling, bumbling bumblebee.

Minuscule mussels must muster muscles.

An itch which itches an inch itches which witch?

Percy seeks special sea species.

163

CULTURE
CONNECTION

Children in San Francisco, California, U.S.A., wear face paint and colorful clothes in celebration of Día de los Muertos (Day of the Dead).

CELEBRATIONS

LUNAR NEW YEAR
January 29

Also called Chinese New Year, this holiday marks the new year according to the lunar calendar. Families celebrate with parades, feasts, and fireworks. Young people may receive gifts of money in red envelopes.

RAMADAN AND EID AL-FITR
February 28*–March 31**

A Muslim holiday, Ramadan is a month long, ending in the Eid al-Fitr celebration. Observers fast during this month—eating only after sunset. People pray for forgiveness and hope to purify themselves through observance.

SONGKRAN
April 13–16**

Marking the Thai New Year, Songkran welcomes a fresh start with a splash. Water plays a big part in the festival, which includes traditions such as cleaning homes and sprinkling droplets on Buddha statues and the hands of elders. Outside, celebrants take part in street parties and a giant friendly water fight.

EASTER
April 20†

A Christian holiday that celebrates the resurrection of Jesus Christ, Easter is celebrated by giving baskets filled with gifts, decorated eggs, or candy to children.

MIDSUMMER
June 21

Celebrating the longest day of the year, the summer festival in Sweden is marked by making flower crowns, singing and dancing, and lunching on foods such as pickled herring and potatoes.

LAMMAS
August 1

Also known as Loaf Mass Day, this holiday is celebrated by some people in England, Scotland, Wales, and Ireland and marks the first wheat harvest. It's common for people to bake loaves of bread to eat—and offer to the church.

ROSH HASHANAH
September 22*–24

A Jewish holiday marking the beginning of a new year on the Hebrew calendar. Celebrations include prayer, ritual foods, and a day of rest.

Around the World

HERITAGE DAY
September 24

South Africans show their patriotic pride on this holiday, which celebrates the diverse cultures throughout the country. It's tradition for families and friends to gather around a wood fire—an event known as a *braai*—to cook and then feast on barbecued meats.

DIWALI
October 20**

To symbolize the inner light that protects against spiritual darkness, people light their homes with clay lamps for India's largest and most important holiday.

HANUKKAH
December 14*-22

This Jewish holiday is eight days long. It commemorates the rededication of the Temple in Jerusalem. Hanukkah celebrations include the lighting of menorah candles for eight days and the exchange of gifts.

CHRISTMAS DAY
December 25

A Christian holiday marking the birth of Jesus Christ, Christmas is usually celebrated by decorating trees, exchanging presents, and having festive gatherings.

*Begins at sundown.
**Dates may vary slightly by location.
†Orthodox Easter is also on April 20.

2025 CALENDAR

JANUARY

S	M	T	W	T	F	S
			1	2	3	4
5	6	7	8	9	10	11
12	13	14	15	16	17	18
19	20	21	22	23	24	25
26	27	28	29	30	31	

FEBRUARY

S	M	T	W	T	F	S
						1
2	3	4	5	6	7	8
9	10	11	12	13	14	15
16	17	18	19	20	21	22
23	24	25	26	27	28	

MARCH

S	M	T	W	T	F	S
						1
2	3	4	5	6	7	8
9	10	11	12	13	14	15
16	17	18	19	20	21	22
23	24	25	26	27	28	29
30	31					

APRIL

S	M	T	W	T	F	S
		1	2	3	4	5
6	7	8	9	10	11	12
13	14	15	16	17	18	19
20	21	22	23	24	25	26
27	28	29	30			

MAY

S	M	T	W	T	F	S
				1	2	3
4	5	6	7	8	9	10
11	12	13	14	15	16	17
18	19	20	21	22	23	24
25	26	27	28	29	30	31

JUNE

S	M	T	W	T	F	S
1	2	3	4	5	6	7
8	9	10	11	12	13	14
15	16	17	18	19	20	21
22	23	24	25	26	27	28
29	30					

JULY

S	M	T	W	T	F	S
		1	2	3	4	5
6	7	8	9	10	11	12
13	14	15	16	17	18	19
20	21	22	23	24	25	26
27	28	29	30	31		

AUGUST

S	M	T	W	T	F	S
					1	2
3	4	5	6	7	8	9
10	11	12	13	14	15	16
17	18	19	20	21	22	23
24	25	26	27	28	29	30
31						

SEPTEMBER

S	M	T	W	T	F	S
	1	2	3	4	5	6
7	8	9	10	11	12	13
14	15	16	17	18	19	20
21	22	23	24	25	26	27
28	29	30				

OCTOBER

S	M	T	W	T	F	S
			1	2	3	4
5	6	7	8	9	10	11
12	13	14	15	16	17	18
19	20	21	22	23	24	25
26	27	28	29	30	31	

NOVEMBER

S	M	T	W	T	F	S
						1
2	3	4	5	6	7	8
9	10	11	12	13	14	15
16	17	18	19	20	21	22
23	24	25	26	27	28	29
30						

DECEMBER

S	M	T	W	T	F	S
	1	2	3	4	5	6
7	8	9	10	11	12	13
14	15	16	17	18	19	20
21	22	23	24	25	26	27
28	29	30	31			

awes8me

THESE EIGHT SUPER SPECTACLES WILL PUT YOU IN A PARTY MOOD.

1 NIGHT-LIGHTS Boca Ciega Bay in St. Petersburg, Florida, U.S.A., comes alive with lighted boats during a floating celebration of the winter holidays. Participants in the annual St. Pete Beach holiday boat parade also donate toys to kids in need. Sounds like a perfect parade!

Festive Parades

2 FLOWER POWER

For more than a century, fantastic flower-covered floats and marching bands have dazzled crowds at the annual Rose Parade in Pasadena, California, U.S.A., on New Year's Day. Not a fan of flowers? Stick around for the college football game that follows the parade.

4 COLORFUL RITUAL

Millions of people of the Hindu faith come together to take a ritual dip in one of four sacred rivers in India as part of the Kumbh Mela festival. The religious procession can include elephants and camels, and festival organizers often provide music and dance performances.

5 BALLOON BONANZA

More than three million people lined the streets of New York City to watch the debut of this Hello Kitty balloon in the Macy's Thanksgiving Day Parade. The parade has been held on the morning of Thanksgiving almost every year since 1924.

3 BLAZING BOAT

The Up Helly Aa festival in Lerwick, Scotland, ends every January in a blaze. Harking back to a Viking ritual, hundreds of torchbearers march through the town's streets before setting a 30-foot (9-m)-long galley—a type of ship—on fire.

DANCE PARTY 6

With fancy headdresses and costumes, dancers perform the samba, an Afro-Brazilian group dance, in front of a crowd at the Carnival parade in Rio de Janeiro, Brazil. Carnival, a festival of merrymaking and feasting, allows people to let loose.

7 FLOATING FESTIVAL

People in Venice, Italy, take their parades to the water. That's because this city is built in a lagoon with canals for streets. Revelers float down the Grand Canal in decorated gondolas, like this giant rat gondola, and other boats during the annual Carnival festival.

8 CLOWN REVELRY

Giant jesters parade through the streets of the historic French Quarter in New Orleans, Louisiana, U.S.A. During the annual Mardi Gras celebration, nearly a hundred krewes— or festive groups— toss goodies, including toys, stuffed animals, and Mardi Gras beads, to the people who come to watch.

What's Your Chinese Horoscope?
Locate your birth year to find out.

In Chinese astrology, the zodiac runs on a 12-year cycle, based on the lunar calendar. Each year corresponds to one of 12 animals, each representing one of 12 personality types. Read on to find out which animal year you were born in and what that might say about you.

RAT
1972, '84, '96, 2008, '20
Say cheese! You're attractive, charming, and creative. When you get mad, you can have really sharp teeth!

HORSE
1966, '78, '90, 2002, '14
Being happy is your *mane* goal. And though you're smart and hardworking, your teacher may get upset if you talk too much.

OX
1973, '85, '97, 2009, '21
You're smart, patient, and as strong as an … well, you know. Though you're a leader, you never brag.

SHEEP
1967, '79, '91, 2003, '15
Gentle as a lamb, you're also artistic, compassionate, and wise. You're often shy.

TIGER
1974, '86, '98, 2010, '22
You may be a nice person, but no one should ever enter your room without asking—you might attack!

MONKEY
1968, '80, '92, 2004, '16
No "monkey see, monkey do" for you. You're a clever problem-solver with an excellent memory.

RABBIT
1975, '87, '99, 2011, '23
Your ambition and talent make you jump at opportunity. You also keep your ears open for gossip.

ROOSTER
1969, '81, '93, 2005, '17
You crow about your adventures, but inside you're really shy. You're thoughtful, capable, brave, and talented.

DRAGON
1976, '88, 2000, '12, '24
You're on fire! Health, energy, honesty, and bravery make you a living legend.

DOG
1970, '82, '94, 2006, '18
Often the leader of the pack, you're loyal and honest. You can also keep a secret.

SNAKE
1977, '89, 2001, '13, '25
You may not speak often, but you're very smart. You always seem to have a stash of cash.

PIG
1971, '83, '95, 2007, '19
Even though you're courageous, honest, and kind, you never hog all the attention.

Bet You Didn't Know!

6 winter feast facts to fill up on

1 Deep-fried jelly doughnuts called *sufganiyot* are eaten during Hanukkah to represent an **ancient miracle** involving long-lasting **lamp oil.**

2 A harvest festival called **Basega** honors ancestors of the **Mossi people** in the African country of Burkina Faso.

3 During **Dongzhi,** a festival celebrated in parts of Asia, families eat sweet dumplings called *tangyuan* to symbolize togetherness.

4 During a Japanese celebration called **Toji,** people take **baths filled with citrus fruits** and eat pumpkin for good luck.

5 *Hallacas,* a type of **tamale** eaten in Venezuela on **Christmas Eve,** can be stuffed with as many as 20 different ingredients.

6 Celebrated by many Black Americans, **Kwanzaa** gets its name from the phrase **"first fruits of the harvest"** in Swahili, an African language.

DIWALI
The Hindu Festival of Lights

Diwali is India's biggest and most important holiday. In October or November each year, millions of Hindus, Sikhs, and Buddhists around the world celebrate for five days.

DIWALI, sometimes called Deepavali or Dipawali, means "rows of lights." People use lamps and lanterns to decorate their homes and public spaces. Fireworks fill the skies. The light symbolizes the victory of good over evil. People in different parts of India have different beliefs about the origins of the holiday. In southern India, people celebrate it as the day the Hindu god Krishna defeated a demon. In western India, it marks the day another god, Vishnu, sent the demon king Bali to rule the underworld.

Each of Diwali's five days has its own set of traditions. The first day is considered a lucky day for shopping and cleaning the house. On the second day, people decorate their homes. On the third day, families come together to feast and celebrate. The fourth day is for exchanging gifts. On the last day of Diwali, brothers visit their married sisters, who welcome them with a meal.

Today, setting off fireworks with a hiss and pop is Diwali's biggest tradition. But it's a new addition to this otherwise ancient holiday. Until the 1900s, pyrotechnics were so expensive they were for royals only.

> Some people believe that the sound of Diwali fireworks sends a message to the gods about the joy of people on Earth.

During Diwali, Hindus light rows of small clay lamps called *diyas,* which are filled with oil.

10 TASTY FACTS ABOUT CHOCOLATE

CHOCOLATE IS MADE FROM THE SEEDS OF THE CACAO PLANT, WHICH GROWS ONLY IN AREAS NEAR THE EQUATOR.

HERSHEY, PENNSYLVANIA, U.S.A., SMELLS LIKE CHOCOLATE. WHY? The Hershey's chocolate factory there produces (among other things) about **70 MILLION** HERSHEY'S KISSES A DAY.

WHITE CHOCOLATE IS TECHNICALLY **NOT CHOCOLATE.** THE PALER TREAT IS MADE WITH ONLY COCOA BUTTER— WHILE REAL CHOCOLATE BARS ARE MADE WITH COCOA POWDER.

CHOCOLATE-COVERED **BACON** IS A POPULAR TREAT AT MANY U.S. STATE FAIRS.

A MINIATURE STATUE OF LIBERTY WAS BUILT OUT OF **229** POUNDS (104 KG) OF CHOCOLATE.

A Swiss company invented a chocolate that won't melt until the temperature reaches 131°F (55°C).

CHOCOLATE-COVERED **ANTS** ARE A TREAT IN **MEXICO.**

The average American eats about **12 POUNDS** (5 KG) OF CHOCOLATE **A YEAR.**

People in the United Kingdom eat 1,000 chocolate bars for every one bar eaten in China.

JUST ONE WHIFF OF CHOCOLATE CAN MAKE PEOPLE **FEEL HAPPY.** A CHEMICAL IN CACAO RELEASES FEEL-GOOD VIBES IN THE BRAIN.

The Secret History of
SPIES

These facts are too fun to stay classified.

You might think of spies as well-dressed sneaks with super-techie gadgets. But spying has been around for thousands of years: Ancient Egyptians hired spies to keep an eye on their enemies; so did the Greeks and Romans. Check out this timeline to get the top secret scoop on spies throughout history.

1 **ca 3100 B.C.–332 B.C.**

Ancient Egyptian spies were some of the first to use poisons to get the job done. To silence their enemies, the expert sneaks used killer methods, including toxins derived from plants and snakes.

Historians don't always know the exact dates of long-ago events. That's why you'll see a "ca" next to some of the years listed here. It stands for "circa," meaning "around."

TOP SECRET
HUSH-HUSH MEETING
(SHH!!!!!)

2 **ca 1185–1600**

The Japanese used spies called *shinobi*, also known as ninjas, to secretly gather information from enemies and rivals. Trained since childhood, shinobi were experts in stealth and assassination. Male ninjas wore all black to sneak around, but female ninjas, or *kunoichi*, would sneak into enemy locations by disguising themselves as dancers or servants.

3 **ca 1325–1521**

Aztec spies called *quimichtin* (pronounced KIM-eech-tin), who lived in what's now central Mexico, were nicknamed "mice" because they worked at night to hide while spying. Because their job was especially dangerous—being caught could mean enslavement or death—they were paid more than most Aztec workers.

4 **1573–1590**

Sir Francis Walsingham, principal secretary to Queen Elizabeth I of England, created a network of spies to protect the queen. They included cryptographers to crack coded letters and people who could open and reseal envelopes containing information—without anyone finding out.

6 **1861–1865**

Harriet Tubman is famous for helping enslaved people in the South of the United States escape to the northern states, where the enslavement of people was illegal. But she was also a spy during the Civil War. Using her knowledge of the land, she mapped territory so Union troops could safely travel through Confederate states.

5 **1775–1783**

Before he was elected president of what would soon become the United States, George Washington ran a gang of spies called the Culper Spy Ring during the Revolutionary War. One of its members, Anna Strong, sent coded messages through her laundry. She hung clothes according to color and number to tell soldiers where secret messages were hidden. (For example, a black dress and two handkerchiefs might have meant "check the second closest creek.")

7 **1916**

During World War I, the French military captured a message that claimed one of their spies was working for their enemy, Germany. A Dutch dancer called Mata Hari was accused of being a double agent, someone who pretended to spy for one country while actually working for another. She was found guilty of telling the Germans secrets. She was executed by firing squad in 1917. However, people today question whether she really was guilty after all, due to lack of any evidence.

8 **1960s**

Things were tense between the United States and the Soviet Union (now Russia). Neither country trusted the other, and spy activities on both sides increased. To help, intelligence agencies developed sneaky gadgets for spies to eavesdrop and collect information. One popular device was the buttonhole camera. The spy simply squeezed a cable that could be hidden inside a coat pocket. That opened a fake button on the coat and snapped a secret photo.

9 **Present day**

Today, spies don't even need to leave their homes to collect classified information. They use computer programs called spyware from anywhere in the world to track activity and access sensitive information on faraway devices such as computers, tablets, and smartphones. Some 20 percent of surveyed companies consider cyber espionage to be their number-one threat.

MONEY AROUND THE WORLD!

In 2022, the U.S. Mint began issuing quarters with notable American women on one side. The first two were poet **MAYA ANGELOU** and astronaut **SALLY RIDE**, the first American woman in space.

IN THE 1600s, SWEDEN ISSUED A plate-size COIN that weighed nearly **44 pounds** (20 kg).

The **colón banknotes** of **Costa Rica** show native animals like the **brown-throated sloth.**

In the United States, more **$100 bills** are in circulation than **$1 bills.**

SOME ANCIENT CHINESE COINS WERE SHAPED LIKE KNIVES AND KEYS.

In Norway, **butter** was once accepted as **currency**.

The **Australian dollar** is also called a **BUCK** or the **AUSSIE.**

During the Middle Ages, people in Italy paid each other with wheels of **PARMESAN CHEESE.**

The new design on British banknotes features **King Charles III** instead of his mother, **Queen Elizabeth II,** who died in 2022.

KING TUT APPEARS ON THE EGYPTIAN ONE-POUND COIN.

The Aztec of ancient Mexico used **CACAO BEANS** as money.

A BRITISH ARTIST MADE A DRESS OUT OF USED **BANKNOTES** FROM AROUND THE **WORLD.**

MONEY TIP! CLIP COUPONS FOR YOUR PARENTS. Ask if they'll put the money they save into your piggy bank.

SAVING
Languages at Risk

Today, there are more than 7,000 languages spoken on Earth. But by 2100, more than half of these may disappear. In fact, some experts say one language dies every two weeks as a result of the increasing dominance of languages such as English, Spanish, and Mandarin.

So what can be done to keep dialects from disappearing altogether? To start, several National Geographic Explorers have embarked on various projects around the planet. Together, they are part of the race to save some of the world's most threatened languages, and to protect and preserve the cultures they belong to. Here are some of the Explorers' stories.

The Explorer: Tam Thi Ton
The Language: Bahnar

TON IN A BAHNAR CLASSROOM

The Work: By gathering folklore like riddles and comics, Ton is creating bilingual learning materials for elementary students to teach them Bahnar, the language of an ethnic group living in Vietnam's Central Highlands.

The Explorer: Sandhya Narayanan
The Languages: Quechua and Aymara

NARAYANAN SHARES STORIES FROM THE FIELD AT NATIONAL GEOGRAPHIC'S HEADQUARTERS IN WASHINGTON, D.C., U.S.A.

The Work: By immersing herself in the Indigenous languages of the Andean region along the Peru–Bolivia border, Narayanan aims to understand how interactions among Indigenous groups affect language over time.

The Explorer: K. David Harrison
The Language: Koro-Aka

The Work: Harrison led an expedition to India that identified Koro-Aka, a language that was completely new to science. He is also vice president of the Living Tongues Institute for Endangered Languages, dedicated to raising awareness and revitalizing little-documented languages.

HARRISON DOING AN INTERVIEW

The Explorer: Susan Barfield
The Language: Mapudungun

The Work: Barfield shines a light on the language of the Mapuche people of southern Chile with her trilingual children's book, *El Copihue*. The book is based on a Mapuche folktale and is illustrated by Mapuche students.

BARFIELD PRESENTS AN OFFERING DURING A BOOK BLESSING CEREMONY.

PERLIN INTERVIEWS A VILLAGE LEADER.

The Explorer: Ross Perlin
The Language: Seke

The Work: In an effort to preserve the Seke language of northern Nepal, Perlin has been working closely with speakers both in their villages and in New York, where many now live, including young speakers determined to document their own language.

The Explorer: Lal Rapacha
The Language: Kiranti-Kõits

The Work: As the founder and director of the Research Institute for Kiratology in Kathmandu, Nepal, Rapacha carries out research on the lesser known languages of Indigenous Himalayan people, including Kiranti-Kõits, his endangered mother tongue.

RAPACHA WORKING IN THE FIELD IN NEPAL

Monster
MASH

Before there was Frankenstein's monster or King Kong, there were the magnificent creatures of Greek mythology. Some had sharp teeth and claws and breathed fire, and others made you solve riddles and brainteasers. These Greek beasties could be pretty scary—especially if you had to fight them—but they're kind of cool, too!

FROM THE HIT PODCAST AND BOOK GREEKING OUT!

THE SPHINX

This giant monster had the body of a lion, the head of a woman, wings of an eagle, and, depending upon who you ask, a snake's tail. She would pounce upon her unsuspecting victims and force them to solve a riddle: Which creature has only one voice, but has four legs in the morning, two legs in the afternoon, and three legs at night? Anyone who didn't answer the riddle correctly was devoured. P.S. Should you ever encounter the Sphinx, the answer is: a human. (The times of day represent important stages of human life!)

TYPHON

Often described as the "father of all monsters," Typhon was one of Gaea's children. He was an incredibly tall giant with multiple dragon heads, snakes for legs, and hundreds of wings. Oh, and he could breathe fire. He once tried to destroy the gods, but Zeus was able to defeat Typhon and imprison him deep inside the Underworld. Then Zeus plopped a mountain on top of the prison for good measure.

HARPIES

These ferocious creatures had the body of a bird but the face of a woman. They used their sharp claws to grab people from Earth and bring them to certain gods or goddesses. They were known to work with Hades and would often torture people on the way to the Underworld. Other stories describe them as wind spirits that carried people away on the breezes.

SIRENS

Sirens were beautiful, alluring creatures that were half bird, half human. They would sit on top of rocks near the ocean and sing for any passing ships. Sounds kinda nice, right? Well, the songs were actually enchanted. Anyone who heard them would jump off the ship and swim through the water to the sirens, providing them with a nice meal for lunch. And if sirens sound familiar, it's because they served as inspiration for what we now call mermaids.

World Religions

Around the world, religion takes many forms. Some belief systems, such as Christianity, Islam, and Judaism, are monotheistic, meaning that followers believe in just one supreme being. Others, like Hinduism, Shintoism, and most Native belief systems, are polytheistic, meaning that their followers believe in multiple gods.

All of the major religions have their origins in Asia, but they have spread around the world. Christianity, with the largest number of followers, has three divisions—Roman Catholic, Eastern Orthodox, and Protestant. Islam, with about one-quarter of all believers, has two main divisions—Sunni and Shiite. Hinduism and Buddhism account for about another one-fifth of believers. Judaism, dating back some 4,000 years, has some 15 million followers, about 2 percent of all believers.

CHRISTIANITY

Based on the teachings of Jesus Christ, who was born some 2,000 years ago in the area of modern-day Israel, Christianity has spread worldwide and actively seeks converts. Followers in Switzerland (above) participate in an Easter season procession with lanterns and crosses.

BUDDHISM

Founded about 2,400 years ago in northern India by the Hindu prince Gautama Buddha, Buddhism spread throughout East and Southeast Asia. Buddhist temples have statues, such as the Mihintale Buddha (above) in Sri Lanka.

HINDUISM

Dating back more than 4,000 years, Hinduism is practiced mainly in India. Hindus follow sacred texts known as the Vedas and believe in reincarnation. During the festival of Navratri, which honors the goddess Durga, the Garba dance is performed (above).

Honoring the Harvest

As part of the Jewish harvest holiday Sukkot, many families eat meals in a sukkah, a temporary outdoor structure, to give thanks to nature and Earth's bounty. A woman from the Samaritan religion decorates with fruits and vegetables.

ISLAM

Muslims believe that the Quran, Islam's sacred book, records the words of Allah (God) as revealed to the Prophet Muhammad beginning around A.D. 610. Believers circle the Kaaba (above) in the Grand Mosque in Mecca, Saudi Arabia, the spiritual center of the faith.

JUDAISM

The traditions, laws, and beliefs of Judaism date back to Abraham (the patriarch) and the Torah (the first five books of the Old Testament). Followers pray before the Western Wall (above), which stands below Islam's Dome of the Rock in Jerusalem.

QUIZ WHIZ

How vast is your knowledge about the world around you? Quiz yourself!

Write your answers on a piece of paper. Then check them below.

1 In medieval Japan, spies called *shinobi* were also known as what?
a. samurai
b. ninjas
c. quimichtin
d. moles

2 How much chocolate does the average American eat each year?
a. 2 ounces (56 g)
b. 12 ounces (340 g)
c. 12 pounds (5 kg)
d. 22 pounds (10 kg)

3 **True or false?** In Greek mythology, creatures called harpies could grab and carry away humans with their sharp claws.

4 Often lit to celebrate Diwali, a *diya* is a small clay lamp filled with what?
a. oil
b. paint
c. water
d. wax

5 The brown-throated sloth appears on some colón banknotes in which country?
a. Egypt
b. Sweden
c. Thailand
d. Costa Rica

Not **STUMPED** yet? Check out the *NATIONAL GEOGRAPHIC KIDS QUIZ WHIZ* collection for more fun **CULTURE** questions!

ANSWERS: 1. b; 2. c; 3. True; 4. a; 5. d

HOMEWORK HELP

Explore a New Culture

STAMPS OF BRAZIL

CURRENCY AND COINS OF BRAZIL

FLAG OF BRAZIL

YOU'RE A STUDENT, but you're also a citizen of the world. Writing a report on another country or your own country is a great way to better understand and appreciate how different people live. Pick the country of your ancestors, one that's been in the news, or one that you'd like to visit someday.

Passport to Success

A country report follows the format of an expository essay because you're "exposing" information about the country you choose.

The following step-by-step tips will help you with this international task.

1 **RESEARCH.** Gathering information is the most important step in writing a good country report. Look to internet sources, encyclopedias, books, magazine and newspaper articles, and other sources to find important and interesting details about your subject.

2 **ORGANIZE YOUR NOTES.** Put the information you gather into a rough outline. For example, sort everything you found about the country's system of government, climate, etc.

3 **WRITE IT UP.** Follow the basic structure of good writing: introduction, body, and conclusion. Remember that each paragraph should have a topic sentence that is then supported by facts and details. Incorporate the information from your notes, but make sure it's in your own words. And make your writing flow with good transitions and descriptive language.

4 **ADD VISUALS.** Include maps, diagrams, photos, and other visual aids.

5 **PROOFREAD AND REVISE.** Correct any mistakes, and polish your language. Do your best!

6 **CITE YOUR SOURCES.** Be sure to keep a record of your sources.

Surprised students react to an explosion of foam during a classroom science experiment.

SCIENCE and
TECHNOLOGY

10 FUTURISTIC FACTS ABOUT TECHNOLOGY

The Int-Ball is an **adorable drone,** slightly larger than a softball, **that floats** aboard the International Space Station.

The **HENN NA HOTEL** in Japan **has robots on its staff,** including a **dinosaur robot** receptionist that checks you in.

Alpha 1S robots broke a world record for the **largest number of** robots dancing at the same time: **1,372.**

Harry the **robot** knows **how to play the trumpet.**

A **band of** music-performing **robots** called Z-Machines has a guitarist with **78 fingers** and a drummer with **22 arms.**

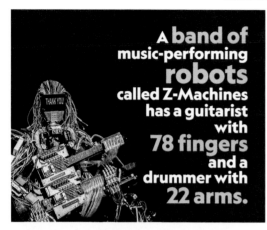

Robear is a **robot nurse** with the **face of a bear** that helps care for patients by **lifting them** out of bed and into a wheelchair.

Researchers **study geckos** to learn how to **help robots** and **astronauts** maneuver around space structures.

Russia once **built a computer** powered by **water.**

There is a **Rubik's Cube robot** that can **solve itself.**

The world's **largest walking robot** is a **dragon** measuring 51 feet 6 inches (15.7 m) long and 26 feet 10 inches (8.2 m) tall that can **blow flames.**

6 COOL INVENTIONS

SUPERSMART COASTERS, ROBOTS, AND GADGETS THAT COULD CHANGE YOUR LIFE

① OCEAN COASTER

Turn a relaxing ocean cruise into a thrilling ride with **BOLT: Ultimate Sea Coaster,** the first roller coaster built on a cruise ship. Starting **18 decks above the ocean's surface,** the ride takes you and a friend around more than 800 feet (244 m) of track. Choose how fast or slow your car moves as it zips up, down, and around the ship up to **35 miles an hour (56 km/h),** about as fast as a car on a city street. Parts of the ride even fly out **beyond the ship's deck,** 187 feet (57 m) above the water. This coaster really rides the waves!

② DIY VIDEO GAMES

Think your doodles and art projects would make a cool video game? **Pixicade** can turn them into one. The toy comes with markers that help **create the design:** Black is for walls, floors, and platforms; green is for avatars; purple, obstacles; red, hazards; and blue is for collectibles. A user can draw a picture, snap a pic of their creation using the Pixicade app, and **start playing** 30 seconds later. Pixicade even lets users share their game with friends. Now that's **leveling up.**

③ TALKING TEXT MACHINE

Turn any printed or digital words into your own audiobook. Just point the **OrCam Read** at the words you want to read—a web page, a menu, or even this book—and the gadget's camera will capture the text and **read the words aloud**. The marker-size device can read fast or slow, and it's small enough to fit in any pencil case. The inventors hope that people who are visually impaired, struggle to read, or are just learning to read will be helped by the device.

④ MUSICAL CLOTHING

With **SoundShirt,** you can literally *feel* the music. Made of stretchy fabric with tiny components that move, this shirt can either **capture sound waves from the air** or connect to a phone app. Then it translates the music into pulses and vibrations that the wearer can feel: You might sense the thrumming of a **violin on your arms** while the **drumbeat rolls across your shoulders.** The inventors hope the device will be especially useful for people who are hard of hearing or deaf. **That rocks!**

⑤ 10-SECOND TOOTHBRUSH

Brushing your teeth for **two whole minutes** can feel like a drag. Cut the time with **Y-Brush,** a toothbrush shaped like a mouthguard. Just pop it in, press the button, and gently chew on the brush while moving the handle from side to side for **five seconds each** on your top and bottom teeth. The tooth technology includes **35,000 nylon bristles** that buzz to shake off yucky bacteria and get you out the door (or into bed) faster.

⑥ ROBOT KITTY

If you're allergic to cats but still think they're adorable, you might want to "adopt" **MarsCat,** a bionic animal companion. Just like a real cat, MarsCat **reacts to your touch and voice,** wiggling when you pet it and even **meowing back** if you talk to it. Each MarsCat has a unique body shape and personality, and it will respond differently depending on how you play with it. The bot will also obey commands— sometimes (just like most real cats!). The best part? No **stinky litter boxes** to clean.

193

WHAT IS LIFE?

This seems like such an easy question to answer. Everybody knows that singing birds are alive and rocks are not. But when we start studying bacteria and other microscopic creatures, things get more complicated.

SO WHAT EXACTLY IS LIFE?

Most scientists agree that something is alive if it can reproduce, grow in size to become more complex in structure, take in nutrients to survive, give off waste products, and respond to external stimuli, such as increased sunlight or changes in temperature.

KINDS OF LIFE

Biologists classify living organisms by how they get their energy. Organisms such as algae, green plants, and some bacteria use sunlight as an energy source. Animals (like humans), fungi, and some single-celled microscopic organisms called Archaea use chemicals to provide energy. When we eat food, chemical reactions within our digestive system turn our food into fuel.

Living things inhabit land, sea, and air. In fact, life thrives deep beneath the oceans, embedded in rocks miles below Earth's crust, in ice, and in other extreme environments. The life-forms that thrive in these challenging environments are called extremophiles. Some of these draw directly upon the chemicals surrounding them for energy. Because these are very different forms of life from what we're used to, we may not think of them as alive, but they are.

HOW IT ALL WORKS

To understand how a living organism works, it helps to look at one example of its simplest form—the single-celled bacterium called *Streptococcus*. There are many kinds of these tiny organisms, and some are responsible for human illnesses. What makes us sick or uncomfortable are the toxins the bacteria give off in our bodies.

A single *Streptococcus* bacterium is so small that at least 500 of them could fit on the dot above this letter *i*. These bacteria are some of the simplest forms of life we know. They have no moving parts, no lungs, no brain, no heart, no liver, and no leaves or fruit. Yet this life-form reproduces. It grows in size by producing long-chain structures, takes in nutrients, and gives off waste products. This tiny life-form is alive, just as you are alive.

What makes something alive is a question scientists grapple with when they study viruses, such as the ones that cause the common cold and COVID-19. They can grow and reproduce within host cells, such as those that make up your body. Because viruses lack cells and cannot metabolize nutrients for energy or reproduce without a host, scientists ask if they are indeed alive. And don't go looking for them without a strong microscope— viruses are a hundred times smaller than bacteria.

Scientists think life began on Earth more than four billion years ago, but no fossils exist from that time. The earliest fossils ever found are from the primitive life that existed 3.5 billion years ago. Other life-forms, some of which are shown below, soon followed. Scientists continue to study how life evolved on Earth and whether it is possible that life exists on other planets.

MICROSCOPIC ORGANISMS

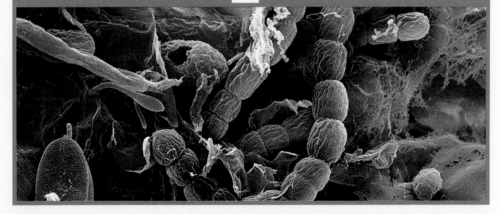

The Three Domains of Life

Biologists divide all living organisms into three domains, or groups: Bacteria, Archaea, and Eukarya. Archaea and Bacteria cells do not have nuclei—cellular parts that are essential to reproduction and other cell functions—but they are different from each other in many ways. Because human cells have a nucleus, we belong to the Eukarya domain.

1 BACTERIA

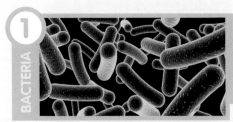

DOMAIN BACTERIA: These single-celled microorganisms are found almost everywhere in the world. Bacteria are small and do not have nuclei. They can be shaped like rods, spirals, or spheres. Some of them are helpful to humans, and some are harmful.

2 ARCHAEA

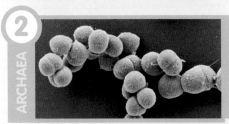

DOMAIN ARCHAEA: These single-celled micro-organisms are often found in extremely hostile environments. Like Bacteria, Archaea do not have nuclei, but they have some genes in common with Eukarya. For this reason, scientists think the Archaea living today most closely resemble the earliest forms of life on Earth.

3 EUKARYA

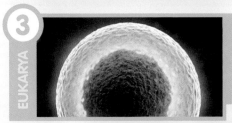

DOMAIN EUKARYA: This diverse group of life-forms is more complicated than Bacteria and Archaea, as Eukarya have one or more cells with nuclei. These are the tiny cells that make up your whole body. Eukarya are divided into four groups: fungi, protists, plants, and animals.

FYI

WHAT IS A DOMAIN? Scientifically speaking, a domain is a major taxonomic division into which natural objects are classified (see page 44 for "What Is Taxonomy?").

FUNGI

KINGDOM FUNGI: Mainly multicellular organisms, fungi cannot make their own food. Mushrooms and yeast are fungi.

PLANTS

KINGDOM PLANTAE: Plants are multicellular, and many can make their own food using photosynthesis.

PROTISTS

PROTISTS: Once considered a kingdom, this group is a "grab bag" that includes unicellular and multicellular organisms of great variety.

ANIMALS

KINGDOM ANIMALIA: Most animals, which are multicellular, have their own organ systems. Animals do not make their own food.

Freaky Plants

Wondering what could be so peculiar about a plant? Then you'll be amazed by these strange sprouts with odd smells, funny "faces," and more.

The fruit on the doll's eye plant looks like human eyeballs.

THE POISON GARDEN in northern England is a public garden filled with **DEADLY PLANTS.**

THE POISON GARDEN
THESE PLANTS CAN KILL   THESE PLANTS CAN KILL

ANTS THAT LIVE ON BULLHORN ACACIAS SWARM ANY INTRUDING BUGS AND THROW THEM OFF THE TREE.

Petals of the skeleton flower become see-through when wet, then turn back to white as they dry.

The trunk of the **baobab tree** swells into the **shape of a bottle** as it collects **rainwater.**

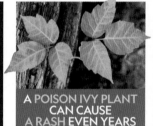

A POISON IVY PLANT CAN CAUSE A RASH EVEN YEARS AFTER IT HAS DIED.

AFTER CLOSING ITS "MOUTH" AROUND AN INSECT, A CARNIVOROUS VENUS FLYTRAP CAN TAKE UP TO 12 DAYS TO REOPEN.

The **Darth Vader flower** from Central America **resembles** the *Star Wars* villain.

Green Scene

Create a Hummingbird Garden!

More than a dozen different species of hummingbirds live throughout the United States—some probably near you. These tiny birds with iridescent feathers are fun to watch as they dart from flower to flower.

Use plants native to your area to create a garden that will attract hummingbirds to your yard. By growing native plants, you'll have a garden that thrives naturally and is good for the environment.

Their wings beat 40 to 80 times a second.

Hummingbirds are the only birds that can fly backward.

BROAD-BILLED HUMMINGBIRD

HOW TO ATTRACT HUMMINGBIRDS

Hovering all day can be exhausting, so hummingbirds need to refuel often. They feed on flowers' nectar, which has lots of energy. And a hummingbird can drink half its weight in just one day.

Hummingbirds will feed from any nectar-producing flower, regardless of its shape or color. The below flowers are examples of "flight fuel" flowers that will attract hummingbirds:

These birds can hover in midair.

BUTTERFLY BUSH

SCARLET SAGE

PENSTEMON

TRUMPET CREEPER

TRUMPET HONEYSUCKLE

Your Amazing Body!

HUMANS ARE THE ONLY SPECIES KNOWN TO BLUSH.

The human body is a complicated mass of systems—nine systems, to be exact. Each has a unique and critical purpose in the body, and we wouldn't be able to survive without all of them.

The **NERVOUS** system controls the body.

The **MUSCULAR** system makes movement possible.

The **SKELETAL** system supports the body.

The **CIRCULATORY** system moves blood throughout the body.

The **RESPIRATORY** system provides the body with oxygen.

The **DIGESTIVE** system breaks down food into nutrients and gets rid of waste.

The **IMMUNE** system protects the body against disease and infection.

The **ENDOCRINE** system regulates the body's functions.

The **REPRODUCTIVE** system enables people to produce offspring.

weird but true!

THE LEFT LUNG IS ABOUT 10 PERCENT SMALLER THAN THE RIGHT ONE.

THE NAILS ON YOUR WRITING HAND LIKELY GROW FASTER THAN THE ONES ON YOUR OTHER HAND.

WHEN MUSIC IS PLAYING, YOUR HEARTBEAT QUICKENS OR SLOWS DEPENDING ON THE SONG'S TEMPO.

FINGERPRINT **FACTS**

Take a look at your fingers. See anything special?
It's your fingerprint! This unique set of ridges and swirls is yours—and yours alone. Grab on to these fascinating fingerprint facts.

THE AVERAGE FINGERPRINT CAN HAVE AS MANY AS

150

INDIVIDUAL RIDGE CHARACTERISTICS.

THINK YOU CAN FIND A MATCH? DON'T BET ON IT! THERE'S ONLY A

1 IN 64 BILLION

CHANCE THAT YOUR FINGERPRINT WILL MATCH UP EXACTLY WITH SOMEONE ELSE'S.

FINGERPRINTS HAVE BEEN USED TO CATCH CRIMINALS SINCE

200 B.C.

FINGERPRINTS ARE TRULY UNIQUE! EVEN

IDENTICAL TWINS

HAVE DIFFERENT FINGERPRINTS.

YOUR FINGERPRINTS WERE THERE BEFORE YOU WERE BORN! A FETUS BEGINS DEVELOPING FINGERPRINTS AFTER

3 MONTHS

IN THE WOMB.

THERE ARE **THREE DIFFERENT KINDS** OF PATTERNS IN FINGERPRINTS. LOOPS, THE MOST COMMON PATTERN, ARE FOUND IN

60–70%

OF ALL FINGERPRINTS.

Why do our teeth fall out?

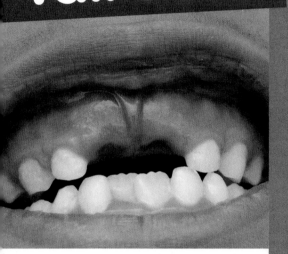

Do animals lose baby teeth, too?

Animals, they're just like us! Well, some of them. Most mammals are born with two sets of teeth, like humans. Puppies, kittens, and even lion cubs have tiny baby teeth that will fall out and be replaced with stronger ones. But there are some exceptions. Manatees, elephants, and kangaroos all have multiple sets of teeth that they go through in a lifetime. Other animals lose and grow new teeth almost constantly. Take the shark, for example, which can go through thousands of teeth in its lifetime!

Wriggly baby teeth are commonplace among kids, but did you ever wonder why you lose those tiny chompers? Most of us are born with a full set of 20 baby teeth, which are embedded in the jaw and eventually grow in when we're between five months and two years old. These teeth help you chew and formulate speech patterns as you learn to talk, but they're not meant to stick around forever. Instead, they're placeholders until our adult teeth, which become permanent, are ready to come in. Adult teeth are stronger and more durable than baby teeth. (After all, they're meant to last for a very, very long time!) As you grow, so does your jaw, creating more space in your mouth for your permanent teeth. When adult teeth push on your baby teeth, the baby teeth get loose. Soon enough, they'll fall out one by one—and maybe with a little help from you, if you can't resist wiggling them back and forth!

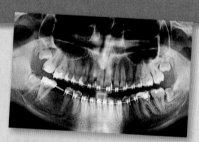

Will wisdom teeth make me smarter?

Despite their name, wisdom teeth have nothing to do with your smarts! These teeth are your third and final set of molars—the flat teeth at the back of your mouth that help you crush and grind food. And they're named for the time they usually appear in your life. This set of four teeth tends to crop up in your late teens or early twenties—when you're thought to have more, well, wisdom! And it's a good thing they don't provide any intellectual value: Dentists often remove wisdom teeth if they're crowding your other teeth or causing other issues in your mouth.

WHY can't I USE my left hand as well as my right one (or the other way around)?

About nine out of 10 of you reading this book will turn its pages with your right hand— the same hand you use to write a note or chuck a fastball. About 90 percent of humans are right-handed, meaning their right hand is their dominant hand. The other 10 percent are left-handed. Activities that feel natural with the dominant hand are awkward or difficult with the other one. Ever try to sign your name with your nondominant hand? Not so easy!

Cave paintings going back more than 5,000 years show humans favoring their right or left hand according to the same nine-to-one ratio we see today. And the same goes for the stone tools our evolutionary ancestors used 1.5 million years ago: Studies show a similar dominance of the right hand long before the human species, *Homo sapiens*, appeared in the fossil record.

So why is one hand dominant?

Scientists have discovered a sequence of genes linked to hand dominance, making it a trait that's passed along to children just like hair color or dimples. These traits determine how our brains are wired. How? The brain is split into two symmetrical halves known as hemispheres. In about 90 percent of people, the left side of the brain processes language skills. These people are typically right-handed. People born with genes for left-handedness—about 10 percent of the population—typically have brains that process speech on the right side.

So whichever side of the brain controls speech usually corresponds with a dominant hand on the opposite side. Because the left side of the brain controls the right side of the body and vice versa, scientists suspect that the evolution of our dominant hand is somehow connected to the development of our language capabilities. Humans can have a dominant eye, foot, and ear, too—but scientists aren't quite sure why. That's just one of many reasons the human brain is considered the most complex object in the universe.

$$NaOH + HCl \longrightarrow NaCl + H_2O$$

ARE YOU "mixed-handed"?

What about people who can use their nondominant hand almost as well as their dominant? They're called mixed-handed. (Scientists don't like using the term "ambidextrous," which implies neither hand is dominant.) About one percent of people are elite lefties/righties. Are you? Grab a piece of scratch paper and find out!

201

How Viruses Spread

IMAGINE YOU'RE AT BASKETBALL PRACTICE when your teammate coughs. He covers his mouth, but tiny droplets—hardly visible to the naked eye—escape. You don't notice, and you keep playing. The next day, your teammate stays home from school. A few days later, you have a fever and a sore throat. Did you get sick from your teammate?

It's hard to pinpoint the source of a virus. Some germs spread through the air, while others can be picked up from surfaces, such as doorknobs, light switches, and desks. If you're around someone who's carrying a virus and that person coughs, sneezes, or even talks near you, you could be in the virus's direct line of fire. Once you're exposed to infectious particles, your immune system will do its best to protect you from getting sick.

But if the virus muscles its way past your body's line of defense, it then has to find a host to stay alive. If it does, the virus invades the host cells in your body and begins to replicate, or make copies of itself. This causes a disease (such as the flu or COVID-19) that usually makes you feel sick. Meanwhile, your immune system continues to work hard against the virus. For example, you might get a fever, which is a sign that your body's fighting off those germs.

What can you do? It's best to rest, hydrate, and lay low while your body rids itself of the virus. Then hopefully within a few days, both you and your teammate will be back on the basketball court!

Germy Terms!

BACTERIA: Microorganisms that can cause sicknesses like ear infections or strep throat. But some are good for your health, like the kind that break down food in your gut.

EPIDEMIC: A sudden increase in the number of people in a certain area—like a town, city, or state—with the same disease.

PANDEMIC: A worldwide outbreak of a disease. This happens when a virus spreads easily and infects a lot of people.

VIRUS: Tiny organisms found all around— in dirt, water, and the air—that need a host's energy to grow and survive. Once inside a host, a virus can multiply and attack cells.

WHAT'S YOUR TYPE?

Everyone's blood is made of the same basic elements, but not all blood is alike. There are four main blood types. If a person needs to use donated blood, the donated blood can react with their body's immune system if it's not the right type. This diagram shows which types of blood are compatible with each other.

 GROUP O can donate red blood cells to anybody. It's the universal donor.

 GROUP A can donate red blood cells to A's and AB's.

 GROUP B can donate red blood cells to B's and AB's.

 GROUP AB can donate to other AB's, but can receive from all others.

 O+ is the most common blood type:

38%

of people in the U.S. have this type.

Blood types can be positive or negative. Only **18%** of people in the U.S. have a negative blood type.

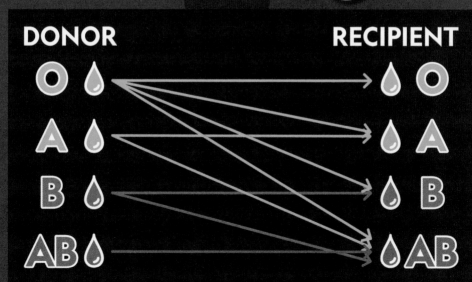

DONOR

RECIPIENT

The Science of Cute

How these adorable animals affect your brain

Waking from a nap, a fluffy kitten blinks its big blue eyes and yawns to reveal a tiny pink tongue. Then it stretches its body, exposing a furry little tummy. Curling back into a ball, the kitten lets out a soft meow and goes back into snooze mode. *So adorable!*

Whether it's a sleepy kitty or a bumbling baby elephant, certain traits drive our cute-o-meters wild. And it turns out that science can explain our need to squee over critters.

Scientists think our tendency to value cuteness has to do with species survival. Human babies are born helpless—they need adults to look after them. Having features that grown-ups find irresistible helps make sure that a baby is cared for and played with so that it's healthy and learns social skills. So over hundreds of thousands of years, humans developed a fondness for certain traits in babies. And when we see similar characteristics in animals, we find them *aw*-worthy as well.

What is it about human babies and animals that we find so adorable? In 1943, Austrian zoologist Konrad Lorenz came up with a list of cuteness traits—from big eyes to clumsiness—that make us feel affection.

"People have an automatic response to these features," says Sookyung Cho, a scientist at Northern Kentucky University. Discover which traits give us warm fuzzies, and why.

head-to-head

Adorable Animal: An arctic fox pokes its fluffy head out from behind a snowbank. Living in its rugged habitat on the Arctic tundra, the animal sports a thick layer of fur in winter that makes its head look big.

Cuteness Factor: A large head is one of the traits that humans find adorable. Some scientists believe that we're drawn to animals with big heads because they remind us of a human baby's noggin. When humans are born, their brains are more developed than other parts of their bodies. Their skulls must then be big enough to hold those brains. So when humans see other animals with similarly large heads, we feel the need to protect them.

round it out

Adorable Animal: A koala rests its rump on a tree branch in an Australian forest as it munches eucalyptus leaves. Its body looks like a furry ball clinging to a branch. The koala swallows the last of its leafy snack.

Cuteness Factor: One quality that people tend to find irresistible in koalas is **a rounded body,** rather than a sharp one like a sea urchin has. In general, humans prefer curving geometric shapes. "We're more drawn to roundness than sharp lines," says researcher Hiroshi Nittono of Japan's Osaka University.

eye got it

Adorable Animal: A baby giraffe on the African savanna blinks, showing off its huge peepers. Lots of young animals have large eyes, from giraffes to puppies to gorillas. Baby humans do, too—a human's eyes grow fastest during the first few years of life, then slow down while the body catches up.

Cuteness Factor: Large eyes are often associated with sweetness and innocence, creating a major adorable alert in your brain. Looking at the big peepers of certain animals and human babies can even prompt some people to produce natural chemicals called dopamine and oxytocin, which boost feelings of happiness.

sweet sounds

Adorable Animal: An emperor penguin chick nestles underneath its father for warmth. The chick opens its beak and squeaks—it's now toasty beneath the dad's belly.

Cuteness Factor: Squeals and trills from animals can make a human want to coo. "Unlike a loud roar or sharp squawk, the sounds made by baby animals aren't threatening," says Joshua Paul Dale, a professor at Japan's Chuo University who studies the concept of cuteness. So humans are able to see the critters as lovable.

205

FUTURE WORLD:

A few decades from now, how will you get to the store? Maybe you'll take a drone to go shopping—or, if it's raining, you might go for a ride in a driverless cube car.

"The sky's no longer the limit in terms of where transportation is headed," says Tom Kurfess, a mechanical engineering professor at the Georgia Institute of Technology. Take a peek at these possible wild rides of the future.

GOING UP ... WAY UP!

The space elevator doors open—welcome to the space station lobby. It's possible that people will one day ride a space elevator from Earth to a space station that orbits our planet from 22,370 miles (36,000 km) above. The elevator could carry passengers and cargo into space without burning huge amounts of fuel, unlike today's rockets. Aboard the station, travelers might stay in a hotel room with a truly out-of-this-world view. Then those heading to, say, Mars can transfer to a spaceship to continue their journey.

NO DRIVER NEEDED

Picture this: You exit your high-rise apartment balcony into your own private glass elevator, take a seat, and say your destination. The elevator car descends 205 floors to street level before detaching from the building and moving to the street. It's now a cube-shaped car. Another cube carrying your friends is nearby; the vehicles connect while in motion, transforming into one bigger car. The cube drops you off at school and parks itself. According to Tommaso Gecchelin, founder of NEXT Future Transportation, driverless cars will work together to end traffic jams and improve safety.

Transportation

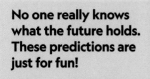

No one really knows what the future holds. These predictions are just for fun!

POWER PLANE

Passenger planes will still be around in the future—they'll just likely travel *much* faster. Today, flying 6,850 miles (11,025 km) from New York City to Beijing, China, takes about 14 hours. But thanks to future technological advancements such as sleeker, more lightweight aircraft, a passenger plane could make the same trip in just under two hours.

FLOWN BY DRONE

Today, drones and robots do deliver meals. But further into the future, helicopter-size drones could also deliver *people*. Some experts even think that cargo drones will be able to lift small houses from a city and carry them to scenic vacation spots.

TOTALLY TUBULAR

Say your friend invites you to her birthday party. It's today—and across the country. No prob. In the future, you could tube it from the West Coast to the East Coast in a couple of hours. You sit in a capsule that looks like a train without rails. Whoosh! The capsule's sucked into a vacuum tube. Like a bullet train, the capsule uses magnets to fly forward in the tube without friction, or resistance. The result: a smooth, fast ride that never slows from 750 miles an hour (1,200 km/h).

FUTURE WORLD:

S cientists are dreaming up ways to cool down Earth. Check out a few of their brainiest— and zaniest!—ideas to slow climate change.

SPACE UMBRELLA

When you get too hot at the beach, you sit under an umbrella, so why not do the same for the planet? Scientists estimate we would need to decrease the sun's glare by only 2 to 4 percent to make the planet's temperature healthy again. One idea is to deploy trillions of butterfly-size robots that would form a sunshade 60,000 miles (96,560 km) wide. But how to launch them is a puzzle—this technology doesn't exist yet.

PAINTING MOUNTAINS

Glaciers help keep the planet cool because their icy white color reflects light and heat from the sun. But as Earth warms, glacier ice melts, which then heats the planet even more. One Peruvian inventor came up with a possible solution: painting a former glacier—now a dark mountain—bright white. Like snow and ice, the white paint would reflect light and heat to help keep the planet cool.

CARBON EATERS

Carbon dioxide—a heat-trapping gas released by burning coal, oil, and natural gas—is dangerously warming the planet. Luckily, phytoplankton (microscopic plantlike creatures that live on the surface of the ocean) suck small amounts of this gas out of the air for food. So scientists dumped iron, which phytoplankton need to grow, into an area of the ocean. The result? A huge growth of hungry phytoplankton that gobbled up the CO_2, causing levels in the area to drop.

Climate Tech

CREATING CLOUDS

When volcanoes erupt, the ash can form a shield that reflects the sun's heat into space and lowers Earth's temperature by one degree Fahrenheit (.55°C) for a short time. This inspired scientists to look into spraying sea salt into the sky from airplanes. There, water vapor would collect on the salt particles and form clouds that would help reflect the sun's heat. But once started, the process would have to go on forever, or the planet would quickly rewarm.

QUIZ WHIZ

Test your science and technology smarts by taking this quiz!

Write your answers on a piece of paper. Then check them below.

1 **Where would you find the softball-size drone known as Int-Ball?**

a. Amazon rainforest in South America

b. Giza Pyramids in Egypt

c. Great Barrier Reef in Australia

d. International Space Station

2 **True or false?** A hummingbird can drink half its weight in nectar in one day.

3 **By what age do all of a human's baby teeth usually grow in?**

a. six months

b. one year

c. two years

d. four years

4 **Which of the following is not one of the three domains of life?**

a. Animalia

b. Archaea

c. Bacteria

d. Eukarya

5 **Petals on the skeleton flower become _____ when wet.**

a. white

b. bones

c. see-through

d. glow in the dark

Not **STUMPED** yet? Check out the *NATIONAL GEOGRAPHIC KIDS QUIZ WHIZ* collection for more fun **SCIENCE AND TECHNOLOGY** questions!

ANSWERS: 1. d; 2. True; 3. c; 4. a; 5. c.

This Is How It's Done!

Sometimes, the most complicated problems are solved with step-by-step directions. These "how-to" instructions are also known as a process analysis essay. Although scientists and engineers use this tool to program robots and write computer code, you also use process analysis every day, from following a recipe to putting together a new toy or gadget. Here's how to write a basic process analysis essay.

Step 1: Choose Your Topic Sentence

Pick a clear and concise topic sentence that describes what you're writing about. Be sure to explain to the readers why the task is important—and how many steps there are to complete it.

Step 2: List Materials

Do you need specific ingredients or equipment to complete your process? Mention these right away so the readers will have all they need to do the activity.

Step 3: Write Your Directions

Your directions should be clear and easy to follow. Assume that you are explaining the process for the first time, and define any unfamiliar terms. List your steps in the exact order the readers will need to follow to complete the activity. Try to keep your essay limited to no more than six steps.

Step 4: Restate Your Main Idea

Your closing idea should revisit your topic sentence, drawing a conclusion relating to the importance of the subject.

EXAMPLE OF A PROCESS ANALYSIS ESSAY

Downloading an app is a simple way to enhance your tablet. Today, I'd like to show you how to search for and add an app to your tablet. First, you will need a tablet with the ability to access the internet. You'll also want to ask a parent for permission before you download anything onto your tablet. Next, select the specific app you want by going to the app store on your tablet and entering the app's name into the search bar. Once you find the app you're seeking, select "download" and wait for the app to load. When you see that the app has fully loaded, tap on the icon and you will be able to access it. Now you can enjoy your app and have more fun with your tablet.

In a mangrove forest in Panama, aquatic animals swim below the water's surface.

WONDERS of NATURE

Biomes

A BIOME, OFTEN CALLED A MAJOR LIFE ZONE, is one of the natural world's major communities where plants and animals adapt to their specific surroundings. Biomes are classified depending on the predominant vegetation, climate, and geography of a region. They can be divided into six major types: forest, freshwater, marine, desert, grassland, and tundra. Each biome consists of many ecosystems.

Biomes are extremely important. Balanced ecological relationships among biomes help to maintain the environment and life on Earth as we know it. For example, an increase in one species of plant, such as an invasive one, can cause a ripple effect throughout a whole biome.

FOREST

Forests occupy about one-third of Earth's land area. There are three major types of forests: tropical, temperate, and boreal (taiga). Forests are home to a diversity of plants, some of which may hold medicinal qualities for humans, as well as thousands of animal species, some still undiscovered. Forests can also absorb carbon dioxide, a greenhouse gas, and give off oxygen.

Certain trees in a temperate forest can grow up to 100 feet (30 m) tall—as high as a seven-story building.

FRESHWATER

Most water on Earth is salty, but freshwater ecosystems—including lakes, ponds, wetlands, rivers, and streams—usually contain water with less than one percent salt concentration. The countless animal and plant species that live in freshwater biomes vary from continent to continent, but they include algae, frogs, turtles, fish, and the larvae of many insects.

The largest freshwater habitat in the world is the Everglades, 1.5 million acres (607,028 ha) of wetlands in southern Florida, U.S.A.

MARINE

The marine biome covers almost three-fourths of Earth's surface, making it the largest habitat on our planet. Oceans make up the majority of the saltwater marine biome. Coral reefs are considered to be the most biodiverse of any of the biome habitats. The marine biome is home to more than one million plant and animal species.

Scientists think that there could be as many as 700,000 marine species—but about 90 percent of them have not yet been identified!

DESERT

Covering about one-fifth of Earth's surface, deserts are places where precipitation is less than 10 inches (25 cm) a year. Although most deserts are hot, there are other kinds as well. The four major kinds of deserts are hot, semiarid, coastal, and cold. Far from being barren wastelands, deserts are biologically rich habitats.

Even though it's covered in snow and ice, Antarctica is a desert because it rarely rains or snows there.

GRASSLAND

Biomes called grasslands are characterized by having grasses instead of large shrubs or trees. Some of the world's largest land animals, such as elephants, live there. Grasslands generally have precipitation for only about half to three-fourths of the year. If it were more, they would become forests. Grasslands can be divided into two types: tropical (savannas) and temperate.

One of the largest grasslands in the world, the Eurasian Steppe stretches from Hungary to China—almost one-fifth of the way around the world.

TUNDRA

The coldest of all biomes, a tundra is characterized by an extremely cold climate, simple vegetation, little precipitation, poor nutrients, and a short growing season. There are two types of tundra: Arctic and alpine. A tundra is home to few kinds of vegetation. Surprisingly, though, quite a few animal species can survive the tundra's extremes, such as wolves and caribou, and even mosquitoes.

Arctic poppies bloom across the tundra in the summer—when a thin layer of soil on the top of the permafrost thaws—making the ground bright yellow.

ANTARCTICA

HERE'S THE THING ABOUT ANTARCTICA— IT'S BIG.

No, not just big—vast! Dictionaries define "vast" as immense, empty, and boundless. All of these words describe Antarctica. But so do these words—fantastic, awesome, otherworldly, and beautiful.

When I first stepped from the plane onto the Antarctic ice, I knew I was in a place like no other. I was struck by the sameness of my surroundings. A nearly flat plain of ice stretched to the horizon in most directions. We were on an island, but you'd never know it. Thick sea ice connected the island to the mainland about 45 miles (72 km) away.

The dry air was crystal clear, making the sky overhead a deep blue. Brilliant sunshine reflected off the landscape. Sunglasses were a must—both day and night. It was summer, and the sun would not be setting the entire three weeks of the expedition.

The constant sunshine did little to warm the air. Temperatures mostly stayed in the negative numbers. Lows were down to minus 30°F (-34°C). Strange things happen when it gets that cold.

The slightest amount of moisture glazes ropes with ice. That makes them tricky to hold. Eating is a challenge, too. My parents used to say, "Eat your food before it gets cold." Here we say, "Eat your food before it freezes." You might end up chiseling frozen soup from a bowl that was hot from the stove a few minutes earlier.

The vastness of Antarctica really makes you feel exposed to the weather, especially when the wind blows. I often had to turn away from the stinging ice crystals that the wind whipped at us. During some days (or were they nights?), the tents rattled and flapped so much I thought for sure they were going to fly away.

Everything about Antarctica was extreme and beautiful. But the sight I'll remember most occurred several days into the expedition. We took a short helicopter ride from our base camp. We landed about halfway up a mountain. I stepped off. I looked up. I don't know how long I gawked at the steaming volcano, Mount Erebus, that loomed before me.

A LAVA LAKE STEAMS INSIDE MOUNT EREBUS.

Expert Tips

STAY HYDRATED! That's the advice of polar explorers such as Will Steger. He should know. His team was the first to cross Antarctica by dogsled: Despite the cold, Antarctica is a desert. The air is dry, and very little precipitation falls. The body loses moisture easily to the dry air. Walking and working on ice can be exhausting. You sweat, breathe heavily, and lose more moisture. As explorers, we make sure we keep our water bottles full. How? By melting ice and snow and then, while the water is hot, pouring it into thermoses!

A SEAL PUP ON ANTARCTICA'S ROSS ISLAND

Gear & Gadgets

WHEN IT COMES TO STAYING WARM, the point isn't to keep cold air out. It's to keep your body heat in. Sometimes when sleeping on the tent floor, the heat from my body melted the ice beneath my sleeping bag. To keep my body heat from escaping, I dress in layers. I sleep in layers, too. In Antarctica, my "bed" consisted of a fleece liner inside a sleeping bag stuffed inside another sleeping bag. I laid the double bags on top of a sheepskin rug on top of an air mattress on top of a foam mat. It took six layers of bedding and as many layers of clothing to keep me warm.

USING A GIANT DRILL, SCIENTISTS ON ROSS ISLAND GATHER A CORE SAMPLE OF ICE.

SCIENTISTS EXPLORE THE CRATER OF MOUNT EREBUS.

In Antarctica, there's a 30-30-30 rule: When the temperature is minus 30°F (-34°C) and the wind is 30 miles an hour (48 km/h), human skin freezes in 30 seconds.

In some parts of Antarctica, the ice is three miles (4.8 km) thick.

217

THE OCEANS

PACIFIC OCEAN

STATS

Surface area
65,100,000 sq mi (168,600,000 sq km)

Percentage of all oceans
46 percent

Surface temperatures
**Summer high:
90°F (32°C)
Winter low: 28°F (-2°C)**

Tides
**Highest: 30 ft (9 m)
near Korean Peninsula
Lowest: 1 ft (0.3 m) near Midway Islands**

Cool creatures: **giant Pacific octopus, bottlenose whale, clownfish, great white shark**

Clownfish

ATLANTIC OCEAN

STATS

Surface area
33,100,000 sq mi (85,600,000 sq km)

Percentage of all oceans
24 percent

Surface temperatures
**Summer high: 90°F (32°C)
Winter low: 28°F (-2°C)**

Tides
**Highest: 52 ft (16 m)
Bay of Fundy, Canada
Lowest: 1.5 ft (0.5 m)
Gulf of Mexico and Mediterranean Sea**

Cool creatures **blue whale, Atlantic spotted dolphin, sea turtle, bottlenose dolphin**

Bottlenose dolphin

INDIAN OCEAN

STATS

Surface area
27,500,000 sq mi (71,200,000 sq km)

Percentage of all oceans
20 percent

Surface temperatures
Summer high: 93°F (34°C)
Winter low: 28°F (-2°C)

Tides
Highest: 36 ft (11 m)
Lowest: 2 ft (0.6 m)
Both along Australia's west coast

Cool creatures: **humpback whale, Portuguese man-of-war, dugong (sea cow), leatherback turtle**

Leatherback turtle

ARCTIC OCEAN

STATS

Surface area
6,100,000 sq mi (15,700,000 sq km)

Percentage of all oceans
4 percent

Surface temperatures
Summer high:
41°F (5°C)
Winter low: 28°F (-2°C)

Tides
Less than 1 ft (0.3 m)
variation throughout the ocean

Cool creatures:
beluga whale, orca, harp seal, narwhal

Narwhal

SOUTHERN OCEAN

STATS

Surface area
8,500,000 sq mi (21,900,000 sq km)

Percentage of all oceans
6 percent

Surface temperatures
Summer high: 50°F (10°C)
Winter low: 28°F (-2°C)

Tides
Less than 2 ft (0.6 m)
variation throughout the ocean

Cool creatures: **emperor penguin, colossal squid, mackerel icefish, Antarctic toothfish**

Emperor penguin

To see the major oceans and bays in relation to landmasses, look at the map on pages 272 and 273.

12 WAYS
TO SAVE THE OCEAN

No matter where you are, you're connected to the ocean.

Plants in the ocean such as plankton and seaweed create at least half the world's oxygen, so you can thank the ocean when you take a deep breath. And the local creek or stream in your neighborhood eventually flows into a river before heading into the ocean. Plus, the ocean is full of animals we love.

Problems caused by people are putting the ocean and the creatures that live there at risk. But you can help. Follow these tips to protect the ocean, whether you're beachside or bedroom-bound.

2 FIX THE TURTLE TRAP

Learn about the animals that depend on the beach you're visiting. For example, the habitat might host nesting sea turtles! If so, fill in the holes that you dig into the sand. Mama turtles or their hatchlings can become trapped in deep holes as they make their way back to the water. (Plus, a deep hole might give a fellow human a sprained ankle.)

4 COOL CREEK

Choose a nearby creek or stream and help keep it clean. Hold cleanups with your family and friends, and make posters to remind your neighbors not to litter.

5 LOW ENERGY

Climate change is creating warmer and more acidic oceans, which changes the way that animals behave, reproduce, and grow. You can help by biking or walking to school instead of riding in a car, hanging up washed clothes instead of putting them in the dryer, and turning off lights and other appliances when you leave the room.

1 BAN BALLOONS

Talk to your teacher about using paper chains, streamers, and pom-poms for party decorations instead of balloons. An escaped balloon eventually falls back to Earth—and can end up in waterways. A recent study found that balloons are the most dangerous trash for seabirds.

3 DON'T BUY SEA LIFE

Don't purchase jewelry or other products made of animals or their parts, including dried-out seahorses, scales, teeth, feathers, coral, and turtle shells. Fake versions of these products are OK. But if you think the product *might* be real, don't buy it.

6 STOP STRAWS

You know plastic straws can't be recycled, can easily blow away, and might be mistaken for food. They're especially dangerous at beachside restaurants. Ask your waiter to skip the straw, then use our guide to request that the eatery stop using plastic straws forever. natgeokids.com/KidsVsPlastic

7 FLOWER POWER

Ask your parents to put native plants and flowers in your yard instead of grass: Grass lawns use lots of water, need gas-powered mowers, and might be fertilized with chemicals that could create toxic algae blooms in nearby waterways.

8 PICKY EATER

Some seafood is caught in ways that hurt other animals when they get trapped in nets or on hooks. When you're out to eat, ask the waiter if the seafood was caught sustainably. Seafood Watch is an online guide that has more information.

9 WILD WATCH

If you see a wild animal, watch from a distance so it doesn't have to waste energy getting away from you. That interrupts behaviors like hunting, nursing, or resting. If you see other people feeding, chasing, or touching an animal like a sea lion or sea turtle, ask an adult to call for help. (The National Oceanic and Atmospheric Administration has a special hotline people can call to report a problem.)

10 SEA SPEAK

Spread the word to your friends and classmates about these sea-saving tips. Want to do more? Form an ocean club at school to make big changes.

NON TOXIC FOR ECOSYSTEM!
100% OXYBENZONE AND OCTINOXATE FREE

11 CLEAN SUNSCREEN

Sunscreen keeps your skin safe, but some chemicals can hurt coral reefs. Slather on sunscreens with a "reef safe" label; these don't contain the harmful chemicals oxybenzone and octinoxate.

12 PET PROBLEMS

Pick up your pet's waste when you take it on a walk. (Duh!) It's not just gross to leave it: Pet poo can contain bacteria that wash into creeks, rivers, and then the ocean, spreading diseases to marine animals.

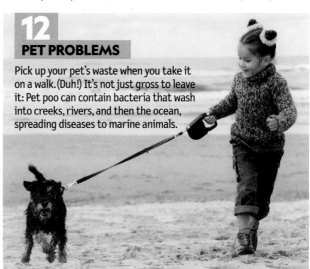

Weather and Climate

Weather is the condition of the atmosphere—temperature, wind, humidity, and precipitation—at a given place at a given time. Climate, however, is the average weather for a particular place over a long period of time. Different places on Earth have different climates, but climate is not a random occurrence.

It is a pattern that is controlled by factors such as latitude, elevation, prevailing winds, the temperature of ocean currents, and location on land relative to water. Climate is generally constant, but evidence indicates that human activity is causing a change in its patterns—a long-term shift called climate change.

WEATHER EXTREMES

LONGEST-LASTING TYPHOON: Typhoon John lasted 31 days between August and September 1994 as it traveled from the eastern to the western Pacific.

HOTTEST MONTH: July 2023, when average temperatures were .43 degrees Fahrenheit (.24 degrees Celsius) higher than any other July on record since 1880.

LONGEST LIGHTNING FLASH: 477 miles (767 km), stretching across Texas, Louisiana, and Mississippi, U.S.A., in 2022

GLOBAL CLIMATE ZONES

Climatologists, people who study climate, have created different systems for classifying climates. One that is often used is called the Köppen system, which classifies climate zones according to precipitation, temperature, and vegetation. It has five major categories—tropical, dry, temperate, cold, and polar—with a sixth category for locations where high elevations override other factors.

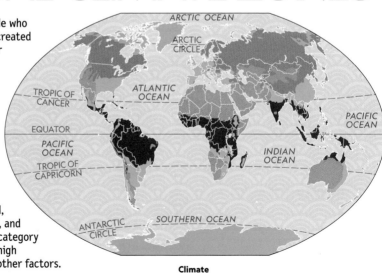

Climate
■ Tropical ☐ Dry ☐ Temperate ☐ Cold ☐ Polar

Climate CHANGE

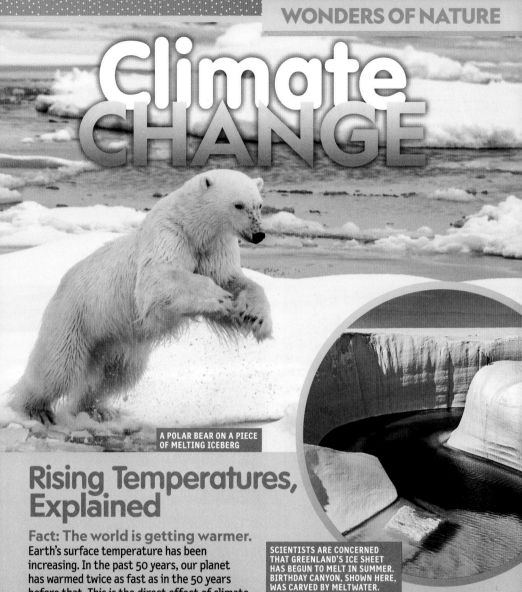

A POLAR BEAR ON A PIECE OF MELTING ICEBERG

SCIENTISTS ARE CONCERNED THAT GREENLAND'S ICE SHEET HAS BEGUN TO MELT IN SUMMER. BIRTHDAY CANYON, SHOWN HERE, WAS CARVED BY MELTWATER.

Rising Temperatures, Explained

Fact: The world is getting warmer.
Earth's surface temperature has been increasing. In the past 50 years, our planet has warmed twice as fast as in the 50 years before that. This is the direct effect of climate change, which refers not only to the increase in Earth's average temperature (known as global warming), but also to its long-term effects on winds, rain, and ocean currents. Global warming is the reason glaciers and polar ice sheets are melting—resulting in rising sea levels and shrinking habitats. This makes survival for some animals a big challenge. Warming also means more flooding along coasts and drought for inland areas.

Why are temperatures climbing?
While some of the recent climate changes can be tied to natural causes—such as changes in the sun's intensity, the unusually warm ocean currents of El Niño, and volcanic activity—human activities are the greatest contributor.

Everyday activities that require burning fossil fuels, such as driving gasoline-powered cars, contribute to global warming. These activities produce greenhouse gases, which enter the atmosphere and trap heat. At the current rate, Earth's global average temperature is projected to rise some 5°F (3°C) or more since 1900, and it will get even warmer after that. And as the climate continues to warm, it will unfortunately continue to affect the environment and our society in many ways.

223

10 FACTS ABOUT FREAKY FORCES OF NATURE

Thousands of small frogs once rained down on a town in Serbia, a country in Europe, sending people scurrying for cover.

A **pyroclastic flow,** which is created by a volcano, is a cloud of gas and rock that can reach temperatures above **1000°F** (538°C).

Flame-throwing tornadoes, called fire whirls, can be **50 feet** (15 m) **wide** and grow as tall as a **40-story** building.

A **hailstorm** in the Himalayan mountain range in Asia **dropped chunks of ice** the size of baseballs **at more than 100 miles an hour** (161 km/h).

Mysterious rogue waves, which can appear without any warning in the open sea, can be **10 STORIES TALL.**

SNOW ROLLERS form when wet snow falls on icy ground that snow can't stick to. Pushed by strong winds, the snow rolls into logs.

Usually seen once a **thunderstorm has passed,** mammatus clouds form from pouches of sinking air.

Underwater hot springs, called hydrothermal vents, occur when water seeps through cracks in the ocean floor after being heated by magma inside Earth.

The fastest wind speed ever recorded— **some 300 miles an hour** (480 km/h)— occurred during a tornado near Oklahoma City, Oklahoma, U.S.A., in 1999.

Vast glowing rings called **AURORAS** often appear far above the North and South Poles. These rings can be more than **12,000 miles** (19,300 km) around.

WATER CYCLE

Precipitation falls

Water storage in ice and snow

Water vapor condenses in clouds

Water filters into the ground

Meltwater and surface runoff

Freshwater storage

Evaporation

Groundwater discharge

Water storage in ocean

The amount of water on Earth is more or less constant—

only the form changes. As the sun warms Earth's surface, liquid water is changed into water vapor in a process called **evaporation.** Water on the surface of plants' leaves turns into water vapor in a process called **transpiration.** As water vapor rises into the air, it cools and changes form again. This time, it becomes clouds in a process called **condensation.** Water droplets fall from the clouds as **precipitation,** which then travels as groundwater or runoff back to the lakes, rivers, and oceans, where the cycle (shown above) starts all over again.

To a meteorologist—a person who studies the weather—a "light rain" is less than 1/48 inch (0.5 mm). A "heavy rain" is more than 1/6 inch (4 mm).

You drink the same water as the dinosaurs! Earth has been recycling water for more than four billion years.

226

Types of Clouds

If you want a clue about the weather, look up at the clouds. They'll tell a lot about the condition of the air and what weather might be on the way. Clouds are made of both air and water. On fair days, warm air currents rise and push against the water in clouds, keeping it from falling. But as the raindrops in a cloud get bigger, it's time to set them free. The bigger raindrops become too heavy for the air currents to hold up, and they fall to the ground.

1 **STRATUS** These clouds make the sky look like a bowl of thick gray porridge. They hang low in the sky, blanketing the day in dreary darkness. Stratus clouds form when cold, moist air close to the ground moves over a region.

2 **CIRRUS** These wispy tufts of clouds are thin and hang high up in the atmosphere where the air is extremely cold. Cirrus clouds are made of tiny ice crystals.

3 **CUMULUS** These white, fluffy clouds make people sing, "Oh, what a beautiful morning!" They form low in the atmosphere and look like marshmallows. They often mix with large patches of blue sky. Formed when hot air rises, cumulus clouds usually disappear when the air cools at night.

4 **CUMULONIMBUS** These are the monster clouds. Rising air currents force fluffy cumulus clouds to swell and shoot upward, as much as 70,000 feet (21,000 m). When these clouds bump against the top of the troposphere, known as the tropopause, they flatten out on top like tabletops.

How Much Does a Cloud Weigh?
A light, fluffy cumulus cloud typically weighs about 216,000 pounds (98,000 kg). That's about the weight of 18 elephants. A rain-soaked cumulonimbus cloud typically weighs 105.8 million pounds (48 million kg), or about the same as 9,000 elephants.

227

COUNTING SNOWFLAKES

Yay! It's a snow day! You've gone sledding at the best hills and built a mighty fine snowperson, but do you know just how many flakes fall from the sky each winter? Put on your mittens and learn more about snow with these frozen facts.

U.S. record for most snowfall in 24 hours:

75.8 INCHES (1.93 m)

Silver Lake, Colorado—April 14–15, 1921

The biggest snowflake on record was

15 INCHES

(38 cm) wide.

MORE THAN

1,000,000,000,000,000,000,000,000

SNOWFLAKES FALL EVERY WINTER.

Tallest snowperson ever built:

122 FEET 1 INCH (37.21 m)

Built by people in Bethel, Maine, U.S.A., over one month in 2008

Bet You Didn't Know!

7 stormy facts to soak up

1 The energy from lightning strikes can create nutrients in soil, helping plants grow.

2 A tornado once traveled 219 miles (352 km) from Missouri to Indiana, U.S.A., in 3.5 hours.

3 At about the same time every day from September to December, a thunderstorm called Hector the Convector breaks out over Australia's Tiwi Islands.

4 The smell in the air after it rains has a name: petrichor.

5 Hailstones can fall faster than a cheetah can run.

6 Virga, also known as phantom rain, is rain that falls from the sky but evaporates before it hits the ground.

7 Before the 1800s, many Europeans thought that ringing church bells could prevent lightning strikes.

229

HURRICANE
HAPPENINGS

A storm is brewing—but is this a tropical cyclone, a hurricane, or a typhoon? These weather events go by different names depending on where they form, how fast their winds get, or both. Strong tropical cyclones are called hurricanes in the Atlantic and parts of the Pacific Ocean; in the western Pacific, they are called typhoons. But any way you look at it, these storms pack a punch. And they all form when warm moist air rises from the ocean, causing air from surrounding areas to be "sucked" in. That air then becomes warm and moist and rises, too, beginning a cycle that forms clouds, which rotate with the spin of Earth. If there is enough warm water to feed the storm, it will result in a hurricane. And the warmer the water and the more moisture in the air, the more powerful the hurricane.

HURRICANE NAMES FOR 2025

Atlantic hurricane names come from six official international lists. The names alternate between male and female. When a storm becomes a hurricane, a name from the list is used, in alphabetical order. (If the hurricane season is especially active and the list runs out, the World Meteorological Organization will provide extra names to draw from.) Each list is reused every six years. A name is "retired" if that hurricane caused a lot of damage or many deaths.

Andrea	Gabrielle	Lorenzo	Rebekah
Barry	Humberto	Melissa	Sebastien
Chantal	Imelda	Nestor	Tanya
Dexter	Jerry	Olga	Van
Erin	Karen	Pablo	Wendy
Fernand			

SCALE OF HURRICANE INTENSITY

CATEGORY	ONE	TWO	THREE	FOUR	FIVE
DAMAGE	Minimal	Moderate	Extensive	Extreme	Catastrophic
WINDS	74–95 mph (119–153 km/h)	96–110 mph (154–177 km/h)	111–129 mph (178–208 km/h)	130–156 mph (209–251 km/h)	157 mph or higher (252+ km/h)
(DAMAGE refers to wind and water damage combined.)					

What Is a Tornado?

THE ENHANCED FUJITA SCALE

The Enhanced Fujita (EF) Scale, named after tornado expert T. Theodore Fujita, classifies tornadoes based on wind speed and the intensity of damage that they cause.

EF0
65–85 mph winds
(105–137 km/h)
Slight damage

EF1
86–110 mph winds
(138–177 km/h)
Moderate damage

EF2
111–135 mph winds
(178–217 km/h)
Substantial damage

EF3
136–165 mph winds
(218–266 km/h)
Severe damage

EF4
166–200 mph winds
(267–322 km/h)
Massive damage

EF5
More than
200 mph winds
(322+ km/h)
Catastrophic
damage

TORNADOES, ALSO KNOWN AS TWISTERS, are funnels of rapidly rotating air that are created during thunderstorms. With wind speeds that can exceed 300 miles an hour (483 km/h), tornadoes have the power to pick up and destroy everything in their path.

THIS ROTATING FUNNEL OF AIR, formed in a cumulus or cumulonimbus cloud, became a tornado when it touched the ground.

TORNADOES HAVE OCCURRED IN ALL 50 U.S. STATES AND ON EVERY CONTINENT EXCEPT ANTARCTICA.

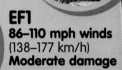

Eruption!

It had been nearly 40 years since Mauna Loa, the world's largest active volcano, had erupted. But while the mega mountain in Volcanoes National Park on Hawaii's Big Island had been dormant for decades, it was far from extinct. And in November 2022, Mauna Loa woke up as lava began flowing from the southwest portion of the volcano's caldera, or crater. The eruption wasn't really a surprise: Volcanologists—scientists who study volcanoes—had been tracking Mauna Loa's activity and warned that a series of earthquakes in the area could trigger lava flows. That's just what happened, with the volcano—which takes up half of the Big Island—erupting for about two weeks, lighting up the molten rock in a bright orange glow.

While ash spewing from Mauna Loa could be seen from space, the eruption did not present a major threat to those who live near the volcano. The lava flowed slowly from Mauna Loa, while the most concerning threat for locals was volcanic smog, or "vog," which is formed by the gases emitted from an erupting volcano and can cause breathing problems and eye irritation. Still, that didn't stop tourists from trekking to the Big Island for a rare glimpse of the volcano in action.

Super Typhoon

On average, several typhoons—powerful storms that start in the northwestern Pacific Ocean—roar through Japan each year. But few have been quite as intense as Super Typhoon Nanmadol, which struck southwest Japan in September 2022. A super typhoon is classified as a storm with sustained surface-wind strength of some 150 miles an hour (240 km/h)—the equivalent of a strong category 4 hurricane—and Nanmadol met that criteria. The storm brought heavy winds, knocking over power lines and causing outages across the region. Rain fell at rates of up to 28 inches (70 cm) in a 24-hour period, triggering landslides and floods and forcing millions of people to evacuate in order to stay safe.

Super Typhoon Nanmadol ultimately weakened to cyclone status before heading out to sea, but not before doing significant damage. Houses were destroyed, businesses and transportation throughout Japan were disrupted, and many people were injured. Ultimately, Japan rebuilt from the super typhoon, but it took plenty of effort to recover from one of the most destructive tropical storms to strike the country in decades.

KOALA RESCUE

A young koala scrambled up a eucalyptus tree. It was not trying to grab one of the tasty leaves it loved snacking on—it was trying to get away from the flames and smoke swirling in the forest beneath it.

In 2019 and 2020, a record number of wildfires raged through woodland habitats in Australia, destroying many of the trees koalas live in and rely on for food. The fires burned across some 65,000 square miles (168,350 sq km), an area the size of Florida, U.S.A. Experts say that some 30,000 koalas might have been killed in these fires, alongside hundreds of millions of other animals.

Koalas aren't endangered, but they face many other threats in addition to wildfires. Starvation, dog attacks, car accidents, and disease have also put the fuzzy mammals in danger. Luckily, brave people step up every day to help these marsupials, like the one described below.

Instead of outrunning fires, koalas usually climb trees to escape.

The raging fire had passed, so the koala cautiously scooted down her eucalyptus tree toward the ground. But before she made it, her paws grasped part of the blackened tree trunk that was still smoldering from the fire. The koala had badly burned her paws and other parts of her body.

Hours later, wildlife rescue organization Wildcare Australia sent a team to find animals injured in the bushfire. They spotted and captured the koala—now named Maddie—and rushed her to Currumbin Wildlife Hospital.

Maddie also had burns on her nose and ears, so her caregivers applied a cooling ointment to her injuries. She was also starving. "When a koala's in pain, it won't eat," says Michael Pyne, the senior veterinarian at the hospital. "So we need her burns to heal quickly."

Less than a week later, Maddie was ready for a meal. But not just any eucalyptus leaf would do. "Koalas all have their favorite," Pyne says. Leaves that they're not used to eating are harder for them to digest, or just taste yucky. But Maddie finished off the batch of leaves she was given.

A month after the fire, she was still recovering at the hospital, but Pyne was hopeful that Maddie would be released soon. "It won't be long before she's taking naps in a forest instead of a hospital," he says.

MADDIE

MADDIE BREATHES IN SLEEPING GAS WHILE DOCTORS TREAT HER SO SHE WON'T BE IN ANY PAIN.

QUIZ WHIZ

Quiz yourself to find out if you're a natural when it comes to nature knowledge!

Write your answers on a piece of paper. Then check them below.

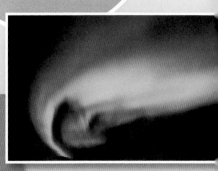

1 **True or false?** The biggest snowflake ever recorded was five inches (12.7 cm) wide.

2 **What do you call the colorful glowing rings that often appear above the North and South Poles?**
a. auroras
b. fire whirls
c. hydrothermal vents
d. rogue waves

3 **When Mauna Loa erupted in 2022, how long had it been since its last eruption?**
a. 4 years
b. 40 years
c. 400 years
d. 4,000 years

4 **In which body of water would you find narwhals?**
a. Amazon River
b. Arctic Ocean
c. Caspian Sea
d. Southern Ocean

5 **True or false?** "Taiga" is another name for a boreal forest.

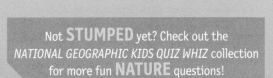

Not **STUMPED** yet? Check out the *NATIONAL GEOGRAPHIC KIDS QUIZ WHIZ* collection for more fun **NATURE** questions!

ANSWERS: 1. False: It was 15 inches (38 cm) wide; **2.** a; **3.** b; **4.** b; **5.** True

HOMEWORK HELP

Oral Reports Made Easy

TIP: Make sure you practice your presentation a few times. Stand in front of a mirror or have a friend or family member record you so you can see if you need to work on anything, such as eye contact.

Does the thought of public speaking start your stomach churning like a tornado? Would you rather get caught in an avalanche than give a speech?

Giving an oral report does not have to be a natural disaster. The basic format is very similar to that of a written essay. There are two main elements that make up a good oral report—the writing and the presentation. As you write your oral report, remember that your audience will be hearing the information as opposed to reading it. Follow the guidelines below, and there will be clear skies ahead.

Writing Your Material

Follow the steps in the "How to Write a Perfect Essay" section on page 127, but prepare your report to be spoken rather than written.

Try to keep your sentences short and simple. Long, complex sentences are harder to follow. Limit yourself to just a few key points. You don't want to overwhelm your audience with too much information. To be most effective, hit your key points in the introduction, elaborate on them in the body, and then repeat them once again in your conclusion.

AN ORAL REPORT HAS THREE BASIC PARTS:

- **Introduction**—This is your chance to engage your audience and really capture their interest in the subject you are presenting. Use a funny personal experience or a dramatic story, or start with an intriguing question.

- **Body**—This is the longest part of your report. Here you elaborate on the facts and ideas you want to convey. Give information that supports your main idea, and expand on it with specific examples or details. In other words, structure your oral report in the same way you would a written essay, so that your thoughts are presented in a clear and organized manner.

- **Conclusion**—This is the time to summarize the information and emphasize your most important points to the audience one last time.

Preparing Your Delivery

1 Practice makes perfect. Practice! Practice! Practice! Confidence, enthusiasm, and energy are key to delivering an effective oral report, and they can best be achieved through rehearsal. Ask family and friends to be your practice audience and give you feedback when you're done. Were they able to follow your ideas? Did you seem knowledgeable and confident? Did you speak too slowly or too fast, too softly or too loudly? The more times you practice giving your report, the more you'll master the material. Then you won't have to rely so heavily on your notes or papers, and you will be able to give your report in a relaxed and confident manner.

2 Present with everything you've got. Be as creative as you can. Incorporate videos, sound clips, slide presentations, charts, diagrams, and photos. Visual aids help stimulate your audience's senses and keep them intrigued and engaged; they can also help to reinforce your key points. And remember that when you're giving an oral report, you're a performer. Take charge of the spotlight and be as animated and entertaining as you can. Have fun with it.

3 Keep your nerves under control. Everyone gets a little nervous when speaking in front of a group. That's normal. But the more preparation you've done— meaning plenty of researching, organizing, and rehearsing—the more confident you'll be. Preparation is the key. And if you make a mistake or stumble over your words, just regroup and keep going. Nobody's perfect, and nobody expects you to be.

Germany's Eltz Castle, which traces its beginnings to the 12th century, stands tall among the surrounding forest trees.

PHARAOHS RULE!

Meet four mighty royals from ancient Egypt.

Pharaohs, who ruled ancient Egypt from ca 3100 to 30 B.C., weren't just old-timey government officials. Ancient Egyptians believed that pharaohs were gods on Earth who controlled nature, owned all the land, and had a direct connection to all the other deities. Fabulously wealthy, these rulers instructed their people to build the pyramids, temples, and tombs that we can still visit today. Read on to meet a few of these famous pharaohs.

Historians don't always know the exact dates of events from ancient times. That's why you'll see "ca" next to some of the years listed. It stands for "circa," meaning "around."

HATSHEPSUT

Reign: ca 1479–1458 B.C.

Claim to Fame The daughter of a pharaoh, Hatshepsut (pronounced hat-SHEP-sut) became queen when she married another pharaoh. After her husband died, she was allowed to rule Egypt temporarily until her toddler-age stepson became old enough to rule. But as the boy grew older, Hatshepsut held on to power and eventually declared *herself* pharaoh. Since almost all Egyptian rulers were male, she began calling herself king and often instructed her royal sculptors and artists to depict her with a traditional pharaoh's beard and a man's body. And she was good at her job: In 21 years on the throne, Hatshepsut organized a trading expedition to faraway lands, constructed a temple called Djeser-Djeseru (dedicated to herself, of course!) that still stands today, and kept Egypt peaceful and wealthy.

PYRAMID POWER

Most people think of ancient Egyptian pharaohs and their treasures being entombed forever in pyramids. But the earliest rulers were simply buried in the ground. Check out how the pyramid shape developed over time.

ca 3100 B.C.

Rulers are buried underneath **mastabas,** which are flat, rectangular structures made of mud bricks. (*Mastaba* means "bench" in the Arabic language.)

ca 2780 B.C.

Pharaoh Djoser commissions a **step pyramid** for his tomb— basically six mastabas stacked on top of each other.

RAMSES II
Reign: 1279–1213 B.C.

Claim to Fame If you believe the murals that Ramses II had created, you'd think he single-handedly defeated an invading army accompanied by a pet lion named Slayer of His Foes. In reality, the battles lasted 16 years, and Ramses eventually signed a peace treaty to end the war. But this ruler understood the importance of telling a good story—about how great *he* was. Ramses II built more monuments to himself than any other pharaoh. One temple at the southern edge of the Egyptian Empire, named Abu Simbel, includes four 66-foot (20-m)-tall statues of Ramses, plus much smaller statues of his family. But he didn't need to exaggerate much: Ramses II reigned for an incredible 66 years, had more than a hundred children, and was considered "Ramses the Great" by the Egyptians who came after him.

TAHARQA
Reign: 690–664 B.C.

Claim to Fame Taharqa (TUH-har-kuh) belonged to a dynasty (or family) of rulers from the kingdom of Kush, which today is in Sudan, a country in Africa just south of Egypt. Kush was a separate state from Egypt, but its rulers believed in the same gods and had similar traditions. At the time, many rulers throughout Egypt were fighting to claim the throne. That's when Taharqa's father, the Kush king, marched north with his army to defeat the warring kings and lead Egypt himself. For nearly a hundred years, this dynasty ruled over the ancient Egyptians and the people of Kush, and Taharqa was the most powerful and wealthy of them all. He started a massive project to repair crumbling temples and build new ones; he even began building pyramids again for the first time in about 800 years.

CLEOPATRA VII
Reign: 51–30 B.C.

Claim to Fame Cleopatra was like the smartest kid in your class: She loved to learn, and experts think she spoke multiple languages. In fact, she was the only pharaoh in her family line who could speak the Egyptian language. (Her ancestors were from Macedonia—now part of Greece—and had conquered ancient Egypt more than 200 years earlier.) While Cleopatra was alive, the Roman Empire was gaining power. At the start of her reign, she convinced Roman general Julius Caesar to support her instead of her younger brother. But later, she lost a war with another Roman ruler. Egypt became part of the Roman Empire, and it never had another pharaoh.

 We don't know for sure what the pharaohs really looked like, so these portraits are just for fun!

ca 2600 B.C.

Pharaoh Snefru needs three attempts to build a smooth-sided pyramid. The second—now called the **Bent Pyramid**—had to be changed halfway through!

ca 2550 B.C.

Snefru's son Khufu constructs the **Great Pyramid,** Egypt's largest tomb structure. Khufu's son and grandson build the two other Giza pyramids nearby.

ca 690 B.C.

About 800 years after the last pharaoh was buried in a pyramid, pharaohs from Kush begin building smaller and steeper **sandstone pyramids** in what's now Sudan.

Brainy Questions

HEY, SMARTY-PANTS!

GOT BIG, WEIRD QUESTIONS?

WE'VE GOT ANSWERS!

Why are ancient statues and buildings always white?

The paint has come off! Ancient Greeks and Romans painted their statues and temples in many different colors, but over the past few thousand years, the paint has worn away. Ancient artists mixed colorful minerals—like crushed-up malachite for green or azurite for blue—with beeswax or egg yolks to create paint. Today, archaeologists are using ultraviolet and infrared lamps, along with chemical analysis, to discover the traces of colors and patterns left behind on statues. We know ancient people would approve: A line in one Greek play implies that wiping color off a statue would make it uglier.

What's inside the Great Pyramid of Giza?

Not much, anymore! The Great Pyramid was built about 4,570 years ago as the final resting place of Khufu, an Egyptian pharaoh. It also stored all the stuff he'd need in the afterlife, like bread, fruit, furniture, clothes, and jewelry. The 481-foot (147-m)-tall stone structure was Khufu's way of telling people that he was super important. But it also screamed, "Hey, stuff to steal inside!" Today, you can walk through a passageway deep into the center of the pyramid until you reach the King's Chamber, which has a granite sarcophagus—but nothing else.

awes8me
BURIED TREASURE

1 BYGONE BLING

SPEAR

These remains from a shipwreck dating to about 60 B.C. were discovered more than a century ago by divers near the Greek island of Antikythera. Pictured here are a bronze spear from a statue and a marble bust of the Greek god Hermes (inset).

2 WATERY RICHES

This jewel-encrusted gold belt was recovered from the wreck of a Spanish ship called the *Nuestra Señora de Atocha* that sank in 1622 off the coast of what is now Florida, U.S.A.

4 METAL MIRACLE

More than a hundred Viking treasures, including the thousand-year-old gold pin seen here, were discovered by a retired businessman using a metal detector in a field in southwest Scotland!

3 TOMB OF TREASURES

A tomb dating back to the Zhou dynasty (1046–256 B.C.) was discovered under a hospital in China's Henan Province. This bronze drinking vessel was among the incredible finds.

5 SPECTACULAR STASH

Pieces of jewelry dating back 2,000 years were uncovered during a department store renovation near London. Archaeologists believe a Roman woman stashed her treasure here for safekeeping during a British tribe's revolt against Roman rule in A.D. 61.

6 DIVING FOR GOLD

Nearly 2,000 gold coins were discovered by amateur scuba divers off the coast of the ancient city of Caesarea, in modern-day Israel. Members of the diving club first thought the thousand-year-old coins were toys!

THIS GOLD ARMLET WAS AMONG THE DISCOVERIES.

8 SHOCKING STOCKPILE

A collection of 108 gold coins was found under a floor tile in these ancient ruins north of Tel Aviv, Israel. Researchers believe that the treasure was hidden to keep it safe from invaders in the mid-13th century.

7 UNDERSEA SWAG

This black granite sphinx—believed to have represented Ptolemy XII, the father of Cleopatra—was one of many treasures uncovered during excavations in the harbor of Alexandria, Egypt.

HISTORY'S MYSTERIES:
THE ANCIENT
MAYA
THE CIVILIZATION THAT WENT THE WAY OF THE DINOSAURS

THE BACKGROUND

The ancient Maya flourished in the Central American rainforest about 3,500 years ago. Their civilization was centuries before its time. They had vast cities, grand stone temples, and advances in writing, astronomy, and mathematics. The Maya were even responsible for discovering the concept of zero! In its heyday, the civilization had dozens of cities, stretching across the areas of modern-day Guatemala, Belize, El Salvador, Honduras, and Mexico.

Then about 2,400 years ago, the Maya people vanished, leaving their giant stone pyramids eerily abandoned in the jungle. How could such a sophisticated society just disappear? And what happened to them? To this day, nobody knows for sure.

THE DETAILS

Archaeologists dig, chisel, sweep, and ponder artifacts left behind—from piles of stone to ruins of entire cities and palaces. The Maya were known for having a sophisticated written language, spectacular art, amazing architecture, and complex mathematical and astronomical systems, which is evident from treasures unearthed from the time when they thrived. Their civilization also developed advanced agricultural techniques such as irrigation, composting, and terracing. Historians have pieced together a history of people rich in knowledge and resources. So, if their cities and temples stood the test of time, why didn't they?

THE CLUES

Over the past few decades, archaeologists have discovered hidden ruins that shed light on the destruction of individual Maya villages. And even more recently, they've used advanced technology to study the world at the time when the Maya lived—and perhaps uncover what happened to them. These three clues stand out as possible indicators of what went wrong.

JAGUAR PAW TEMPLE IN GUATEMALA

DEFORESTATION MIGHT HAVE CONTRIBUTED TO THE DOWNFALL OF THE MAYA.

MAYA ARCHAEOLOGICAL SITE IN YUCATÁN STATE, MEXICO

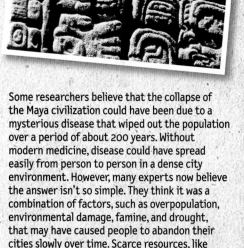

MAYA STONE CARVING

MAYA WRITING

BURIED IN ASH In 1978, archaeologists first set eyes on Joya de Cerén, a lost village in El Salvador that was accidentally discovered by construction workers. They dug through 16 feet (5 m) of volcanic ash before hitting the roof of a preserved thatched Maya house.

ALL DRIED UP In 2009, scientists studying environmental conditions in Mexico's Yucatán Peninsula discovered there had been a sharp reduction in rainfall in the areas where the Maya lived at about the same time their numbers started to dwindle.

CROP COLLAPSE NASA conducted computer simulations and collected data that indicate there was serious deforestation during the time of the Maya—meaning the Maya people cut down a huge amount of trees. This could have affected local climate, caused erosion, and depleted the soil of its nutrients.

THE THEORIES

The question of what happened to the Maya has fascinated researchers and the public since 19th-century explorers began discovering these imposing lost cities in the jungles of Central America.

Some evidence, like the volcanic ash discovered at Joya de Cerén, suggests a sudden catastrophe, like a mega earthquake, hurricane, or volcanic eruption, led to the end of the Maya.

Some researchers believe that the collapse of the Maya civilization could have been due to a mysterious disease that wiped out the population over a period of about 200 years. Without modern medicine, disease could have spread easily from person to person in a dense city environment. However, many experts now believe the answer isn't so simple. They think it was a combination of factors, such as overpopulation, environmental damage, famine, and drought, that may have caused people to abandon their cities slowly over time. Scarce resources, like water and food, could have caused the system to crumble and led to catastrophic violence and wars with nearby civilizations.

Millions of people in Guatemala today are direct descendants of the ancient Maya. Many of them still use an ancient Maya dialect as their first language. If only they also knew the secrets of what happened to this fascinating civilization.

ARE YOU A MIDDLE AGES ACE?

The Middle Ages lasted for roughly 1,000 years, from about A.D. 476 to around 1500. In fact, the word "medieval" comes from Latin words that mean "middle age." During this time period, great empires were rising around the globe. Try your hand at this quiz to see how much you already know about the people and places of this era. Don't worry, you won't be graded—it's just for fun!

Sow unfair.

In medieval times, everyone thought the world was flat. It took Christopher Columbus's voyage in 1492 to prove the world was round.

FALSE! Some folks in the Middle Ages may have wondered if the world was flat, but great thinkers of ancient times wrote that Earth was like a giant ball in space. And educated people in the Middle Ages thought so, too. But it is true that European medieval mapmakers didn't know exactly what the rest of the world looked like—or that the Americas, Australia, and Antarctica even existed!

Animals in the Middle Ages could be arrested if they hurt humans.

TRUE! Animals such as dogs and pigs could be arrested and brought to court if they hurt people or destroyed property.

In A.D. 1000, London was the world's largest city.

FALSE! With a population of about nine million today, London is one big city. But in medieval times, it was just a tiny town compared to Kaifeng, China. In the year 1000, one million people lived in Kaifeng.

Ivar the Boneless, Harald Bluetooth, and Alfonso the Slobberer were all European warriors or rulers during medieval times.

TRUE! Nicknames come in all flavors—they can be funny or cruel or describe a person's looks. Many medieval rulers ended up with nicknames, though today we may not know exactly where those nicknames came from.

Ivar the Boneless was a Viking warrior who, in 865, led a raid on England and captured chunks of land there. He wasn't really boneless, of course—otherwise he couldn't have picked up a sword! But some stories say he had a bone disease and had to be carried into battle.

Harald Bluetooth was a 10th-century Danish king who spread Christianity in his land. Some historians say a bad tooth—one that was actually black, not blue—led to his nickname. Many centuries later, in honor of Harald, Bluetooth was chosen as the name for a wireless system used by smartphones and computers.

Starting at the end of the 12th century, Alfonso IX ruled the kingdoms of Leon and Galicia, in what is today Spain. He earned the Spanish nickname *"Baboso,"* which can mean "slobberer" in English. It was said that Alfonso foamed at the mouth when he got angry.

If you needed medical help in medieval Europe, you might go see the local barber.

TRUE! Barbers back then were often called barber-surgeons because they might cut you open along with cutting your hair. They often did something called bloodletting—cutting a person to let blood flow out was thought to cure some illnesses. The red and white stripes on today's barbershop poles represent the blood that flowed in the medieval shops, and the white bandages used to stop it. Oh, and medieval barbers also pulled teeth.

Thirteenth-century explorer Marco Polo brought pasta to Italy from China.

FALSE! Marco (Polo!) did travel to China, and he later wrote about food that was something like pasta. But Italians had already been eating a mixture of flour and water that they molded into different shapes and cooked.

PIRATE QUEEN

CHING SHIH
FIERCE LEADER AND SAVVY NEGOTIATOR

WHEN: circa A.D. 1775 to 1844

WHERE: South China Sea

WHO: Ching Shih, whose masterful leadership made the massive Red Flag Fleet indomitable, commanded more ships and more pirates than any other pirate in history.

ALIASES: Ching Shih aka Cheng I Sao aka Zheng Yi Sao aka Madame Ching

TAKING OVER

Sailing the South China Sea, Ching Shih and her husband shared command of the powerful Red Flag Fleet. They had been married for six years when he died suddenly. Ching Shih—or Cheng I Sao, as she was sometimes called, which means "wife of Cheng I"—commandeered their pirate business, supposedly telling her fleet, "We shall see how you prove yourselves under the hand of a woman."

DREAM TEAM

The convincing new commander persuaded rival pirates to work together under her leadership. As a result, she united an enormous squadron of an estimated 1,800 ships with more than 80,000 pirates. She appointed her adopted son, Cheung Po Tsai, as captain of the fleet, which freed her to focus on business and military strategy. Before long, her pirates were not only pillaging and plundering at sea, but also expanding to schemes on land, such as extortion and blackmail. They also took over several coastal villages.

As more money flowed in, Ching Shih set up a pirates' bank to ensure her crew had savings to support their families.

LAW AND ORDER

Ching Shih wrote a set of laws for her crew to follow, and those who broke them were severely punished. Anyone caught disobeying a superior's orders, for example, faced the threat of having their ears cut off—or worse, they'd be beheaded. Often, at sea, pirates would bring women aboard their ships as enslaved people. Ching Shih refused to allow this mistreatment. She mandated that male pirates could only bring their wives on board and punished anyone who dared mistreat them.

SOVEREIGN OF THE SEAS

By 1807, the Red Flag Fleet was more organized than the Chinese navy. Chinese officials tried to stop the fleet with the help of British and Portuguese warships, but the Red Flag Fleet defeated that armada. Outmaneuvered and outnumbered at every turn, the Chinese government had no choice but to forgive Ching Shih's crimes. In exchange, they asked Ching Shih to stop pirating. She agreed, but on the condition that her entire crew be pardoned, too.

She got what she wanted—along with a small fleet of ships for her new husband to command, offers of military employment for her crew members, and money for their new life onshore. They also got to keep their loot.

A LEADER'S LEGACY

A life on land didn't mean laying low for Ching Shih. Instead, she used her fortune to start new business enterprises, which by all accounts were pretty successful. She died peacefully at the age of about 69. This shrewd commander defied stereotypes and used her smarts and resourcefulness to create one of the most formidable pirate fleets the world has ever known.

SHREWD MOVES

She's often called history's most successful pirate. So just how prosperous was Ching Shih? To put it in perspective, her fleet of 1,800 ships and 80,000 men was hundreds of times larger than those of other well-known raiders of the time, like Captain Blackbeard. Managing such a colossal fleet couldn't have been easy, and it's said that Ching Shih's business savvy helped her be a better boss. Aside from overseeing the day-to-day schedules of her own army of ruffians, she was able to devise military strategy, manage the finances of her fleet, and broker business deals. One of Ching Shih's most impressive alliances? Developing a partnership with local farmers, who agreed to supply her men with food. And with 80,000 mouths to feed, that deal was certainly no small potatoes.

10 REGAL FACTS ABOUT ROYALTY

The name of the ancient **Egyptian queen Nefertiti** means "the beautiful one has arrived."

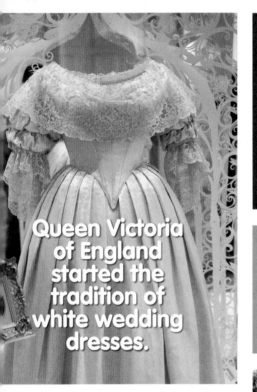

Queen Victoria of England started the tradition of **white wedding dresses.**

A barrier of **PRICKLY PLANTS** protected the **Royal Palaces of Abomey,** built in the 17th century in West Africa.

Only royalty in the **Inca Empire—** a civilization that ruled parts of South America during the 15th and 16th centuries— **could wear fleece from an alpaca.**

The Imperial Palace in Tokyo, Japan, is home to **20 percent of the city's trees.**

The **jaguar** was a symbol of royalty to some ancient Central American people who believed the cat protected them from evil.

In 17th-century India, some garments worn by royalty were decorated with **beetle wings.**

Flatulists— people who **passed gas** on **command—** entertained royals in France.

TOPKAPI PALACE in Türkiye (Turkey) was built by Sultan Mehmed II and is home to an **86-carat diamond** called the **Spoonmaker's Diamond.**

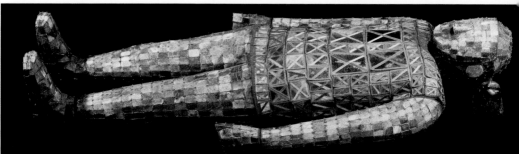

Royalty in ancient China wore **burial suits made of jade.** They believed the mineral **preserved their bodies.**

GOING TO WAR

Since the beginning of time, different countries, territories, and cultures have feuded with each other over land, power, and politics. Major military conflicts include the following wars:

1095–1291 THE CRUSADES
Starting late in the 11th century, these wars over religion were fought in the Middle East for nearly 200 years.

1337–1453 HUNDRED YEARS' WAR
France and England battled over rights to land for more than a century before the French eventually drove the English out in 1453.

1754–1763 FRENCH AND INDIAN WAR (part of Europe's Seven Years' War)
A nine-year war between the British and French for control of North America.

1775–1783 AMERICAN REVOLUTION
Thirteen British colonies in America united to reject the rule of the British government and to form the United States of America.

1861–1865 AMERICAN CIVIL WAR
This war occurred when the northern states (the Union) went to war with the southern states, which had seceded, or withdrawn, to form the Confederate States of America. Slavery was one of the key issues in the Civil War.

1910–1920 MEXICAN REVOLUTION
The people of Mexico revolted against the rule of dictator President Porfirio Díaz, leading to his eventual defeat and to a democratic government.

1914–1918 WORLD WAR I
The assassination of Austria's Archduke Ferdinand by a Serbian nationalist sparked this wide-spreading war. The U.S. entered after Germany sank the British ship *Lusitania,* killing more than 120 Americans.

1918–1920 RUSSIAN CIVIL WAR
Following the 1917 Russian Revolution, this conflict pitted the Communist Red Army against the foreign-backed White Army. The Red Army won, leading to the establishment of the Union of Soviet Socialist Republics (U.S.S.R.) in 1922.

1936–1939 SPANISH CIVIL WAR
Aid from Italy and Germany helped Spain's Nationalists gain victory over the Communist-supported Republicans. The war resulted in the loss of more than 300,000 lives and increased tension in Europe leading up to World War II.

1939–1945 WORLD WAR II
This massive conflict in Europe, Asia, and North Africa involved many countries that aligned with the two sides: the Allies and the Axis. After the bombing of Pearl Harbor in Hawaii in 1941, the U.S. entered the war on the side of the Allies. More than 50 million people died during the war.

WARTIME INVENTIONS

1946-1949 CHINESE CIVIL WAR
Also known as the "War of Liberation," this war pitted the Communist and Nationalist Parties in China against each other. The Communists won.

1950-1953 KOREAN WAR
Kicked off when the Communist forces of North Korea, with backing from the Soviet Union, invaded their democratic neighbor to the south. A coalition of 16 countries from the United Nations stepped in to support South Korea. An armistice, or temporary truce, ended active fighting in 1953.

1950s-1975 VIETNAM WAR
This war was fought between the Communist North, supported by allies including China, and the government of South Vietnam, supported by the United States and other anticommunist nations.

1967 SIX-DAY WAR
This was a battle for land between Israel and the states of Egypt, Jordan, and Syria. The outcome resulted in Israel's gaining control of coveted territory, including the Gaza Strip and the West Bank.

1991-PRESENT SOMALI CIVIL WAR
The war began when Somalia's last president, a dictator named Mohamed Siad Barre, was overthrown. This has led to years of fighting and anarchy.

2001-2014 WAR IN AFGHANISTAN
After attacks in the U.S. by the terrorist group al Qaeda, a coalition that eventually included more than 40 countries invaded Afghanistan to find Osama bin Laden and other al Qaeda members and to dismantle the Taliban. Bin Laden was killed in a U.S. covert operation in 2011. The North Atlantic Treaty Organization (NATO) took control of the coalition's combat mission in 2003. That combat mission officially ended in 2014. The United States completed its withdrawal of troops in 2021.

2003-2011 WAR IN IRAQ
A coalition led by the U.S., and including Britain, Australia, and Spain, invaded Iraq over suspicions that Iraq had weapons of mass destruction.

2022-PRESENT RUSSIA-UKRAINE WAR
Military forces led by Russian president Vladimir Putin crossed the border into Ukraine, seeking to take control of the country. Russia launched attacks on major cities across the country, including the capital city of Kyiv.

It's said that necessity is the mother of invention. And in wartime, necessity—or at least the need for making life easier—is especially key. So it's not too surprising that some of the more useful things in our world today were created during times of conflict—in particular, during World War I, when industrialization led to innovations across the board.

Take, for example, Kleenex tissues. What we use today to blow our noses was born out of what was first meant to be a thin, cottony liner used in a gas mask. In 1924, the company Kimberly-Clark started selling the same tissue liners as a disposable makeup remover for women. But when an employee with hay fever started blowing his nose in the wipes, Kimberly-Clark saw an opportunity—and sold the Kleenex as an alternative to cloth handkerchiefs.

Then there are zippers: Originally known as "hookless fasteners," they first widely appeared on the flying suits of aviators during World War I. Before then, buttons were the fashionable way to fasten shirts, pants, and boots, but the new invention was much more, well, zippy. In 1923, the B.F. Goodrich Company coined the term zipper, and the name stuck.

And whenever you check the time on your wristwatch, you can thank World War I soldiers for making this type of timepiece trendy. At the time of the war, wristwatches were popular with women, while men mostly kept the time on pocket watches, which they'd have tucked away on a chain. But during the war, male soldiers switched to wristwatches for easier access to the time (and to keep both hands free in the trenches). After the war, the wristwatch became a common look for all genders—and remains so today.

251

THE CONSTITUTION & THE BILL OF RIGHTS

The United States Constitution was written in 1787 by a group of political leaders from the 13 states that made up the United States at the time. Thirty-nine men, including Benjamin Franklin and James Madison, signed the document to create a national government. While some feared the creation of a strong federal government, all 13 states eventually ratified, or approved, the Constitution, making it the law of the land. The Constitution has three major parts: the preamble, the articles, and the amendments.

Here's a summary of what topics are covered in each part of the Constitution. The Constitution can be found online or at your local library for the full text.

THE PREAMBLE outlines the basic purposes of the government: *We the People of the United States, in order to form a more perfect Union, establish justice, insure domestic tranquility, provide for the common defense, promote the general welfare, and secure the blessings of liberty to ourselves and our posterity, do ordain and establish this Constitution for the United States of America.*

SEVEN ARTICLES outline the powers of Congress, the president, and the court system:

Article I outlines the legislative branch—the Senate and the House of Representatives—and its powers and responsibilities.

Article II outlines the executive branch—the presidency—and its powers and responsibilities.

Article III outlines the judicial branch—the court system—and its powers and responsibilities.

Article IV describes the individual states' rights and powers.

Article V outlines the amendment process.

Article VI establishes the Constitution as the law of the land.

Article VII gives the requirements for the Constitution to be approved.

THE AMENDMENTS, or additions to the Constitution, were put in later as needed. In 1791, the first 10 amendments, known as the Bill of Rights, were added. Since then, another 17 amendments have been added. This is the Bill of Rights:

1st Amendment: guarantees freedom of religion, speech, and the press, and the right to assemble and petition. The U.S. may not have a national religion.

2nd Amendment: discusses the militia and the right of people to bear arms

3rd Amendment: prohibits the military or troops from using private homes without consent

4th Amendment: protects people and their homes from search, arrest, or seizure without probable cause or a warrant

5th Amendment: grants people the right to have a trial and prevents punishment before prosecution; protects private property from being taken without compensation

6th Amendment: guarantees the right to a speedy and public trial

7th Amendment: guarantees a trial by jury in certain cases

8th Amendment: forbids "cruel and unusual punishments"

9th Amendment: states that the Constitution is not all-encompassing and does not deny people other unspecified rights

10th Amendment: grants the powers not covered by the Constitution to the states and the people

The full text version is online at the National Constitution Center.

White House

BRANCHES OF GOVERNMENT

The **UNITED STATES GOVERNMENT** is divided into three branches: executive, legislative, and judicial. This system of checks and balances is a way to control power and to make sure one branch can't take the reins of government. For example, most of the president's actions require the approval of Congress. Likewise, the laws passed in Congress must be signed by the president before they can take effect.

Executive Branch

The Constitution lists the central powers of the president: to serve as commander in chief of the armed forces; make treaties with other nations; grant pardons; inform Congress on the state of the union; and appoint ambassadors, officials, and judges. The executive branch includes the president and the 15 governmental departments.

Legislative Branch

This branch is made up of Congress—the Senate and the House of Representatives. The Constitution grants Congress the power to make laws. Congress is made up of elected representatives from each state. Each state has two representatives in the Senate, while the number of representatives in the House is determined by the size of the state's population. Washington, D.C., and the territories elect nonvoting representatives to the House of Representatives. The Founding Fathers set up this system as a compromise between big states—which wanted representation based on population—and small states—which wanted all states to have equal representation rights.

The U.S. Capitol in Washington, D.C.

Judicial Branch

The U.S. Supreme Court Building in Washington, D.C.

The judicial branch is composed of the federal court system—the U.S. Supreme Court, the courts of appeals, and the district courts. The Supreme Court is the most powerful court. Its motto is "Equal Justice Under Law." This influential court is responsible for interpreting the Constitution and applying it to the cases that it hears. The decisions of the Supreme Court are absolute—they are the final word on any legal question.

There are nine justices on the Supreme Court. They are appointed by the president of the United States and confirmed by the Senate.

253

The Native American Experience

Native Americans are Indigenous

to North and South America—they are the people who were here before Columbus and other European explorers came to these lands. They live in nations, tribes, and bands across both continents. For decades following the arrival of Europeans in 1492, Native Americans clashed with the newcomers who had ruptured the Indigenous people's ways of living.

Tribal Land

During the 19th century, both United States legislation and military action restricted the movement of Native Americans, forcing them to live on reservations and attempting to dismantle tribal structures. For centuries, Native Americans were displaced or killed. In 1924, the Indian Citizenship Act granted citizenship to all Native Americans. Unfortunately, this was not enough to end the social discrimination and mistreatment that many Indigenous people have faced. Today, Native Americans living in the United States still face many challenges.

Healing the Past

Many members of the 570-plus recognized tribes in the United States live primarily on reservations. Some tribes have more than one reservation, while others have none. Together these reservations make up less than 3 percent of the nation's land area. The tribal governments on reservations have the right to form their own governments and to enforce laws, similar to individual states. Many feel that this sovereignty is still not enough to right the wrongs of the past: They hope for a change in the U.S. government's relationship with Native Americans.

An annual powwow in New Mexico features more than 3,000 dancers from more than 500 North American tribes.

Navajo is the most commonly spoken Native American language in the United States.

Top: A Navajo teenager holds her pet lamb.

Middle: A Monacan girl dances in a traditional jingle dress.

Bottom: Navajo siblings ride their horses.

The president of the United States is the chief of the executive branch, the commander in chief of the U.S. armed forces, and head of the federal government. Elected every four years, the president is the highest policymaker in the nation. The 22nd Amendment (1951) says that no person may be elected to the office of president more than twice. There have been 46 presidencies and 45 presidents.

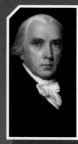

JAMES MADISON
4th President of the United States ★ 1809–1817
BORN March 16, 1751, at Belle Grove, Port Conway, VA
POLITICAL PARTY Democratic-Republican
NO. OF TERMS two
VICE PRESIDENTS 1st term: George Clinton
2nd term: Elbridge Gerry
DIED June 28, 1836, at Montpelier, Orange County, VA

GEORGE WASHINGTON
1st President of the United States ★ 1789–1797
BORN Feb. 22, 1732, in Pope's Creek, Westmoreland County, VA
POLITICAL PARTY Federalist
NO. OF TERMS two
VICE PRESIDENT John Adams
DIED Dec. 14, 1799, at Mount Vernon, VA

JAMES MONROE
5th President of the United States ★ 1817–1825
BORN April 28, 1758, in Westmoreland County, VA
POLITICAL PARTY Democratic-Republican
NO. OF TERMS two
VICE PRESIDENT Daniel D. Tompkins
DIED July 4, 1831, in New York, NY

JOHN ADAMS
2nd President of the United States ★ 1797–1801
BORN Oct. 30, 1735, in Braintree (now Quincy), MA
POLITICAL PARTY Federalist
NO. OF TERMS one
VICE PRESIDENT Thomas Jefferson
DIED July 4, 1826, in Quincy, MA

JOHN QUINCY ADAMS
6th President of the United States ★ 1825–1829
BORN July 11, 1767, in Braintree (now Quincy), MA
POLITICAL PARTY Democratic-Republican
NO. OF TERMS one
VICE PRESIDENT John Caldwell Calhoun
DIED Feb. 23, 1848, at the U.S. Capitol, Washington, D.C.

JOHN ADAMS entered Harvard University at the age of 15.

ANDREW JACKSON
7th President of the United States ★ 1829–1837
BORN March 15, 1767, in the Waxhaw region, NC and SC
POLITICAL PARTY Democrat
NO. OF TERMS two
VICE PRESIDENTS 1st term: John Caldwell Calhoun
2nd term: Martin Van Buren
DIED June 8, 1845, in Nashville, TN

THOMAS JEFFERSON
3rd President of the United States ★ 1801–1809
BORN April 13, 1743, at Shadwell, Goochland (now Albemarle) County, VA
POLITICAL PARTY Democratic-Republican
NO. OF TERMS two
VICE PRESIDENTS 1st term: Aaron Burr
2nd term: George Clinton
DIED July 4, 1826, at Monticello, Charlottesville, VA

MARTIN VAN BUREN
8th President of the United States ★ 1837–1841
BORN Dec. 5, 1782, in Kinderhook, NY
POLITICAL PARTY Democrat
NO. OF TERMS one
VICE PRESIDENT Richard M. Johnson
DIED July 24, 1862, in Kinderhook, NY

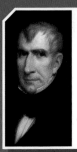

WILLIAM HENRY HARRISON
9th President of the United States ★ 1841
BORN Feb. 9, 1773, in Charles City County, VA
POLITICAL PARTY Whig
NO. OF TERMS one (died while in office)
VICE PRESIDENT John Tyler
DIED April 4, 1841, in the White House, Washington, D.C.

JOHN TYLER
10th President of the United States ★ 1841–1845
BORN March 29, 1790, in Charles City County, VA
POLITICAL PARTY Whig
NO. OF TERMS one (partial)
VICE PRESIDENT none
DIED Jan. 18, 1862, in Richmond, VA

JAMES K. POLK
11th President of the United States ★ 1845–1849
BORN Nov. 2, 1795, near Pineville, Mecklenburg County, NC
POLITICAL PARTY Democrat
NO. OF TERMS one
VICE PRESIDENT George Mifflin Dallas
DIED June 15, 1849, in Nashville, TN

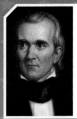

ZACHARY TAYLOR
12th President of the United States ★ 1849–1850
BORN Nov. 24, 1784, in Orange County, VA
POLITICAL PARTY Whig
NO. OF TERMS one (died while in office)
VICE PRESIDENT Millard Fillmore
DIED July 9, 1850, in the White House, Washington, D.C.

MILLARD FILLMORE
13th President of the United States ★ 1850–1853
BORN Jan. 7, 1800, in Cayuga County, NY
POLITICAL PARTY Whig
NO. OF TERMS one (partial)
VICE PRESIDENT none
DIED March 8, 1874, in Buffalo, NY

FRANKLIN PIERCE
14th President of the United States ★ 1853–1857
BORN Nov. 23, 1804, in Hillsborough (now Hillsboro), NH
POLITICAL PARTY Democrat
NO. OF TERMS one
VICE PRESIDENT William Rufus De Vane King
DIED Oct. 8, 1869, in Concord, NH

JAMES BUCHANAN
15th President of the United States ★ 1857–1861
BORN April 23, 1791, in Cove Gap, PA
POLITICAL PARTY Democrat
NO. OF TERMS one
VICE PRESIDENT John Cabell Breckinridge
DIED June 1, 1868, in Lancaster, PA

JAMES BUCHANAN is the only president who never MARRIED.

ABRAHAM LINCOLN
16th President of the United States ★ 1861–1865
BORN Feb. 12, 1809, near Hodgenville, KY
POLITICAL PARTY Republican (formerly Whig)
NO. OF TERMS two (assassinated)
VICE PRESIDENTS 1st term: Hannibal Hamlin
2nd term: Andrew Johnson
DIED April 15, 1865, in Washington, D.C.

ANDREW JOHNSON
17th President of the United States ★ 1865–1869
BORN Dec. 29, 1808, in Raleigh, NC
POLITICAL PARTY Democrat
NO. OF TERMS one (partial)
VICE PRESIDENT none
DIED July 31, 1875, in Carter's Station, TN

ULYSSES S. GRANT
18th President of the United States ★ 1869–1877

BORN April 27, 1822, in Point Pleasant, OH
POLITICAL PARTY Republican
NO. OF TERMS two
VICE PRESIDENTS 1st term: Schuyler Colfax
2nd term: Henry Wilson
DIED July 23, 1885, in Mount McGregor, NY

RUTHERFORD B. HAYES
19th President of the United States ★ 1877–1881

BORN Oct. 4, 1822, in Delaware, OH
POLITICAL PARTY Republican
NO. OF TERMS one
VICE PRESIDENT William Almon Wheeler
DIED Jan. 17, 1893, in Fremont, OH

JAMES A. GARFIELD
20th President of the United States ★ 1881

BORN Nov. 19, 1831, near Orange, OH
POLITICAL PARTY Republican
NO. OF TERMS one (assassinated)
VICE PRESIDENT Chester A. Arthur
DIED Sept. 19, 1881, in Elberon, NJ

CHESTER A. ARTHUR
21st President of the United States ★ 1881–1885

BORN Oct. 5, 1829, in Fairfield, VT
POLITICAL PARTY Republican
NO. OF TERMS one (partial)
VICE PRESIDENT none
DIED Nov. 18, 1886, in New York, NY

GROVER CLEVELAND
*22nd and 24th President of the United States
1885–1889 ★ 1893–1897*

BORN March 18, 1837, in Caldwell, NJ
POLITICAL PARTY Democrat
NO. OF TERMS two (nonconsecutive)
VICE PRESIDENTS 1st administration:
Thomas Andrews Hendricks
2nd administration:
Adlai Ewing Stevenson
DIED June 24, 1908, in Princeton, NJ

BENJAMIN HARRISON
23rd President of the United States ★ 1889–1893

BORN Aug. 20, 1833, in North Bend, OH
POLITICAL PARTY Republican
NO. OF TERMS one
VICE PRESIDENT Levi Parsons Morton
DIED March 13, 1901, in Indianapolis, IN

WILLIAM MCKINLEY
25th President of the United States ★ 1897–1901

BORN Jan. 29, 1843, in Niles, OH
POLITICAL PARTY Republican
NO. OF TERMS two (assassinated)
VICE PRESIDENTS 1st term:
Garret Augustus Hobart
2nd term:
Theodore Roosevelt
DIED Sept. 14, 1901, in Buffalo, NY

THEODORE ROOSEVELT
26th President of the United States ★ 1901–1909

BORN Oct. 27, 1858, in New York, NY
POLITICAL PARTY Republican
NO. OF TERMS one, plus balance of
McKinley's term
VICE PRESIDENTS 1st term: none
2nd term: Charles
Warren Fairbanks
DIED Jan. 6, 1919, in Oyster Bay, NY

WILLIAM HOWARD TAFT
27th President of the United States ★ 1909–1913

BORN Sept. 15, 1857, in Cincinnati, OH
POLITICAL PARTY Republican
NO. OF TERMS one
VICE PRESIDENT James Schoolcraft
Sherman
DIED March 8, 1930, in Washington, D.C.

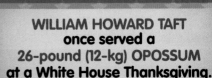

**WILLIAM HOWARD TAFT
once served a
26-pound (12-kg) OPOSSUM
at a White House Thanksgiving.**

WOODROW WILSON
28th President of the United States ★ 1913–1921

BORN Dec. 29, 1856, in Staunton, VA
POLITICAL PARTY Democrat
NO. OF TERMS two
VICE PRESIDENT Thomas Riley Marshall
DIED Feb. 3, 1924, in Washington, D.C.

WARREN G. HARDING
29th President of the United States ★ 1921–1923
BORN Nov. 2, 1865, in Caledonia (now Blooming Grove), OH
POLITICAL PARTY Republican
NO. OF TERMS one (died while in office)
VICE PRESIDENT Calvin Coolidge
DIED Aug. 2, 1923, in San Francisco, CA

CALVIN COOLIDGE
30th President of the United States ★ 1923–1929
BORN July 4, 1872, in Plymouth, VT
POLITICAL PARTY Republican
NO. OF TERMS one, plus balance of Harding's term
VICE PRESIDENTS 1st term: none
2nd term: Charles Gates Dawes
DIED Jan. 5, 1933, in Northampton, MA

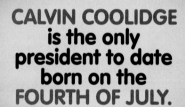

CALVIN COOLIDGE is the only president to date born on the FOURTH OF JULY.

HERBERT HOOVER
31st President of the United States ★ 1929–1933
BORN Aug. 10, 1874, in West Branch, IA
POLITICAL PARTY Republican
NO. OF TERMS one
VICE PRESIDENT Charles Curtis
DIED Oct. 20, 1964, in New York, NY

FRANKLIN D. ROOSEVELT
32nd President of the United States ★ 1933–1945
BORN Jan. 30, 1882, in Hyde Park, NY
POLITICAL PARTY Democrat
NO. OF TERMS four (died while in office)
VICE PRESIDENTS 1st & 2nd terms: John Nance Garner; 3rd term: Henry Agard Wallace; 4th term: Harry S. Truman
DIED April 12, 1945, in Warm Springs, GA

HARRY S. TRUMAN
33rd President of the United States ★ 1945–1953
BORN May 8, 1884, in Lamar, MO
POLITICAL PARTY Democrat
NO. OF TERMS one, plus balance of Franklin D. Roosevelt's term
VICE PRESIDENTS 1st term: none
2nd term: Alben William Barkley
DIED Dec. 26, 1972, in Independence, MO

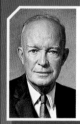

DWIGHT D. EISENHOWER
34th President of the United States ★ 1953–1961
BORN Oct. 14, 1890, in Denison, TX
POLITICAL PARTY Republican
NO. OF TERMS two
VICE PRESIDENT Richard Nixon
DIED March 28, 1969, in Washington, D.C.

JOHN F. KENNEDY
35th President of the United States ★ 1961–1963
BORN May 29, 1917, in Brookline, MA
POLITICAL PARTY Democrat
NO. OF TERMS one (assassinated)
VICE PRESIDENT Lyndon B. Johnson
DIED Nov. 22, 1963, in Dallas, TX

LYNDON B. JOHNSON
36th President of the United States ★ 1963–1969
BORN Aug. 27, 1908, near Stonewall, TX
POLITICAL PARTY Democrat
NO. OF TERMS one, plus balance of Kennedy's term
VICE PRESIDENTS 1st term: none
2nd term: Hubert Horatio Humphrey
DIED Jan. 22, 1973, near San Antonio, TX

RICHARD NIXON
37th President of the United States ★ 1969–1974
BORN Jan. 9, 1913, in Yorba Linda, CA
POLITICAL PARTY Republican
NO. OF TERMS two (resigned)
VICE PRESIDENTS 1st term & 2nd term (partial): Spiro Theodore Agnew; 2nd term (balance): Gerald R. Ford
DIED April 22, 1994, in New York, NY

GERALD R. FORD
38th President of the United States ★ 1974–1977
BORN July 14, 1913, in Omaha, NE
POLITICAL PARTY Republican
NO. OF TERMS one (partial)
VICE PRESIDENT Nelson Aldrich Rockefeller
DIED Dec. 26, 2006, in Rancho Mirage, CA

GERALD R. FORD was a star FOOTBALL PLAYER in college.

JIMMY CARTER
39th President of the United States ★ 1977–1981
BORN Oct. 1, 1924, in Plains, GA
POLITICAL PARTY Democrat
NO. OF TERMS one
VICE PRESIDENT Walter Frederick (Fritz) Mondale

RONALD REAGAN
40th President of the United States ★ 1981–1989
BORN Feb. 6, 1911, in Tampico, IL
POLITICAL PARTY Republican
NO. OF TERMS two
VICE PRESIDENT George H. W. Bush
DIED June 5, 2004, in Los Angeles, CA

GEORGE H. W. BUSH
41st President of the United States ★ 1989–1993
BORN June 12, 1924, in Milton, MA
POLITICAL PARTY Republican
NO. OF TERMS one
VICE PRESIDENT James Danforth (Dan) Quayle III
DIED Nov. 30, 2018, in Houston, TX

BILL CLINTON
42nd President of the United States ★ 1993–2001
BORN Aug. 19, 1946, in Hope, AR
POLITICAL PARTY Democrat
NO. OF TERMS two
VICE PRESIDENT Albert Arnold Gore, Jr.

GEORGE W. BUSH
43rd President of the United States ★ 2001–2009
BORN July 6, 1946, in New Haven, CT
POLITICAL PARTY Republican
NO. OF TERMS two
VICE PRESIDENT Richard Bruce Cheney

BARACK OBAMA
44th President of the United States ★ 2009–2017
BORN Aug. 4, 1961, in Honolulu, HI
POLITICAL PARTY Democrat
NO. OF TERMS two
VICE PRESIDENT Joe Biden

DONALD TRUMP
45th President of the United States ★ 2017–2021
BORN June 14, 1946, in Queens, NY
POLITICAL PARTY Republican
NO. OF TERMS one
VICE PRESIDENT Mike Pence

JOE BIDEN
46th President of the United States ★ 2021–
BORN November 20, 1942, in Scranton, PA
POLITICAL PARTY Democrat
VICE PRESIDENT Kamala Harris

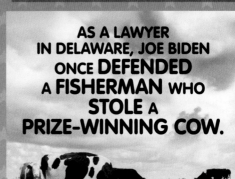

AS A LAWYER IN DELAWARE, JOE BIDEN ONCE DEFENDED A FISHERMAN WHO STOLE A PRIZE-WINNING COW.

THIS CAR IS CONFIDENTIAL

But we've got some secrets about the president's ride.

The president of the United States doesn't take the bus or fly coach. For long trips, the commander in chief boards the presidential plane, called Air Force One, or the official helicopter, Marine One. But once the leader lands, he or she climbs inside the Beast.

The Beast is the nickname of the official state vehicle that carries the president in comfort and safety using the latest in science and technology. It's based off a Cadillac CT6 (the model rolled out in 2018), but the Beast is more like an armored truck—President Barack Obama called it a "Cadillac on a tank frame." And like a tank, the 10-ton (9-t) Beast was designed to be nearly indestructible.

Many of the Beast's features are classified. But according to reports, it's loaded with James Bond–style tricks, including the ability to create a smoke screen or oil slick as well as launch tear gas. Check out these other sort-of-secret details about the president's ride.

HOW TO GO UNDERCOVER

The Beast is like an extremely large-and-in-charge bodyguard. But spies—who also help protect the country—are more secretive. Want to try out your spy skills? Check out these tricks for going undercover.

COVER STORY

Invent a boring backstory (aka your legend). Tell people you're a distant relative in your family or a student from far away. The legend should be believable but forgettable. Make it more convincing by highlighting specific phony experiences.

DRESS FOR SUCCESS

Look for outfits that won't seem out of place with the group or event you're trying to snoop on. (Wear a superhero T-shirt if you're going to a sci-fi convention, for instance.) Throw people off by borrowing duds from an older sibling or close buddy.

BEHIND THE WHEEL

The Beast's most impressive feature isn't any of its high-tech gadgets—it's the human driver, trained for making getaways and handling dangerous situations. The driver even has access to night-vision technology to keep on rolling if the headlights go out.

MORE THAN FREE WI-FI

The president has access to a state-of-the-art communications system that keeps them connected to the world. The leader can even place a call to a nuclear submarine on the other side of the world.

WINDOW TREATMENT

Up to seven people can ride inside the Beast. Several passengers are Secret Service agents, who protect the president in case of an attack. The Beast typically is part of a convoy that includes Secret Service vehicles, a backup Beast, and a communications truck.

AIR FORCED

The interior of the Beast can be sealed off and supplied with its own air in case of a chemical attack or if the vehicle crashes into water. It can basically turn into a submarine!

DOOR BUSTERS

The Beast's doors are rumored to be at least eight inches (20 cm) thick—about as thick as the doors of a commercial airplane. That's one reason you never see the president open their car door. It's too heavy!

FLAT CHANCE

The Beast's tires are called run-flat tires, meaning they're designed to keep rolling even if they're damaged.

BEASTLY HIDE

The Beast's skin is made of layers of aluminum, steel, and ceramic armors, designed to withstand any sort of attack—even from rockets!

FACING FACTS

Forget the fake beards and eye patches. Dark sunglasses are an easy way to disguise your eyes, one of your most recognizable features.

PLAY THE PART

Do your hair in a way that doesn't look like you. Part it a different way or slick it back. Make a bun. Braid it.

WALK THIS WAY

Keep people from recognizing you by walking in a new way. Try moving your arms more or taking longer steps. You can even put pebbles in your shoes.

CIVIL RIGHTS

Although the Constitution protects the civil rights of American citizens, it has not always been able to protect all Americans from persecution or discrimination. During the first half of the 20th century, many Americans, particularly Black Americans, were subjected to widespread discrimination and racism. By the mid-1950s, many people were eager to end the barriers caused by racism and bring freedom to all men and women.

The civil rights movement of the 1950s and 1960s sought to end racial discrimination against Black people, especially in the southern states. The movement wanted to give the fundamentals of economic and social equality to those who had been oppressed.

Woolworth Counter Sit-in

On February 1, 1960, four Black college students walked into a Woolworth's "five-and-dime" store in Greensboro, North Carolina. They planned to have lunch there, but were refused service as soon as they sat down at the counter. In a time of pervasive racism, the Woolworth's manager had a strict whites-only policy. But the students wouldn't take no for an answer. The men—later dubbed the "Greensboro Four"—stayed seated, peacefully and quietly, at the lunch counter until closing. The next day, they returned with 15 additional college students. The following day, even more. By February 5, some 300 students gathered at Woolworth's, forming one of the most famous sit-ins of the civil rights movement. The protest—which sparked similar sit-ins throughout the country—worked: Just six months later, restaurants across the South began to integrate.

Key Events in the Civil Rights Movement

1954	The Supreme Court case *Brown* v. *Board of Education* declares school segregation illegal.
1955	Rosa Parks refuses to give up her bus seat to a white passenger and spurs a bus boycott.
1957	The Little Rock Nine help to integrate schools.
1960	Four Black college students begin sit-ins at a restaurant in Greensboro, North Carolina.
1961	Freedom Rides to southern states begin as a way to protest segregation in transportation.
1963	Martin Luther King, Jr., leads the famous March on Washington.
1964	The Civil Rights Act, signed by President Lyndon B. Johnson, prohibits discrimination based on race, color, religion, sex, and national origin.
1967	Thurgood Marshall becomes the first Black American to be named to the Supreme Court.
1968	President Lyndon B. Johnson signs the Civil Rights Act of 1968, which prohibits discrimination in the sale, rental, and financing of housing.

STONE OF HOPE:
THE LEGACY OF MARTIN LUTHER KING, JR.

On April 4, 1968, Martin Luther King, Jr., was shot by James Earl Ray while standing on a hotel balcony in Memphis, Tennessee, U.S.A. The news of his death sent shock waves throughout the world: King, a Baptist minister and founder of the Southern Christian Leadership Conference, was the most prominent civil rights leader of his time. His nonviolent protests and marches against segregation, as well as his powerful speeches—including his famous "I Have a Dream" speech—motivated people to fight for justice for all.

More than 50 years after his death, King's dream lives on through a memorial on the National Mall in Washington, D.C. Built in 2011, the memorial features a 30-foot (9-m) statue of King carved into a granite boulder named the "Stone of Hope."

Today, King continues to inspire people around the world with his words and his vision for a peaceful world without racism. He will forever be remembered as one of the most prominent leaders of the civil rights movement.

"The time is always right to do what is right."

Martin Luther King, Jr., Memorial in Washington, D.C.

JOHN LEWIS: GETTING IN GOOD TROUBLE

John Lewis joins hands with President Barack Obama as they lead a commemorative march across the Edmund Pettus Bridge in Selma, Alabama, in 2015.

On March 7, 1965, a 25-year-old man linked arms with five other people, including Martin Luther King, Jr., as they led hundreds in a march across the Edmund Pettus Bridge in Selma, Alabama, U.S.A. It was a simple act, but it carried a very loud message: Those marching along the bridge were marching for racial justice and equality during a time when Black people were treated unjustly by many and were denied the same basic rights as white people, including the right to vote.

That young man was John Lewis. And, after crossing the bridge, Lewis was attacked by state troopers and beaten badly. The scene was so shocking that it made national news and created a public outcry. An act that prevented Black people from being denied the right to vote was passed just five months later. From then on, Lewis, who survived the attack, became a legend in the civil rights movement for his quiet yet powerful ability to create change. He called it getting in "good trouble": Standing up for what you believe is right and just, even if it means ruffling feathers along the way.

Lewis went on to serve in the U.S. House of Representatives for 33 years until his death in 2020. Before he passed, he was able to speak about the Black Lives Matter movement, once again encouraging people to fight for justice. "We must use our time and our space on this little planet that we call Earth to make a lasting contribution, to leave it a little better than we found it," said Lewis. "And now that need is greater than ever before."

263

WOMEN

FIGHTING FOR EQUALITY

Women in New York City cast their votes for the first time in November 1920.

Today, women make up about half of the workforce in the United States. But a little over a century ago, less than 20 percent worked outside the home. In fact, they didn't even have the right to vote!

That began to change in the mid-1800s when women, led by pioneers like Elizabeth Cady Stanton and Susan B. Anthony, started speaking up about inequality. They organized public demonstrations, gave speeches, published documents, and wrote newspaper articles to express their ideas. In 1848, about 300 people attended the Seneca Falls Convention in New York State to address the need for equal rights. By the late 1800s, the National American Woman Suffrage Association had made great strides toward giving women the freedom to vote. One by one, states began allowing women to vote. By 1920, the U.S. Constitution was amended, giving women across the country the ability to cast a vote during any election.

But the fight for equality did not end there. In the 1960s and 1970s, the women's rights movement experienced a rebirth, as feminists protested against injustices in areas such as the workplace and in education.

While these efforts enabled women to make great strides in our society, the efforts to even the playing field among men and women continue today.

New Zealand gave women the right to vote in 1893, becoming the world's first country to do so.

In 2020, Katie Sowers became the first woman to coach in the Super Bowl.

KAMALA HARRIS IS SWORN
IN AS VICE PRESIDENT
ON JANUARY 20, 2021.

Key Events in U.S. Women's History

1848: **Elizabeth Cady Stanton** and **Lucretia Mott** organize the Seneca Falls Convention in New York. Attendees rally for equitable laws, equal educational and job opportunities, and the right to vote.

1920: The 19th Amendment, which granted women the right to vote, is ratified.

1964: Title VII of the Civil Rights Act of 1964, which prohibits employment discrimination on the basis of sex, is successfully amended.

1971: Gloria Steinem heads up the National Women's Political Caucus, which encourages women to be active in government. She also launches *Ms.,* a magazine about women's issues.

1972: Congress approves **the Equal Rights Amendment** (ERA), proposing that women and men have equal rights under the law. It is ratified by 35 of the necessary 38 states, and is still not part of the U.S. Constitution.

1981: President Ronald Reagan appoints **Sandra Day O'Connor** as the first female Supreme Court justice.

2009: President Obama signs **the Lilly Ledbetter Fair Pay Act** to protect against pay discrimination among men and women.

2013: The **ban against women in military combat positions** is removed, overturning a 1994 Pentagon decision restricting women from combat roles.

2016: Democratic presidential nominee **Hillary Rodham Clinton** becomes the first woman to lead the ticket of a major U.S. party.

2021: Kamala Harris is sworn in as vice president of the United States, becoming the first woman to hold that office.

Jessica Nabongo
BLACK AMERICAN TRAVEL EXPERT
Have a yearning to see the world? Jessica Nabongo took that passion a step further (well, many steps further) and became the first Black woman to visit every country on Earth. The historic feat included more than 450 flights, over one million air miles, and visits to 195 countries. The journey, which Jessica documents in her book *The Catch Me If You Can,* wasn't just about seeing new sights: The writer collected stories and took photos of her experiences and now shares them in writing and at public speaking events to foster a global community and inspire others to see the world, too.

Greta Thunberg
CLIMATE CHANGE ACTIVIST
Greta Thunberg isn't afraid to speak up for what she believes in. Her biggest cause of concern? Climate change. At just 15 years old, Thunberg—who was born in Stockholm, Sweden—began a strike outside the Swedish Parliament to notify politicians about the dangerous threats of carbon emissions. Her courage caught the attention of millions of people around the world, and ultimately inspired the largest climate demonstration in human history. For her efforts, which include a book of essays by experts across the world on how to tackle the climate crisis, Greta has been nominated for a Nobel Peace Prize four years in a row.

265

QUIZ WHIZ

Go back in time to seek the answers to this history quiz!

Write your answers on a piece of paper. Then check them below.

1 **True or false?** The name of the ancient Egyptian queen Nefertiti means "glory of the noble one."

2 About how many years ago did the ancient Maya people vanish from Central America?
a. 1,300
b. 2,400
c. 3,500
d. 4,600

3 _____ once discovered nearly 2,000 ancient gold coins off the coast of Israel.
a. Amateur scuba divers
b. Retired teachers
c. Hospital workers
d. Store clerks

4 After her husband's death, Ching Shih commanded a group of ships called the _____ Fleet.
a. Green Streamer
b. Purple Pennant
c. Red Flag
d. Blue Banner

5 Where did many people in medieval Europe go to get medical help?
a. grocery store
b. bank
c. barbershop
d. ice-cream parlor

Not **STUMPED** yet? Check out the _NATIONAL GEOGRAPHIC KIDS QUIZ WHIZ_ collection for more fun **HISTORY** questions!

ANSWERS: 1. False: It means "the beautiful one has arrived."; **2.** b; **3.** a; **4.** c; **5.** c

HOMEWORK HELP

Brilliant Biographies

Malala Yousafzai

A biography is the story of a person's life. It can be a brief summary or a long book. Biographers—those who write biographies—use many different sources to learn about their subjects. You can write your own biography of a famous person you find inspiring.

How to Get Started

Choose a subject you find interesting. If you think Cleopatra is cool, you have a good chance of getting your readers interested, too. If you're bored by ancient Egypt, your readers will be snoring after your first paragraph.

Your subject can be almost anyone: an author, an inventor, a celebrity, a politician, or a member of your family. To find someone to write about, ask yourself these simple questions:

1. Who do I want to know more about?
2. What did this person do that was special?
3. How did this person change the world?

Do Your Research

- Find out as much about your subject as possible. Read books, news articles, and encyclopedia entries. Watch video clips and movies. Conduct interviews, if possible.
- Take notes, writing down important facts and interesting stories about your subject.

Write the Biography

- Come up with a title. Include the person's name.
- Write an introduction. Consider asking a probing question about your subject.
- Include information about the person's childhood. When was this person born? Where did they grow up? Who did they admire?
- Highlight the person's talents, accomplishments, and personal attributes.
- Describe the specific events that helped to shape this person's life. Did this person ever have a problem and overcome it?
- Write a conclusion. Include your thoughts about why it is important to learn about this person.
- Once you have finished your first draft, revise and then proofread your work.

Here's a **SAMPLE BIOGRAPHY** of Malala Yousafzai, a human rights advocate and the youngest ever recipient of the Nobel Peace Prize. Of course, there is so much more for you to discover and write about on your own!

Malala Yousafzai

Malala Yousafzai was born in Pakistan on July 12, 1997. Malala's father, Ziauddin, a teacher, made it a priority for his daughter to receive a proper education. Malala loved school. She learned to speak three languages and even wrote a blog about her experiences as a student.

Around the time Malala turned 10, the Taliban—a group of strict Muslims who support terrorism and believe women should stay at home—took over the region where she lived. The Taliban did not approve of Malala's outspoken love of learning. One day, on her way home from school, Malala was shot in the head by a Taliban gunman. Very badly injured, she was sent to a hospital in England.

Not only did Malala survive the shooting—she thrived. She used her experience as a platform to fight for girls' education worldwide. She began speaking out about educational opportunities for all. Her efforts gained worldwide attention, and she was eventually awarded the Nobel Peace Prize in 2014 at the age of 17. She is the youngest person to earn the prestigious prize.

Each year on July 12, World Malala Day honors her heroic efforts to bring attention to human rights issues.

GEOGRAPHY
ROCKS

A hiker explores the Dolomites, a mountain range made up of 18 peaks in the northern Italian Alps.

THE POLITICAL WORLD

Earth's land area is made up of seven continents, but people have divided much of the land into smaller political units called countries. Antarctica is used for scientific research. Australia is a continent made up of a single country, but the other five continents include almost 200 independent countries. The political map shown here depicts boundaries—imaginary lines created by treaties—that separate countries. Some boundaries, such as the one between the United States and Canada, are very stable and have been recognized for many years.

ARCTIC

Beaufort Sea
RUSSIA
Alaska (U.S.)
Bering Sea
60°

Baffin Bay
Greenland (Denmark)

ARCTIC CIRCLE

ICELAND

Hudson Bay
CANADA
Labrador Sea

UNITED KINGDOM

IRELAND (ÉIRE)

UNITED STATES

PORT. SPAIN

See Europe map for more detail.

30°

MOROCCO

TROPIC OF CANCER
MEXICO
Gulf of Mexico
THE BAHAMAS

WESTERN SAHARA (Morocco)
ALG

Hawai'i (U.S.)

CUBA DOMINCAN REP.
BELIZE HAITI **Puerto Rico** (U.S.)
JAMAICA
GUATEMALA HONDURAS *Caribbean Sea*
EL SALVADOR NICARAGUA
COSTA RICA
PANAMA VENEZUELA GUYANA
COLOMBIA

CABO VERDE MAURITANIA MALI
THE GAMBIA SENEGAL BURKINA FASO
GUINEA-BISSAU
GUINEA GHANA
SIERRA LEONE
LIBERIA
CÔTE D'IVOIRE (IVORY COAST)

See North America map for more detail.

French Guiana (France)

PACIFIC OCEAN

0° EQUATOR 150° 120° 90° 30° 0°

KIRIBATI

Galápagos Islands (Ecuador) ECUADOR
PERU
BRAZIL

EQ. GUINEA

SAO TOME AND PRINCIPE

Marquesas Islands (France)

SAMOA
—**American Samoa** (U.S.) **French Polynesia** (France)
TONGA

BOLIVIA

ATLANTIC OCEAN

PARAGUAY

TROPIC OF CAPRICORN

ARGENTINA
URUGUAY

30°

CHILE

0 _____ 2000 Miles
0 _____ 2000 Kilometers
Winkel Tripel Projection

Chatham Is. (N.Z.)

Falkland Islands (Islas Malvinas) (U.K.)

Prime Meridian

SOUTHERN
ANTARCTIC

60°

Weddell Sea

270

Other boundaries, such as the one between Sudan and South Sudan in northeast Africa, are relatively new and still disputed. Countries come in all shapes and sizes. Russia and Canada are giants; others, such as El Salvador and Qatar, are small. Some countries are long and skinny—look at Chile in South America! Still other countries—such as Indonesia and Japan in Asia—are made up of groups of islands. The political map is a clue to the diversity that makes Earth so fascinating.

OCEAN
Svalbard
(Norway)

Barents
Sea

Kara
Sea

East
Siberian Sea

NORWAY
SWEDEN
FINLAND

R U S S I A

Sea of
Okhotsk

Bering
Sea

60°

EST.
LATV.
LITH.

DEN.

GERMANY
POLAND
BELARUS

FRANCE

UKRAINE
MOLD.

KAZAKHSTAN

MONGOLIA

NORTH
KOREA

JAPAN

ITALY
ROMANIA
BULGARIA
GEORGIA

UZBEK.

KYRGYZSTAN

SOUTH
KOREA

GREECE
TÜRKİYE
(TURKEY)
ARM. AZERB.
TURKMEN.
TAJIKISTAN

C H I N A

Mediterranean Sea
SYRIA
AFGHAN.

TAIWAN
30°

TUNISIA
LEBANON
IRAQ
IRAN

The People's Republic of China
claims Taiwan as its 23rd province.
Taiwan's government (Republic of
China) maintains that there are
two political entities.

ERIA
ISRAEL
JORDAN
KUWAIT
PAKISTAN
NEPAL
BHUTAN

LIBYA
EGYPT
BAHRAIN
QATAR
U.A.E.

SAUDI
ARABIA

BANGLADESH

INDIA

MYANMAR
(BURMA)
VIETNAM
LAOS

TAIWAN

South
China
Sea

Philippine
Sea

Northern Mariana
Islands PACIFIC
(U.S.)

Red Sea

NIGER
SUDAN
ERITREA
YEMEN

OMAN

Arabian
Sea

Bay
of
Bengal

THAILAND

CAMBODIA

PHILIPPINES

Guam
(U.S.)

OCEAN

CHAD
DJIBOUTI

PALAU

MARSHALL ISLANDS

BENIN
NIGERIA
CAMEROON
CEN.
AF. REP.
SOUTH
SUDAN
SOMALILAND
ETHIOPIA
SOMALIA

SRI
LANKA

BRUNEI

FEDERATED STATES
OF MICRONESIA

TOGO
MALDIVES

MALAYSIA
SINGAPORE

KIRIBATI

GABON
CONGO
DEM.
REP.
OF THE
CONGO
RWANDA
BURUNDI
UGANDA
KENYA

60°
90°

EQUATOR
150°
0°

NAURU

TANZANIA

INDESIA
I N D O N E S I A

PAPUA
NEW
GUINEA

SOLOMON
ISLANDS

SEYCHELLES

I N D I A N

ANGOLA
ZAMBIA
MALAWI

COMOROS

O C E A N

TIMOR-LESTE

TUVALU

NAMIBIA
ZIMBABWE
BOTSWANA
MOZAMBIQUE
MADAGASCAR

MAURITIUS
Réunion
(France)

Coral
Sea
VANUATU
FIJI

ESWATINI
(SWAZILAND)

SOUTH
AFRICA
LESOTHO

AUSTRALIA

New
Caledonia
(France)

Great
Australian
Bight

Tasman
Sea

30°

NEW
ZEALAND

Kerguelen
Islands
(France)

OCEAN
CIRCLE

60°

A N T A R C T I C A

271

THE PHYSICAL WORLD

Earth is dominated by large landmasses called continents—seven in all—and by an interconnected global ocean that is divided into five parts by the continents. More than 70 percent of Earth's surface is covered by oceans, and the rest is made up of land areas.

Different landforms give variety to the surface of the continents. The Rocky Mountains divide North America, the Andes mark the western edge of South America, and the Himalaya tower above South Asia. The Plateau of Tibet forms the rugged core of Asia,

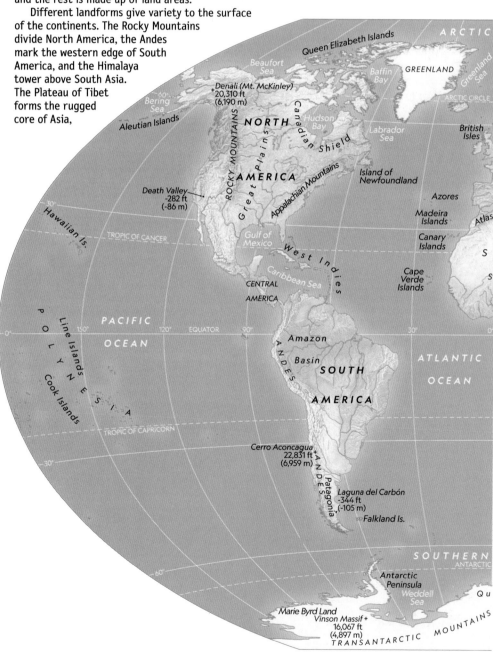

ARCTIC

Queen Elizabeth Islands

Beaufort Sea

GREENLAND

Greenland Sea

Baffin Bay

ARCTIC CIRCLE

Denali (Mt. McKinley) + 20,310 ft (6,190 m)

Bering Sea

Hudson Bay

Labrador Sea

British Isles

Aleutian Islands

NORTH

Canadian Shield

AMERICA

ROCKY MOUNTAINS

Great Plains

Appalachian Mountains

Island of Newfoundland

Death Valley -282 ft (-86 m)

Azores

Madeira Islands

Atlas

Hawaiian Is.

TROPIC OF CANCER

Gulf of Mexico

West Indies

Canary Islands

S

Caribbean Sea

Cape Verde Islands

S

CENTRAL AMERICA

POLYNESIA

Line Islands

PACIFIC

OCEAN

EQUATOR

Amazon

ATLANTIC

Cook Islands

Basin

ANDES

SOUTH

OCEAN

AMERICA

TROPIC OF CAPRICORN

Cerro Aconcagua + 22,831 ft (6,959 m)

ANDES

Patagonia

Laguna del Carbón -344 ft (-105 m)

Falkland Is.

SOUTHERN

ANTARCTIC

Antarctic Peninsula

Weddell Sea

Qu

Marie Byrd Land

Vinson Massif + 16,067 ft (4,897 m)

TRANSANTARCTIC MOUNTAINS

while the Northern European Plain extends from the North Sea to the Ural Mountains. Much of Africa is a plateau, and dry plains cover large areas of Australia. Mountains rise more than 16,000 feet (4,877 m) above Antarctica's massive ice sheets. Mountains and trenches make the ocean floors as varied as any continent. A mountain chain called the Mid-Atlantic Ridge runs the length of the Atlantic Ocean. In the western Pacific, trenches drop deep into the ocean floor.

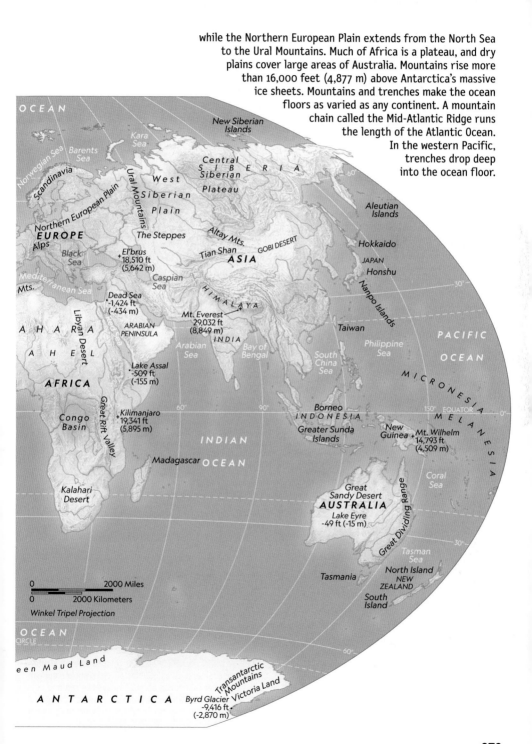

OCEAN

New Siberian Islands

Kara Sea

Barents Sea

Norwegian Sea

Scandinavia

Central SIBERIA

West Siberian

Ural Mountains

Siberian Plateau

Northern European Plain

West Siberian Plain

Aleutian Islands

EUROPE

Alps

The Steppes

Altay Mts.

Hokkaido

Black Sea

El'brus 18,510 ft (5,642 m)

Tian Shan

GOBI DESERT

JAPAN

Honshu

Mediterranean Sea

ASIA

Caspian Sea

Mts.

Dead Sea -1,424 ft (-434 m)

HIMALAYA

Nampo Islands

SAHARA

Libyan Desert

ARABIAN PENINSULA

Mt. Everest 29,032 ft (8,849 m)

INDIA

Taiwan

PACIFIC

SAHEL

Arabian Sea

Bay of Bengal

South China Sea

Philippine Sea

OCEAN

Lake Assal -509 ft (-155 m)

AFRICA

MICRONESIA

Congo Basin

Great Rift Valley

Kilimanjaro 19,341 ft (5,895 m)

INDONESIA

Borneo

MELANESIA

Greater Sunda Islands

New Guinea

Mt. Wilhelm 14,793 ft (4,509 m)

EQUATOR

INDIAN

Madagascar OCEAN

Coral Sea

Kalahari Desert

Great Sandy Desert

AUSTRALIA

Lake Eyre -49 ft (-15 m)

Great Dividing Range

Tasman Sea

0   2000 Miles

0   2000 Kilometers

Winkel Tripel Projection

Tasmania

North Island

NEW ZEALAND

South Island

OCEAN

CIRCLE

een Maud Land

Transantarctic Mountains

Victoria Land

ANTARCTICA

Byrd Glacier -9,416 ft (-2,870 m)

273

KINDS OF MAPS

Maps are special tools that geographers use to tell a story about Earth. Maps can be used to show just about anything related to places. Some maps show physical features, such as mountains or vegetation. Maps can also show climates or natural hazards and other things we cannot easily see. Other maps illustrate different features on Earth—political boundaries, urban centers, and economic systems.

AN IMPERFECT TOOL

Maps are not perfect. A globe is a scale model of Earth with accurate relative sizes and locations. Because maps are flat, they involve distortions of size, shape, and direction. Also, cartographers—people who create maps—make choices about what information to include. Because of this, it is important to study many different types of maps to learn the complete story of Earth. Three commonly found kinds of maps are shown on this page.

PHYSICAL MAPS. Earth's natural features—landforms, water bodies, and vegetation—are shown on physical maps. The map above uses color and shading to illustrate mountains, lakes, rivers, and deserts of central South America. Country names and borders are added for reference, but they are not natural features.

POLITICAL MAPS. These maps represent characteristics of the landscape created by humans, such as boundaries, cities, and place-names. Natural features are added only for reference. On the map above, capital cities are represented with a star inside a circle, while other cities are shown with black dots.

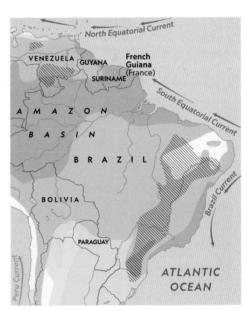

THEMATIC MAPS. Patterns related to a particular topic or theme, such as population distribution, appear on these maps. The map above displays the region's climate zones, which range from tropical wet (bright green) to tropical wet and dry (light green) to semiarid (dark yellow) to arid or desert (light yellow).

MAKING MAPS

Meet a Cartographer!

As a National Geographic cartographer, **Mike McNey** works with maps every day. Here, he shares more about his cool career.

National Geographic staff cartographers Mike McNey and Rosemary Wardley review a map of Africa for the *National Geographic Kids World Atlas*.

What exactly does a cartographer do?

I create maps specifically for books and atlases to help the text tell the story on the page. The maps need to fit into the size and the style of the book, with the final goal being that it's all accurate and appealing for the reader.

What kinds of stories have you told with your maps?

Once, I created a map that showed the spread of the Burmese python population in Florida, U.S.A., around the Everglades National Park. I've also made maps that show data like farmland, food production, cattle density, and fish catch in a particular location, like the United States.

How do you rely on technology in your job?

All aspects of mapmaking are on the computer. This makes it much quicker to make a map. It also makes it easier to change anything on a map. If you want to change the color of the rivers on a map, you just click the mouse.

How do you create your maps?

I work with geographic information systems (GIS), a computer software that allows us to represent any data on a specific location of the world, or even the entire world. Data can be anything, including endangered species, animal ranges, or population of a particular place. We also use remote systems, like satellites and aerial imagery, to analyze Earth's surface.

Satellites in orbit around Earth act as eyes in the sky, recording data about the planet's land and ocean areas. The data are converted to numbers transmitted back to computers specially programmed to interpret the data. They record the information in a form that cartographers can use to create maps.

What will maps of the future look like?

In the future, you'll see more and more data on maps. I also think more online maps are going to be made in a way that you can switch from a world view to a local view to see data at any scale.

What's the best part of your job?

I love the combination of science and design involved in it. It's also fun to make maps interesting for kids.

275

UNDERSTANDING
MAPS

MAKING A PROJECTION

Globes present a model of Earth as it is—a sphere—but they are bulky and can be difficult to use and store. Flat maps are much more convenient, but certain problems can result from transferring Earth's curved surface to a flat piece of paper, a process called projection. Imagine a globe that has been cut in half, like the one to the right. If a light is shined into it, the lines of latitude and longitude and the shapes of the continent will cast shadows that can be "projected" onto a piece of paper, as shown here. Depending on how the paper is positioned, the shadows will be distorted in different ways.

KNOW THE CODE

Every map has a story to tell, but first you have to know how to read one. Maps represent information by using a language of symbols. When you know how to read these symbols, you can access a wide range of information. For example, look at the scale and compass rose or arrow to understand distance and direction (see box below).

To find out what each symbol on a map means, you must use the key. It's your secret decoder—identifying information by each symbol on the map.

There are three main types of map symbols: points, lines, and areas. Points, which can be either dots or small icons, represent the location or the number of things, such as schools, cities, or landmarks. Lines are used to show boundaries, roads, or rivers and can vary in color or thickness. Area symbols use pattern or color to show regions, such as a sandy area or a neighborhood.

SCALE AND DIRECTION

The scale on a map can be shown as a fraction, as words, or as a line or bar. It relates distance on the map to distance in the real world. Sometimes the scale identifies the type of map projection. Maps may include an arrow to indicate north on the map or a compass rose to show all principal directions.

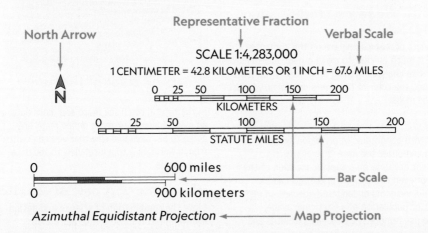

North Arrow

Representative Fraction

Verbal Scale

SCALE 1:4,283,000
1 CENTIMETER = 42.8 KILOMETERS OR 1 INCH = 67.6 MILES

0   25   50   100   150   200
KILOMETERS

0   25   50   100   150   200
STATUTE MILES

0   600 miles
0   900 kilometers

Bar Scale

Azimuthal Equidistant Projection ← Map Projection

GEOGRAPHIC FEATURES

From roaring rivers to parched deserts, from underwater canyons to jagged mountains, Earth is covered with beautiful and diverse environments. Here are examples of the most common types of geographic features found around the world.

WATERFALL

Waterfalls form when rivers reach an abrupt change in elevation. At left, the Iguazú waterfall system—on the border of Brazil and Argentina—is made up of 275 falls.

VALLEY

Valleys, cut by running water or moving ice, may be broad and flat or narrow and steep, such as the Indus River Valley (above) in Ladakh, India.

RIVER

As a river moves through flatlands, it twists and turns. Above, the Rio Los Amigos winds through a rainforest in Peru.

MOUNTAIN

Mountains are Earth's tallest landforms, and Mount Everest (above) rises highest of all, at 29,031.69 feet (8,848.86 m) above sea level.

GLACIER

Glaciers—"rivers" of ice—such as Hubbard Glacier (above) in Alaska, U.S.A., move slowly from mountains to the sea. Global warming is shrinking them.

CANYON

Steep-sided valleys called canyons are created mainly by running water. Buckskin Gulch (above) in Utah, U.S.A., is the deepest "slot" canyon in the American Southwest.

DESERT

Deserts are land features created by climate, specifically by a lack of water. Here, a camel caravan crosses the Sahara in North Africa.

AFRICA

Snow sometimes falls on parts of the Sahara.

Part of the canine family, black-backed jackal pups are usually born from August to October.

Black-backed jackal pups

The massive continent of Africa, where humankind began millions of years ago, is second only to Asia in size. Stretching nearly as far from west to east as it does from north to south, Africa is home to both the longest river in the world (the Nile) and the largest hot desert on Earth (the Sahara).

Luanda, Angola

FIERCE FISH

Fossils from one of the world's deadliest prehistoric fish have been found in South Africa, researchers say. The 360-million-year-old fossils of *Hyneria udlezinye* revealed that the bony fish measured up to nine feet (2.7 m) long, sported a mouthful of razor-sharp teeth, and likely preyed on large creatures.

COOL CANYON

Local legend says that Namibia's Fish River Canyon—the largest canyon in Africa—was carved by a giant serpent when it burrowed deep into the ground while hiding from hunters.

Great Pyramid, Great Numbers
How do the numbers for Earth's biggest pyramid stack up?

Due to erosion, the pyramid is **30 feet (9 m)** shorter than it was originally.

Weight of largest stone blocks: **15 tons (14 t)**

Number of stone blocks: **2.3 million**

Number of builders: **20,000**

Angle at which the sides rise: 51°52″

Height: **451 feet (138 m)**

Average length of each side: **756 feet (230 m)**

REMARKABLE RIVER

Africa is home to one of the longest rivers in the world: the Nile. Flowing south to north along some 4,100 miles (6,600 km), the Nile runs through or along the border of 11 African countries. Throughout history, the Nile has been a key source of fresh water and food for both people and the animals that live nearby, including hippos, turtles, and crocodiles.

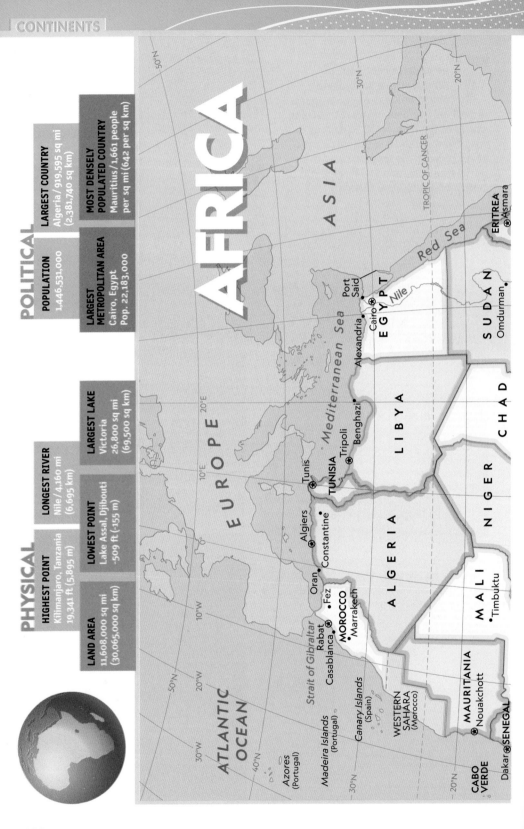

AFRICA

PHYSICAL

HIGHEST POINT
Kilimanjaro, Tanzania
19,341 ft (5,895 m)

LOWEST POINT
Lake Assal, Djibouti
-509 ft (-155 m)

LONGEST RIVER
Nile / 4,160 mi
(6,695 km)

LAND AREA
11,608,000 sq mi
(30,065,000 sq km)

LARGEST LAKE
Victoria
26,800 sq mi
(69,500 sq km)

POLITICAL

POPULATION
1,446,531,000

LARGEST COUNTRY
Algeria / 919,595 sq mi
(2,381,740 sq km)

LARGEST METROPOLITAN AREA
Cairo, Egypt
Pop. 22,183,000

MOST DENSELY POPULATED COUNTRY
Mauritius / 1,661 people
per sq mi (642 per sq km)

ASIA

EUROPE

ATLANTIC OCEAN

Mediterranean Sea

Red Sea

TROPIC OF CANCER

Azores
(Portugal)

Madeira Islands
(Portugal)

Canary Islands
(Spain)

Strait of Gibraltar

CABO VERDE

Dakar ⊛ SENEGAL

MAURITANIA
⊛ Nouakchott

WESTERN SAHARA
(Morocco)

MOROCCO
Rabat ⊛
Casablanca •
• Fez
• Marrakech

Oran •

Algiers
⊛ • Constantine

ALGERIA

MALI
• Timbuktu

Tunis
⊛ TUNISIA

Tripoli •

LIBYA

Benghazi •

NIGER

CHAD

Alexandria •

Cairo ⊛
EGYPT
Port Said

Nile

SUDAN
Omdurman •

ERITREA
⊛ Asmara

50°W 40°N 30°W 30°N 20°W 20°N 10°W 10°E 20°E 20°N 30°N 50°N

280

ATLANTIC OCEAN

INDIAN OCEAN

SOMALIA
Gulf of Aden
SOMALILAND
DJIBOUTI Djibouti
Lake Assal (-155 m) -509 ft
Mogadishu

ETHIOPIA
Khartoum
Addis Ababa

SOUTH SUDAN
Juba

DARFUR

CENTRAL AFRICAN REPUBLIC
Bangui

N'Djamena

UGANDA
Kampala
Lake Victoria
RWANDA
Kigali
BURUNDI
Gitega
Bujumbura

KENYA
Nairobi
Kilimanjaro 19,341 ft (5,895 m)
Mombasa

SEYCHELLES
Victoria

TANZANIA
Dodoma
Dar es Salaam

COMOROS
Moroni

MADAGASCAR
Antananarivo

MAURITIUS
Port Louis
Réunion (France)

Mozambique Channel

DEMOCRATIC REPUBLIC OF THE CONGO
Kisangani
Kinshasa
Mbuji-Mayi
Kananga

CONGO
Brazzaville

GABON
Libreville

CAMEROON
Yaoundé
Douala

EQUATORIAL GUINEA
Malabo

SAO TOME & PRINCIPE
São Tomé

NIGERIA
Abuja
Lagos
Ogbomosho
Kano

BENIN
Porto-Novo
Cotonou

TOGO
Lomé

GHANA
Accra

BURKINA FASO
Ouagadougou

NIGER
Niamey

CÔTE D'IVOIRE (IVORY COAST)
Yamoussoukro
Abidjan

LIBERIA
Monrovia

SIERRA LEONE
Freetown

GUINEA
Conakry

GUINEA-BISSAU
Bissau

THE GAMBIA
Banjul

Bamako

Pointe-Noire
Cabinda (Angola)

ANGOLA
Luanda

NAMIBIA
Windhoek

BOTSWANA
Gaborone

ZAMBIA
Lusaka
Kitwe
Kolwezi

Lubumbashi

MALAWI
Lilongwe

MOZAMBIQUE

ZIMBABWE
Harare

SOUTH AFRICA
Pretoria (Tshwane)
Johannesburg
Bloemfontein
Cape Town
Port Elizabeth
Durban

ESWATINI (SWAZILAND)
Mbabane
Lobamba

LESOTHO
Maseru

Maputo

St. Helena (U.K.)

Ascension (U.K.)

EQUATOR

TROPIC OF CAPRICORN

10°N · 0° · 10°S · 20°S · 30°S
30°E · 40°E · 50°E · 60°E
0° · 10°E · 20°E

Map Key
⊛ National capital
• Other city
▲ Highest point (above sea level)
▼ Lowest point (below sea level)

800 Miles
800 Kilometers
Azimuthal Equal-Area Projection

ANTARCTICA

Humpback whale

> Most of the meteorites found on Earth are in Antarctica.

> In the summer months, humpback whales in Antarctica feed mostly on krill.

This frozen continent may be a cool place to visit, but unless you're a penguin, you probably wouldn't want to hang out in Antarctica for long. The fact that it's the coldest, windiest, and driest continent helps explain why humans never colonized this ice-covered land surrounding the South Pole.

Weddell seal

PENGUIN PATROL

Call it a not-so-stealthy spy mission: In an effort to learn how climate change is impacting animals that live in the Antarctic region, scientists are sending a battery-powered rover to follow penguins. The slow-moving robot records photos, video, and other types of data to get an up-close-and-personal look into penguin colonies.

WARMER THAN EVER

With Antarctica experiencing record-breaking high temperatures, the continent as a whole is getting warmer. Temperatures reached a record high of nearly 65°F (18.3°C) in February 2020, making the area one of the fastest warming regions on Earth.

50	50
40	40
30	30
20	20
10	10
0	0
10	10
20	20
30	30
40	40
50	50

Annual Average Snowfall

17 feet (5 m)

8 feet (2 m)

0.7 foot (0.2 m)

Sapporo, Japan

Buffalo, New York, U.S.A.

South Pole, Antarctica

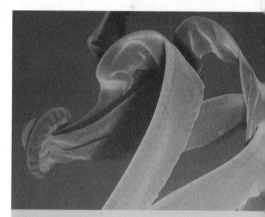

GIANT JELLYFISH

Giant phantom jellyfish were recently spotted by cruise-goers off the coast of Antarctica. With ribbonlike bodies stretching 30 feet (9 m) and umbrellalike heads, the super-rare swimmers are now considered some of the largest invertebrate predators in the sea.

PHYSICAL

LAND AREA
5,100,000 sq mi
(13,209,000 sq km)

HIGHEST POINT
Vinson Massif
16,067 ft (4,897 m)

LOWEST POINT
Byrd Glacier
-9,416 ft (-2,870 m)

COLDEST PLACE
Ridge A, annual
average temperature
-94°F (-70°C)

**AVERAGE
PRECIPITATION ON
THE POLAR PLATEAU**
Less than 2 in (5 cm)

POLITICAL

POPULATION
There are no
Indigenous inhabitants,
but there are both
permanent and
summer-only staffed
research stations.

**NUMBER OF
INDEPENDENT
COUNTRIES** 0

**NUMBER OF
COUNTRIES
CLAIMING LAND** 7

**NUMBER OF
COUNTRIES
OPERATING YEAR-
ROUND RESEARCH
STATIONS** 20

**NUMBER OF YEAR-
ROUND RESEARCH
STATIONS** 40

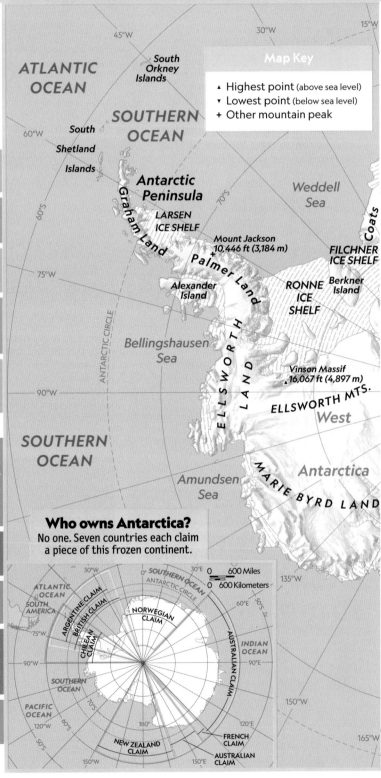

Map Key
▲ Highest point (above sea level)
▼ Lowest point (below sea level)
+ Other mountain peak

ATLANTIC OCEAN

South Orkney Islands

SOUTHERN OCEAN

South Shetland Islands

Antarctic Peninsula

Weddell Sea

Graham Land

LARSEN ICE SHELF

Mount Jackson 10,446 ft (3,184 m)

Coats

FILCHNER ICE SHELF

Palmer Land

Alexander Island

RONNE ICE SHELF

Berkner Island

ANTARCTIC CIRCLE

Bellingshausen Sea

ELLSWORTH LAND

Vinson Massif ▲ 16,067 ft (4,897 m)

ELLSWORTH MTS.

West

SOUTHERN OCEAN

Amundsen Sea

MARIE BYRD LAND

Antarctica

Who owns Antarctica?
No one. Seven countries each claim
a piece of this frozen continent.

ATLANTIC OCEAN

SOUTH AMERICA

SOUTHERN OCEAN

ARGENTINE CLAIM
BRITISH CLAIM
CHILEAN CLAIM

NORWEGIAN CLAIM

ANTARCTIC CIRCLE

INDIAN OCEAN

AUSTRALIAN CLAIM

PACIFIC OCEAN

NEW ZEALAND CLAIM

FRENCH CLAIM

AUSTRALIAN CLAIM

0 600 Miles
0 600 Kilometers

ANTARCTICA

FIMBUL ICE SHELF

0°

SOUTHERN OCEAN

60°E

RIISER-LARSEN ICE SHELF

ENDERBY LAND

QUEEN MAUD LAND

Land

Valkyrie Dome

MacKenzie Bay 75°E

Lambert Glacier

AMERY ICE SHELF

AMERICAN HIGHLAND

Ridge A +

WEST ICE SHELF

POLAR PLATEAU

T R A N S A N T A R C T I C   M O U N T A I N S

★ South Pole

East

Antarctica

90°E

SHACKLETON ICE SHELF

80°S

105°E

ROSS ICE SHELF

Byrd Glacier -9,416 ft (-2,870 m)

Roosevelt Island

Taylor Glacier

Ross Island

W I L K E S   L A N D

70°S

+ **Mount Erebus** 12,448 ft (3,794 m)

V I C T O R I A   L A N D

120°E

Ross Sea

SOUTHERN OCEAN

180°

Talos Dome

60°S

150°E

135°E

INDIAN OCEAN

0   600 Miles

0   600 Kilometers

Azimuthal Equidistant Projection

ASIA

Prayer flags in Tibet

The colors on Tibetan prayer flags represent different elements, such as air, fire, earth, and water.

An annual marathon is run along part of the Great Wall of China.

ade up of 46 countries, Asia is the world's largest continent. Just how big is it? From western Türkiye (Turkey) to the eastern tip of Russia, Asia spans nearly half the globe! Home to more than four billion citizens—that's three out of five people on the planet—Asia's population is bigger than that of all the other continents combined.

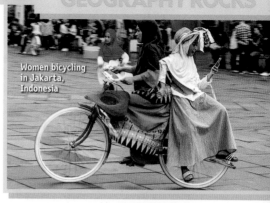

Women bicycling in Jakarta, Indonesia

SAVING THE GIBBONS

Javan gibbons—only found in Java, Indonesia—are extremely endangered due to threats like habitat loss and hunting. But conservation groups are working hard to change that fact. Efforts like rehabilitating captive-born gibbons and releasing them into protected areas are aimed at repopulating the primates.

TREES, PLEASE

Plans are underway for one million trees to be planted throughout Singapore by 2030. The hope? To improve air quality and add more parks, so that everyone in the city will one day be within a 10-minute walk to a green space.

JUNGLE TEMPLE

The 900-year-old temple known as Angkor Wat sits in the jungle of northern Cambodia. Covering more than 400 acres (162 ha), the massive religious structure was built inside the capital of the Khmer Empire, a once powerful civilization in Southeast Asia. Today, the site receives more than two million visitors a year.

World's Deepest Lakes

Lake Baikal (Russia)	Lake Tanganyika (eastern Africa)	Caspian Sea (Central Asia/Europe border)	Lake Malawi (eastern Africa)	Ysyk-Köl (Kyrgyzstan)
			2,316 ft (706 m)	2,297 ft (700 m)
		3,104 ft (946 m)		
	4,708 ft (1,435 m)			
5,369 ft (1,637 m)				

Most of Earth's surface water is stored in lakes. The deepest of all is Asia's Lake Baikal, which contains about 20 percent of Earth's total surface fresh water.

PHYSICAL

LAND AREA
17,208,000 sq mi
(44,570,000 sq km)

HIGHEST POINT
Mount Everest,
China–Nepal
29,032 ft (8,849 m)

LOWEST POINT
Dead Sea,
Israel–Jordan
-1,424 ft (-434 m)

LONGEST RIVER
Yangtze, China
3,880 mi (6,244 km)

**LARGEST LAKE
ENTIRELY IN ASIA**
Lake Baikal, Russia
12,200 sq mi
(31,500 sq km)

POLITICAL

POPULATION
4,698,537,000

**LARGEST
METROPOLITAN AREA**
Tokyo, Japan
Pop. 37,194,000

**LARGEST COUNTRY
ENTIRELY IN ASIA**
China
3,705,405 sq mi
(9,596,960 sq km)

**MOST DENSELY
POPULATED COUNTRY**
Singapore
21,494 people
per sq mi
(8,311 per sq km)

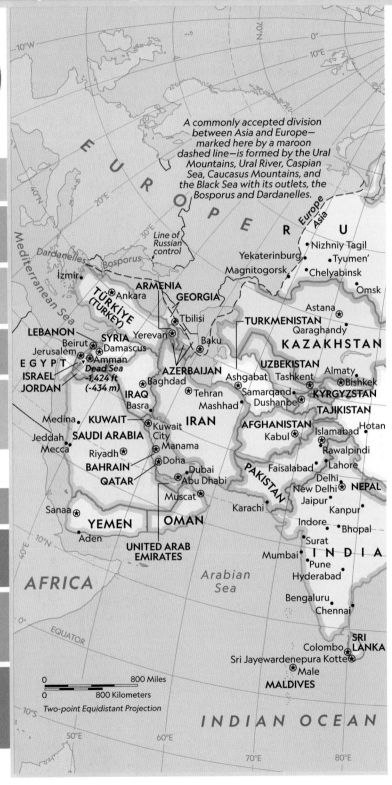

A commonly accepted division between Asia and Europe—marked here by a maroon dashed line—is formed by the Ural Mountains, Ural River, Caspian Sea, Caucasus Mountains, and the Black Sea with its outlets, the Bosporus and Dardanelles.

288

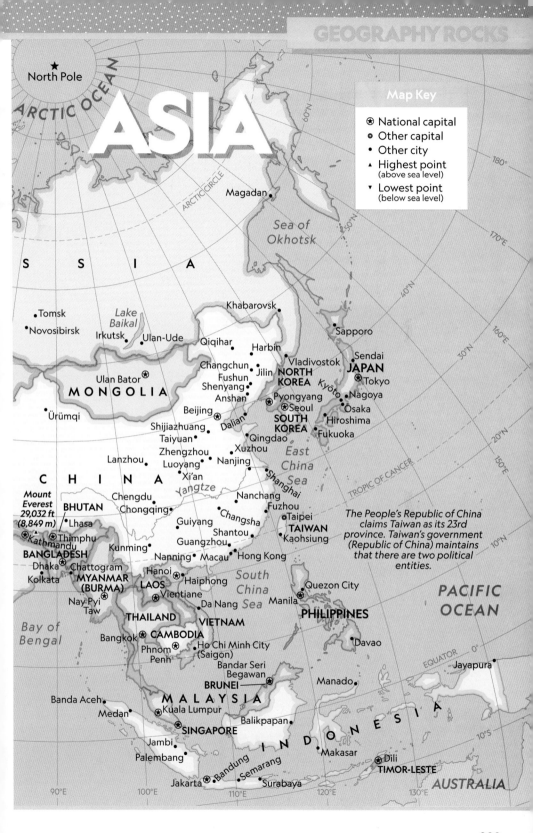

ASIA

North Pole ★

ARCTIC OCEAN

ARCTIC CIRCLE

Map Key

⊗ National capital
⊙ Other capital
• Other city
▲ Highest point
(above sea level)
▼ Lowest point
(below sea level)

Magadan

Sea of Okhotsk

R U S S I A

Tomsk
Novosibirsk
Irkutsk
Ulan-Ude
Qiqihar
Harbin
Khabarovsk
Sapporo
Sendai
Vladivostok
JAPAN
Changchun
Jilin
NORTH KOREA
Kyoto
Tokyo
Fushun
Shenyang
Anshan
Pyongyang
Nagoya
Seoul
Osaka
SOUTH KOREA
Hiroshima
Fukuoka

Lake Baikal

Ulan Bator ⊗
M O N G O L I A

Ürümqi

Beijing ⊗
Shijiazhuang
Dalian
Taiyuan
Qingdao
Xuzhou
East China Sea
Lanzhou
Zhengzhou
Nanjing
Luoyang
Xi'an
Yangtze
Shanghai

C H I N A

Nanchang
Fuzhou

Mount Everest
29,032 ft
(8,849 m) ▲

BHUTAN
Chengdu
Chongqing
Changsha
Taipei
Kathmandu ⊗
Lhasa
Guiyang
TAIWAN
Thimphu ⊙
Shantou
Kaohsiung
BANGLADESH
Kunming
Guangzhou
Dhaka
Chattogram
Nanning
Macau
Hong Kong
Kolkata
MYANMAR
(BURMA)
Hanoi
Haiphong
South China Sea
Nay Pyi
Taw
LAOS
Vientiane
Da Nang
Quezon City
Bay of Bengal
THAILAND
VIETNAM
Manila
Banda Aceh
Bangkok
CAMBODIA
PHILIPPINES
Phnom
Penh
Ho Chi Minh City
(Saigon)
Davao
Bandar Seri Begawan
BRUNEI
Manado
Medan
M A L A Y S I A
Kuala Lumpur
Balikpapan
SINGAPORE ⊗
I N D O N E S I A
Jambi
Makasar
Palembang
Dili
TIMOR-LESTE
Jakarta ⊗
Bandung
Semarang
Surabaya
AUSTRALIA
Jayapura

PACIFIC OCEAN

The People's Republic of China claims Taiwan as its 23rd province. Taiwan's government (Republic of China) maintains that there are two political entities.

TROPIC OF CANCER

EQUATOR

North Pole ★

180°
170°E
160°E
150°E
130°E
120°E
110°E
100°E
90°E
0°
10°S
10°N
20°N
30°N
40°N
50°N
60°N

AUSTRALIA,
NEW ZEALAND, AND OCEANIA

Papua New Guinea is home to the world's third largest tropical rainforest, behind the Amazon and the Congo Basin.

A young red-legged pademelon stays in Mom's pouch for its first six months of life.

Red-legged pademelon

G'day, mate! This vast region, covering almost 3.3 million square miles (8.5 million sq km), includes Australia—the world's smallest and flattest continent—and New Zealand, as well as a fleet of mostly tiny islands scattered across the Pacific Ocean. Also known as "down under," most of the countries in this region are in the Southern Hemisphere, below the Equator.

Maori children of New Zealand in ceremonial clothing

SHIPWRECK CENTRAL

Some 1,600 shipwrecks litter the coastline of Western Australia, giving the area the nickname "Treasure Coast" because of the gold, diamonds, and other booty left behind. Massive tides, hidden coral reefs, and extreme winds make these waters some of the most treacherous for boats to cross.

SINGLE FLOWER

PREHISTORIC BLOOMS

A landowner in southeastern Australia uncovered a football field–size prehistoric rainforest while working on his fields. The area revealed 15-million-year-old fossils, all preserved in a reddish rock—including flowers, worms, spiders, cicadas, and even a tiny wasp with pollen attached to its head.

RAD RUINS

On a tiny island in the middle of the Pacific Ocean, you'll find Nan Madol, the only ancient city ever built atop a coral reef. What's left today—stone walls and columns—are the ruins of a once thriving civilization known as the Saudeleur, a dynasty that ruled the island of Pohnpei.

More Animals Than People

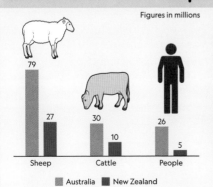

Figures in millions

	Sheep	Cattle	People
Australia	79	30	26
New Zealand	27	10	5

■ Australia ■ New Zealand

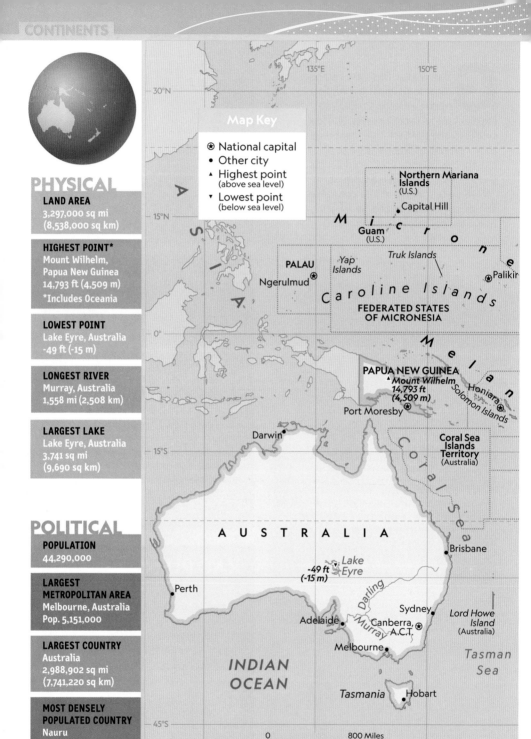

PHYSICAL

LAND AREA
3,297,000 sq mi
(8,538,000 sq km)

HIGHEST POINT*
Mount Wilhelm,
Papua New Guinea
14,793 ft (4,509 m)
*Includes Oceania

LOWEST POINT
Lake Eyre, Australia
-49 ft (-15 m)

LONGEST RIVER
Murray, Australia
1,558 mi (2,508 km)

LARGEST LAKE
Lake Eyre, Australia
3,741 sq mi
(9,690 sq km)

POLITICAL

POPULATION
44,290,000

**LARGEST
METROPOLITAN AREA**
Melbourne, Australia
Pop. 5,151,000

LARGEST COUNTRY
Australia
2,988,902 sq mi
(7,741,220 sq km)

**MOST DENSELY
POPULATED COUNTRY**
Nauru
1,232 people per sq mi
(469 per sq km)

Map Key

⊛ National capital
• Other city
▲ Highest point
   (above sea level)
▼ Lowest point
   (below sea level)

A S I A

M i c r o n e s i a

Northern Mariana
Islands
(U.S.)
Capital Hill

Guam
(U.S.)

PALAU
Ngerulmud ⊛

Yap
Islands

Truk Islands

Caroline Islands

⊛ Palikir

FEDERATED STATES
OF MICRONESIA

M e l a n e s i a

PAPUA NEW GUINEA
▲ Mount Wilhelm
14,793 ft
(4,509 m)

Honiara ⊛
Solomon Islands

Port Moresby ⊛

Coral Sea
Islands
Territory
(Australia)

Darwin •

C o r a l   S e a

AUSTRALIA

Brisbane •

▼ -49 ft
(-15 m)

Lake
Eyre

Darling

Murray

Perth •

Sydney •

Lord Howe
Island
(Australia)

Adelaide •

Canberra ⊛
A.C.T.

Melbourne •

Tasman
Sea

INDIAN
OCEAN

Tasmania   Hobart •

0   800 Miles
0   800 Kilometers
Mercator Projection

30°N
15°N
0°
15°S
45°S

135°E   150°E

120°E   135°E   150°E

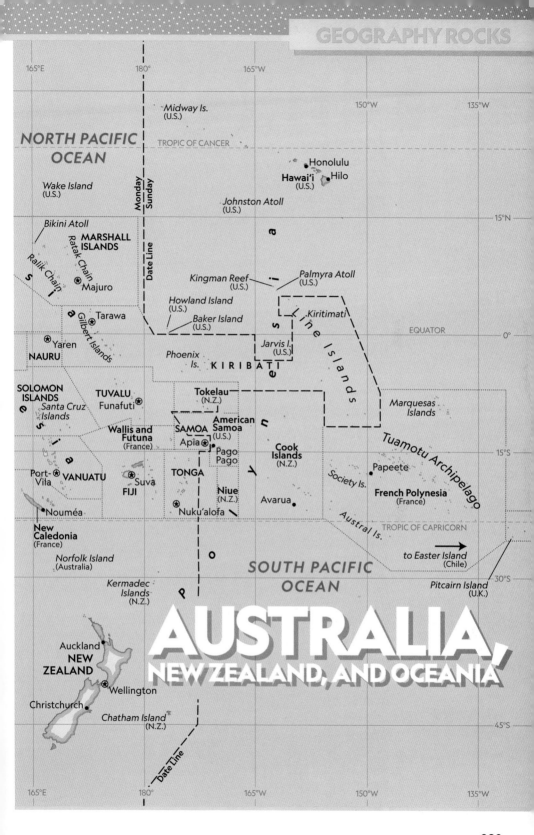

165°E   180°   165°W   150°W   135°W

Midway Is.
(U.S.)

NORTH PACIFIC
OCEAN

TROPIC OF CANCER

Honolulu
Hawai'i
(U.S.)   Hilo

Wake Island
(U.S.)

Johnston Atoll
(U.S.)

15°N

Bikini Atoll

MARSHALL
ISLANDS
Ratak Chain

Kingman Reef
(U.S.)   Palmyra Atoll
(U.S.)

Ralik Chain

Majuro

Howland Island
(U.S.)

Kiritimati

Tarawa

Baker Island
(U.S.)

EQUATOR   0°

Gilbert Islands

Yaren

Phoenix
Is.   Jarvis I.
(U.S.)

NAURU

K I R I B A T I

Line Islands

SOLOMON
ISLANDS

TUVALU

Tokelau
(N.Z.)

Marquesas
Islands

Santa Cruz
Islands

Funafuti

American
Samoa
(U.S.)

SAMOA

Wallis and
Futuna
(France)

Apia

Tuamotu Archipelago

15°S

Port-
Vila   **VANUATU**

Pago
Pago

Cook
Islands
(N.Z.)

Society Is.   Papeete

Suva

TONGA

French Polynesia
(France)

FIJI

Niue
(N.Z.)

Avarua

Nouméa

Nuku'alofa

Austral Is.

TROPIC OF CAPRICORN

New
Caledonia
(France)

Norfolk Island
(Australia)

to Easter Island
(Chile)

SOUTH PACIFIC
OCEAN

30°S

Kermadec
Islands
(N.Z.)

Pitcairn Island
(U.K.)

AUSTRALIA,
NEW ZEALAND, AND OCEANIA

Auckland
NEW
ZEALAND

Wellington

Christchurch

Chatham Island
(N.Z.)

45°S

Date Line

165°E   180°   165°W   150°W   135°W

Monday Sunday

Date Line

EUROPE

European pine marten

A dachshund parade is held each September in Kraków, Poland.

Pine martens, a type of weasel, make nests in hollow trees.

A cluster of peninsulas and islands jutting west from Asia, Europe is bordered by the Atlantic and Arctic Oceans and more than a dozen seas. Here you'll find a variety of scenery, from mountains to countryside to coastlines. Europe is also known for its rich cultures and fascinating history, which make it one of the most visited continents on Earth.

A traditional dance performed in Greece

THE NOSE KNOWS

What's that smell? A museum in Germany pairs scenes with scents as part of its "Follow Your Nose" tour. The tour pairs paintings of items like flowers, perfume bottles, and tablescapes of food with matching scents to offer an immersive experience for its visitors.

SEALED UP

Every fall, hundreds of gray seal pups are born on England's Farne Islands. For more than 70 years, rangers have been counting the seals in the colony. Nowadays, new pups are recorded in part using drone technology, which helps count and track the population.

FLOWERING AGAIN

What's lost has been found again in Türkiye (Turkey), where a plant that supposedly disappeared 2,000 years ago has possibly reemerged. The yellow-flowered silphion was popular in ancient Greece as a spice as well as a cure-all for everything from stomachaches to warts. Though it was thought to have been eaten into extinction, experts are encouraged that it's growing once more—and may once again provide healthy benefits.

Europe's Longest Rivers

Volga	2,294 mi (3,692 km)
Danube	1,770 mi (2,848 km)
Dnieper	1,420 mi (2,285 km)
Rhine	765 mi (1,230 km)
Elbe	724 mi (1,165 km)

PHYSICAL

LAND AREA
3,841,000 sq mi
(9,947,000 sq km)

HIGHEST POINT
El'brus, Russia
18,510 ft (5,642 m)

LOWEST POINT
Caspian Sea
-92 ft (-28 m)

LONGEST RIVER
Volga, Russia
2,294 mi
(3,692 km)

**LARGEST LAKE
ENTIRELY IN EUROPE**
Ladoga, Russia
6,900 sq mi
(17,872 sq km)

POLITICAL

POPULATION
749,943,000

**LARGEST
METROPOLITAN AREA**
Moscow, Russia
Pop. 12,680,000

**LARGEST COUNTRY
ENTIRELY IN EUROPE**
France
248,573 sq mi
(643,801 sq km)

**MOST DENSELY
POPULATED COUNTRY**
Monaco
31,597 people per sq
mi (15,799 per sq km)

Map Key

⊛ National capital
⊛ Capital of Northern
   Ireland, Scotland,
   or Wales
◉ Other capital
• Other city
▫ Small country
▲ Highest point
   (above sea level)
▼ Lowest point
   (below sea level)

296

EUROPE

A commonly accepted division between Asia and Europe—marked here by a maroon dashed line—is formed by the Ural Mountains, Ural River, Caspian Sea, Caucasus Mountains, and the Black Sea with its outlets, the Bosporus and Dardanelles.

Barents Sea

10°E 20°E 30°E 40°E 50°E 60°E

Murmansk

Arkhangel'sk

RUSSIA

Asia
Europe

60°N

N·O·R·W·A·Y

S·W·E·D·E·N

FINLAND

Helsinki

Lake Ladoga

St. Petersburg

Tallinn
Stockholm
ESTONIA

Baltic Sea

Riga
LATVIA

Yaroslavl'
Tver'
Moscow
Ryazan'
Smolensk

Volga
Kazan'
Nizhniy Novgorod
Samara

Ufa

Orenburg

LITHUANIA
Kaunas
Russia
Vilnius
Minsk
Vitsyebsk

Gdańsk

BELARUS

Bryansk

Penza

Saratov

KAZAKHSTAN

50°N

POLAND
Warsaw
Homyel'
Bydgoszcz
Łódź
Wrocław
CZECHIA
(CZECH REP.)
Kraków
Vienna
SLOVAKIA
Bratislava
Budapest
HUNGARY
Zagreb
CROATIA
BOSNIA & HERZEGOVINA
Sarajevo
SERBIA
Belgrade
MONTENEGRO
Podgorica
Tirana
ALBANIA

Kursk

Lviv
UKRAINE
Kyiv
Poltava
Vinnytsia
Dnipro
MOLDOVA
Chisinau
Odesa
Simferopol'
Sevastopol'
ROMANIA
Bucharest

KOSOVO
Pristina
BULGARIA
Sofia
Skopje
N. MAC.
Thessaloníki
Varna

Kharkiv
Donetsk

Volgograd

Rostov na Donu
Line of Russian control
Boundary claimed by Ukraine
CRIMEA

Astrakhan'

Caspian Sea

-92 ft (-28 m)

El'brus (5,642 m) 18,510 ft
Sochi
Groznyy
GEORGIA
AZERBAIJAN
Baku

40°N

Black Sea

Bosporus
Istanbul
Dardanelles

T·Ü·R·K·İ·Y·E
(TURKEY)

GREECE
Athens

Sea

Crete

NORTHERN CYPRUS
Nicosia
CYPRUS

CRIMEA
Russia invaded Crimea in 2014 and, after secession from Ukraine was approved in a disputed and boycotted referendum held in Crimea, the Russian parliament voted to annex Crimea into the Russian Federation. The United Nations General Assembly subsequently adopted a nonbinding resolution declaring the annexation invalid and affirming Ukraine's territorial jurisdiction. Russia administers and controls the peninsula, while Ukraine continues to maintain that Crimea is its sovereign territory.

20°E 30°E 40°E

NORTH AMERICA

Flamingos are the national bird of the Bahamas.

In mariachi bands, there are no lead singers.

Two people dance at a mariachi festival in Guadalajara, Mexico.

298

From the Great Plains of Canada and the United States to the rainforests of Panama, North America stretches 5,500 miles (8,850 km) from north to south. The third largest continent, North America can be divided into five regions: the mountainous west (including parts of Mexico and Central America's western coast), the Great Plains, the Canadian Shield, the varied eastern region (including Central America's lowlands and coastal plains), and the Caribbean.

A Day of the Dead (Día de los Muertos) parade in Mexico City, Mexico

CAVE OF CRYSTALS

Massive, milky white selenite crystals fill Mexico's Cave of Crystals, some 950 feet (290 m) below ground. Discovered in 2000, the cave was untouched by humans for hundreds of thousands of years, and its crystal contents grew big enough to walk on.

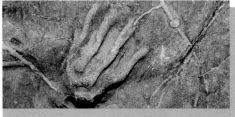

FANTASTIC FOSSILS

Fossils abound near the Bay of Fundy, located between Canada's Nova Scotia and New Brunswick Provinces. Rising up from the bay are the Joggins Fossil Cliffs, which contain fossils from the Coal Age, 50 million years before dinosaurs lived! Some of the ancient creatures encased in the rock: plants, spiders, and a giant millipede that is thought to be one of the largest prehistoric invertebrates.

LONG TRAIL

Imagine walking from Washington State to Washington, D.C.—without ever having to share the road with a car. That may be reality soon, thanks to the 3,700-mile (5,955-km) Great American Rail-Trail. With this extensive project, what were once abandoned railways crossing the United States will soon be safe places for people to walk, bike, and run.

World's Longest Coastlines

Canada	125,567 miles (202,080 km)
Indonesia	33,998 miles (54,716 km)
Russia	23,397 miles (37,653 km)
Philippines	22,549 miles (36,289 km)
Japan	18,486 miles (29,751 km)

PHYSICAL

LAND AREA	HIGHEST POINT
9,449,000 sq mi (24,474,000 sq km)	Denali, Alaska, U.S.A. 20,310 ft (6,190 m)

LONGEST RIVER	LOWEST POINT	LARGEST LAKE
Mississippi–Missouri, U.S.A. 3,710 mi (5,971 km)	Death Valley, California, U.S.A. -282 ft (-86 m)	Lake Superior, U.S.–Canada / 31,700 sq mi (82,100 sq km)

POLITICAL

POPULATION	LARGEST METROPOLITAN AREA
601,251,000	Mexico City, Mexico Pop. 22,281,000

LARGEST COUNTRY	MOST DENSELY POPULATED COUNTRY
Canada 3,855,101 sq mi (9,984,670 sq km)	Barbados / 1,828 people per sq mi (706 per sq km)

Map Key
⊛ National capital
● Other city
▲ Highest point (above sea level)
▼ Lowest point (below sea level)

EUROPE

ARCTIC CIRCLE

Greenland (Denmark)

ARCTIC OCEAN

80°N

C A N A D A

Edmonton
Calgary
Winnipeg
Thunder Bay
Montréal

Seattle
Vancouver
Victoria

ASIA

Alaska (U.S.)

(Mount McKinley) Denali (6,190 m) 20,310 ft ▲
Anchorage

60°N

160°W

180

40°N

40°N

40°W

20°W

800 Miles
800 Kilometers
Azimuthal Equidistant Projection

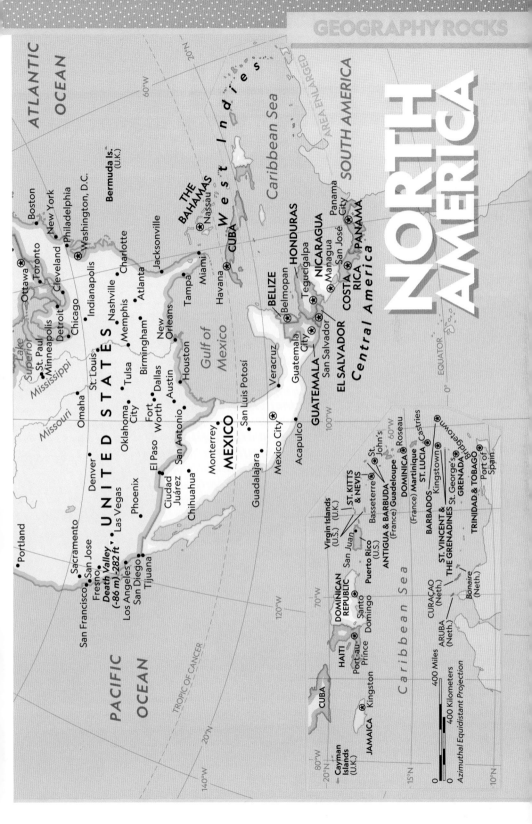

NORTH AMERICA

ATLANTIC OCEAN

PACIFIC OCEAN

Caribbean Sea

Gulf of Mexico

West Indies

Central America

SOUTH AMERICA

AREA ENLARGED

EQUATOR

TROPIC OF CANCER

UNITED STATES

MEXICO

Portland
San Francisco
Sacramento
San Jose
Fresno
Death Valley -282 ft (-86 m)
Los Angeles
San Diego
Tijuana
Phoenix
Las Vegas
Denver
Omaha
St. Louis
Minneapolis
St. Paul
Detroit
Chicago
Indianapolis
Cleveland
Ottawa
Toronto
Boston
New York
Philadelphia
Washington, D.C.
Nashville
Memphis
Birmingham
Atlanta
Charlotte
Jacksonville
Tampa
Miami
New Orleans
Houston
Austin
Dallas
Fort Worth
San Antonio
El Paso
Ciudad Juárez
Chihuahua
Oklahoma City
Tulsa
Monterrey
Guadalajara
Mexico City
San Luis Potosi
Veracruz
Acapulco

Mississippi
Missouri
Lake Superior

Bermuda Is. (U.K.)

THE BAHAMAS
Nassau
CUBA
Havana

Caribbean Sea

BELIZE
Belmopan
GUATEMALA
Guatemala City
San Salvador
EL SALVADOR
HONDURAS
Tegucigalpa
NICARAGUA
Managua
COSTA RICA
San José
Panama City
PANAMA
Panama

Inset map

Virgin Islands (U.S.)
San Juan
Puerto Rico (U.S.)
St. John's
Basseterre
ST. KITTS & NEVIS
ANTIGUA & BARBUDA
Guadeloupe (France)
DOMINICA Roseau
Martinique (France)
Castries
ST. LUCIA
BARBADOS
Kingstown
ST. VINCENT & THE GRENADINES
St. George's
GRENADA
Bridgetown
Port of Spain
TRINIDAD & TOBAGO
Bonaire (Neth.)
CURAÇAO (Neth.)
ARUBA (Neth.)

DOMINICAN REPUBLIC
Santo Domingo
HAITI
Port-au-Prince
CUBA
JAMAICA Kingston
Cayman Islands (U.K.)

Caribbean Sea

400 Miles
400 Kilometers
0
Azimuthal Equidistant Projection

SOUTH AMERICA

A woman in Ecuador sells produce from a market stall.

The *arazá*, also known as an Amazonian pear, is a super-sour fruit.

Capoeira, a sport combining martial arts and dance, was invented in Brazil.

South America is bordered by three major bodies of water—the Caribbean Sea, Atlantic Ocean, and Pacific Ocean. The world's fourth largest continent extends over a range of climates, from tropical in the north to subarctic in the south. South America produces a rich diversity of natural resources, including nuts, fruits, sugar, grains, coffee, and chocolate.

Santiago Cathedral in Santiago, Chile

LARGEST LILY PADS

These leaves are unbelievable! Bolivia's La Rinconada ecological park boasts both the world's largest and strongest lily pads. Growing to be as wide as a garage door, the aquatic pads are sturdy enough to support the weight of a small child without sinking—but it's probably better to view these floating leaves from land!

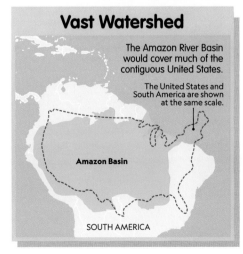

RUNNING WILD

Guanacos, wild relatives of camels that look like small llamas with longer necks, are native to the grasslands of the Andes. Super-speedy animals that can run as fast as 35 miles an hour (56 km/h), guanacos are a protected species in Chile and Peru.

Vast Watershed

The Amazon River Basin would cover much of the contiguous United States.

The United States and South America are shown at the same scale.

Amazon Basin

SOUTH AMERICA

TALL FALLS

Venezuela's Angel Falls, also known as Salto Churún Merú, is the world's highest uninterrupted waterfall. With a height of 3,212 feet (979 m), the falls are named for American aviator Jimmie Angel, the first person to fly over them.

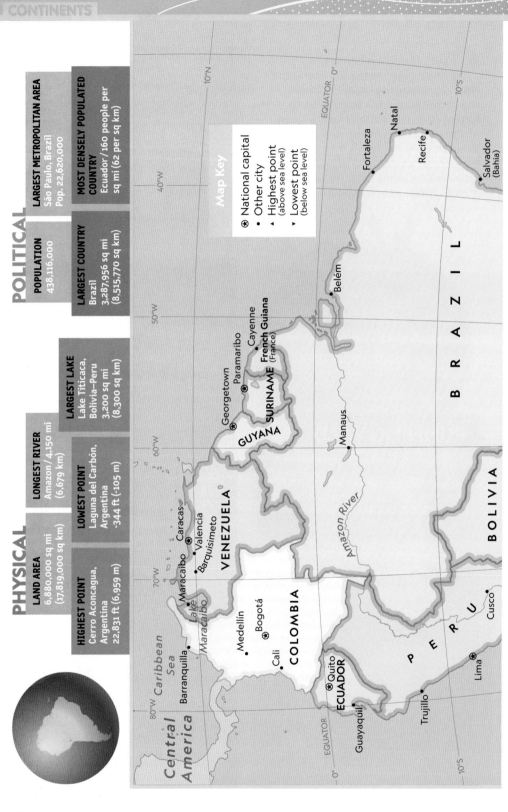

PHYSICAL

LAND AREA
6,880,000 sq mi
(17,819,000 sq km)

HIGHEST POINT
Cerro Aconcagua,
Argentina
22,831 ft (6,959 m)

LOWEST POINT
Laguna del Carbón,
Argentina
-344 ft (-105 m)

LONGEST RIVER
Amazon / 4,150 mi
(6,679 km)

LARGEST LAKE
Lake Titicaca,
Bolivia–Peru
3,200 sq mi
(8,300 sq km)

POLITICAL

POPULATION
438,116,000

LARGEST COUNTRY
Brazil
3,287,956 sq mi
(8,515,770 sq km)

LARGEST METROPOLITAN AREA
São Paulo, Brazil
Pop. 22,620,000

MOST DENSELY POPULATED COUNTRY
Ecuador / 160 people per
sq mi (62 per sq km)

Map Key
⊛ National capital
• Other city
▲ Highest point
  (above sea level)
▼ Lowest point
  (below sea level)

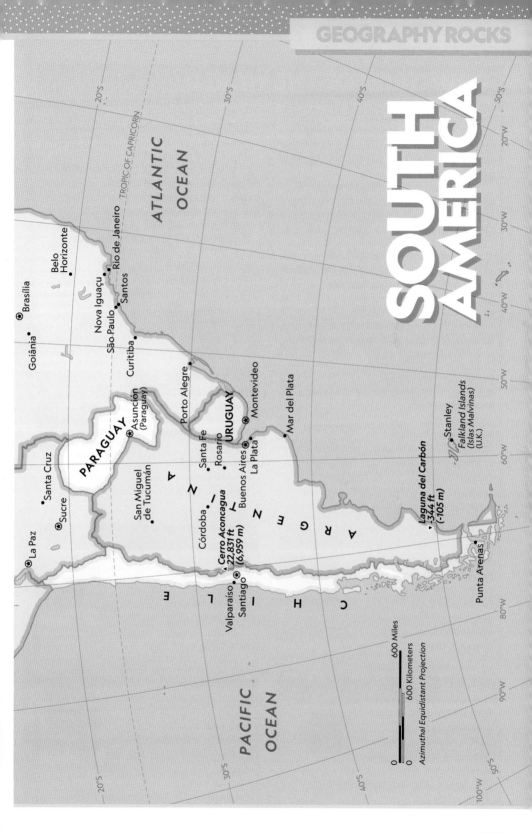

SOUTH AMERICA

ATLANTIC
OCEAN

TROPIC OF CAPRICORN

PACIFIC
OCEAN

Brasília ⊛

Goiânia ·

Belo
Horizonte ·

Rio de Janeiro
Nova Iguaçu ·
Santos ·
São Paulo ·
Curitiba ·

Porto Alegre ·

Montevideo
URUGUAY

Santa Fe ·
Rosario ·
Buenos Aires ⊛
La Plata ·

Mar del Plata ·

La Paz ⊛

Sucre ⊛

Santa Cruz ·

PARAGUAY

Asunción
(Paraguay) ·

San Miguel
de Tucumán ·

Córdoba ·

▲ Cerro Aconcagua
22,831 ft
(6,959 m)

Valparaíso ·
Santiago ⊛

A R G E N T I N A

C H I L E

▾ Laguna del Carbón
-344 ft
(-105 m)

Stanley ·
Falkland Islands
(Islas Malvinas)
(U.K.)

Punta Arenas ·

0   600 Miles
0   600 Kilometers
Azimuthal Equidistant Projection

20°S

30°S

40°S

50°S

20°W

30°W

40°W

50°W

60°W

70°W

80°W

90°W

100°W

305

COUNTRIES OF THE WORLD

The following pages present a general overview of all 195 independent countries recognized by the National Geographic Society, including the newest nation, South Sudan, which gained independence in 2011.

The flags of each independent country symbolize diverse cultures and histories. The statistical data cover highlights of geography and demography and provide a brief overview of each country. They present general characteristics and are not intended to be comprehensive. For example, not every language spoken in a specific country can be listed. Thus, languages shown are the most representative of that area. This is also true of the religions mentioned.

A country is defined as a political body with its own independent government, geographical space, and, in most cases, laws, military, and taxes.

Disputed areas such as Northern Cyprus and Taiwan, and dependencies of independent nations, such as Bermuda and Puerto Rico, are not included in this listing.

Note the color key at the bottom of the pages and the locator map below, which assign a color to each country based on the continent on which it is located. Some capital city populations include that city's metro area. All information is accurate as of press time.

Color Key by Continent

Afghanistan

Area: 251,827 sq mi (652,230 sq km)
Population: 39,232,000
Capital: Kabul, pop. 4,589,000
Currency: afghani (AFN)
Religion: Muslim
Languages: Afghan Persian (Dari), Pashto, Uzbek, English

Albania

Area: 11,100 sq mi (28,748 sq km)
Population: 3,102,000
Capital: Tirana, pop. 520,000
Currency: lek (ALL)
Religions: Muslim, Roman Catholic, Eastern Orthodox
Language: Albanian

Algeria

Area: 919,595 sq mi (2,381,740 sq km)
Population: 44,758,000
Capital: Algiers, pop. 2,902,000
Currency: Algerian dinar (DZD)
Religion: Muslim
Languages: Arabic, French, Berber (Tamazight)

Andorra

Area: 181 sq mi (468 sq km)
Population: 85,000
Capital: Andorra la Vella, pop. 23,000
Currency: euro (EUR)
Religion: Roman Catholic
Languages: Catalan, French, Castilian, Portuguese

Angola

Area: 481,353 sq mi (1,246,700 sq km)
Population: 35,981,000
Capital: Luanda, pop. 9,292,000
Currency: kwanza (AOA)
Religions: Roman Catholic, Protestant
Languages: Portuguese, Umbundu, other African languages

Antigua and Barbuda

Area: 171 sq mi (443 sq km)
Population: 101,000
Capital: St. John's, pop. 21,000
Currency: East Caribbean dollar (XCD)
Religions: Protestant, Roman Catholic, other Christian
Languages: English, Antiguan creole

Argentina

Area: 1,073,518 sq mi
(2,780,400 sq km)
Population: 46,622,000
Capital: Buenos Aires,
pop. 15,490,000
Currency: Argentine peso (ARS)
Religion: Roman Catholic
Languages: Spanish, Italian, English, German, French

3 cool things about ARGENTINA

1. To date, both the hottest (120°F [48.9°C]) and coldest (-27°F [-32.8°C]) temperatures in South America's history were recorded in Argentina.

2. The game of *pato*, a combination of basketball and polo, is the country's national sport.

3. Ushuaia, Argentina —nicknamed "The End of the World"—is considered the southernmost city on Earth.

Armenia

Area: 11,484 sq mi
(29,743 sq km)
Population: 2,989,000
Capital: Yerevan,
pop. 1,095,000
Currency: dram (AMD)
Religion: Oriental Orthodox
Languages: Armenian, Russian

Australia

Area: 2,988,902 sq mi
(7,741,220 sq km)
Population: 26,461,000
Capital: Canberra, A.C.T.,
pop. 472,000
Currency: Australian dollar (AUD)
Religions: Protestant, Roman Catholic
Language: English

Austria

Area: 32,383 sq mi (83,871 sq km)
Population: 8,941,000
Capital: Vienna, pop. 1,975,000
Currency: euro (EUR)
Religions: Roman Catholic, Eastern Orthodox, Muslim
Languages: German, Croatian

Azerbaijan

Area: 33,436 sq mi
(86,600 sq km)
Population: 10,421,000
Capital: Baku, pop. 2,432,000
Currency: Azerbaijani manat (AZN)
Religion: Muslim
Languages: Azerbaijani (Azeri), Russian

Bahamas, The

Area: 5,359 sq mi
(13,880 sq km)
Population: 359,000
Capital: Nassau, pop. 280,000
Currency: Bahamian dollar (BSD)
Religions: Protestant, Roman Catholic, other Christian
Languages: English, Creole

Bahrain

Area: 293 sq mi (760 sq km)
Population: 1,554,000
Capital: Manama, pop. 709,000
Currency: Bahraini dinar (BHD)
Religions: Muslim, Christian
Languages: Arabic, English, Farsi, Urdu

Bangladesh

Area: 57,321 sq mi
(148,460 sq km)
Population: 167,184,000
Capital: Dhaka, pop. 23,210,000
Currency: taka (BDT)
Religions: Muslim, Hindu
Language: Bangla (Bengali)

Barbados

Area: 166 sq mi (430 sq km)
Population: 303,000
Capital: Bridgetown, pop. 89,000
Currency: Barbadian dollar (BBD)
Religions: Protestant, other Christian
Languages: English, Bajan

Belgium

Area: 11,787 sq mi (30,528 sq km)
Population: 11,914,000
Capital: Brussels, pop. 2,122,000
Currency: euro (EUR)
Religions: Roman Catholic, Muslim
Languages: Dutch, French, German

Belarus

Area: 80,155 sq mi
(207,600 sq km)
Population: 9,384,000
Capital: Minsk, pop. 2,057,000
Currency: Belarusian ruble (BYN)
Religions: Eastern Orthodox, Roman Catholic
Languages: Russian, Belarusian

Belize

Area: 8,867 sq mi (22,966 sq km)
Population: 419,000
Capital: Belmopan, pop. 23,000
Currency: Belizean dollar (BZD)
Religions: Roman Catholic, Protestant
Languages: English, Spanish, Creole, Maya

SNAPSHOT Barbados

A sea turtle swims in the Caribbean Sea off the coast of Barbados.

COLOR KEY ● Africa ● Australia, New Zealand, and Oceania

Benin

Area: 43,484 sq mi (112,622 sq km)
Population: 14,220,000
Capitals: Porto-Novo, pop. 285,000; Cotonou, pop. 722,000
Currency: CFA franc BCEAO (XOF)
Religions: Muslim, Roman Catholic, Protestant, Vodou, other Christian
Languages: French, Fon, Yoruba, Indigenous languages

Bhutan

Area: 14,824 sq mi (38,394 sq km)
Population: 876,000
Capital: Thimphu, pop. 203,000
Currency: ngultrum (BTN)
Religions: Buddhist, Hindu
Languages: Sharchhopka, Dzongkha, Lhotshamkha

Bolivia

Area: 424,164 sq mi (1,098,581 sq km)
Population: 12,186,000
Capitals: La Paz, pop. 1,936,000; Sucre, pop. 278,000
Currency: boliviano (BOB)
Religions: Roman Catholic, Protestant
Languages: Spanish, Quechua, Aymara, Guarani

Bosnia and Herzegovina

Area: 19,767 sq mi (51,197 sq km)
Population: 3,808,000
Capital: Sarajevo, pop. 346,000
Currency: convertible mark (BAM)
Religions: Muslim, Eastern Orthodox, Roman Catholic
Languages: Bosnian, Serbian, Croatian

Botswana

Area: 224,607 sq mi (581,730 sq km)
Population: 2,418,000
Capital: Gaborone, pop. 269,000
Currency: pula (BWP)
Religion: Christian
Languages: Setswana, Sekalanga, Shekgalagadi, English

Brazil

Area: 3,287,956 sq mi (8,515,770 sq km)
Population: 218,690,000
Capital: Brasília, pop. 4,873,000
Currency: real (BRL)
Religions: Roman Catholic, Protestant
Language: Portuguese

Brunei

Area: 2,226 sq mi (5,765 sq km)
Population: 485,000
Capital: Bandar Seri Begawan, pop. 267,000
Currency: Bruneian dollar (BND)
Religions: Muslim, Christian, Buddhist, Indigenous beliefs
Languages: Malay, English, Chinese

Bulgaria

Area: 42,811 sq mi (110,879 sq km)
Population: 6,828,000
Capital: Sofia, pop. 1,288,000
Currency: lev (BGN)
Religions: Eastern Orthodox, Muslim
Language: Bulgarian

Burkina Faso

Area: 105,869 sq mi (274,200 sq km)
Population: 22,489,000
Capital: Ouagadougou, pop. 3,204,000
Currency: CFA franc BCEAO (XOF)
Religions: Muslim, Roman Catholic, traditional or animist, Protestant
Languages: French, African languages

Burundi

Area: 10,745 sq mi (27,830 sq km)
Population: 13,163,000
Capitals: Bujumbura, pop. 1,207,000; Gitega, pop. 135,000
Currency: Burundi franc (BIF)
Religions: Roman Catholic, Protestant
Languages: Kirundi, French, English, Swahili

Cabo Verde

Area: 1,557 sq mi (4,033 sq km)
Population: 604,000
Capital: Praia, pop. 168,000
Currency: Cabo Verdean escudo (CVE)
Religions: Roman Catholic, Protestant
Languages: Portuguese, Krioulo

Cambodia

Area: 69,898 sq mi (181,035 sq km)
Population: 16,891,000
Capital: Phnom Penh, pop. 2,281,000
Currency: riel (KHR)
Religion: Buddhist
Language: Khmer

Cameroon

Area: 183,568 sq mi (475,440 sq km)
Population: 30,136,000
Capital: Yaoundé, pop. 4,509,000
Currency: CFA franc BEAC (XAF)
Religions: Roman Catholic, Protestant, other Christian, Muslim
Languages: African languages, English, French

Canada

Area: 3,855,101 sq mi (9,984,670 sq km)
Population: 38,517,000
Capital: Ottawa, pop. 1,437,000
Currency: Canadian dollar (CAD)
Religions: Roman Catholic, Protestant, other Christian
Languages: English, French

Central African Republic

Area: 240,535 sq mi (622,984 sq km)
Population: 5,552,000
Capital: Bangui, pop. 958,000
Currency: CFA franc BEAC (XAF)
Religions: Christian, Muslim
Languages: French, Sangho, Indigenous languages

Chad

Area: 495,755 sq mi (1,284,000 sq km)
Population: 18,523,000
Capital: N'Djamena, pop. 1,592,000
Currency: CFA franc BEAC (XAF)
Religions: Muslim, Protestant, Roman Catholic
Languages: French, Arabic, Sara, Indigenous languages

Chile

Area: 291,932 sq mi (756,102 sq km)
Population: 18,549,000
Capital: Santiago, pop. 6,903,000
Currency: Chilean peso (CLP)
Religions: Roman Catholic, Protestant
Languages: Spanish, English

China

Area: 3,705,405 sq mi (9,596,960 sq km)
Population: 1,413,143,000
Capital: Beijing, pop. 21,766,000
Currency: Renminbi yuan (RMB)
Religions: folk religion, Buddhist, Christian
Languages: Standard Chinese (Mandarin), Yue (Cantonese), Wu, Minbei, Minnan, Xiang, Gan, regional official languages

Colombia

Area: 439,735 sq mi (1,138,910 sq km)
Population: 49,336,000
Capital: Bogotá, pop. 11,508,000
Currency: Colombian peso (COP)
Religions: Roman Catholic, Protestant
Language: Spanish

Comoros

Area: 863 sq mi (2,235 sq km)
Population: 888,000
Capital: Moroni, pop. 62,000
Currency: Comoran franc (KMF)
Religion: Muslim
Languages: Arabic, French, Shikomoro (Comorian)

COLOR KEY ● Africa ● Australia, New Zealand, and Oceania

Congo

Area: 132,047 sq mi (342,000 sq km)
Population: 5,677,000
Capital: Brazzaville, pop. 2,638,000
Currency: CFA franc BEAC (XAF)
Religions: Roman Catholic, other Christian, Protestant
Languages: French, Lingala, Monokutuba, Kikongo, local languages

Côte d'Ivoire (Ivory Coast)

Area: 124,504 sq mi (322,463 sq km)
Population: 29,345,000
Capitals: Abidjan, pop. 5,686,000; Yamoussoukro, pop. 231,000
Currency: CFA franc BCEAO (XOF)
Religions: Muslim, Roman Catholic, Protestant
Languages: French, Diola, Native dialects

Costa Rica

Area: 19,730 sq mi (51,100 sq km)
Population: 5,257,000
Capital: San José, pop. 1,462,000
Currency: Costa Rican colón (CRC)
Religions: Roman Catholic, Protestant
Languages: Spanish, English

Croatia

Area: 21,851 sq mi (56,594 sq km)
Population: 4,169,000
Capital: Zagreb, pop. 684,000
Currency: kuna (HRK)
Religion: Roman Catholic
Languages: Croatian, Serbian

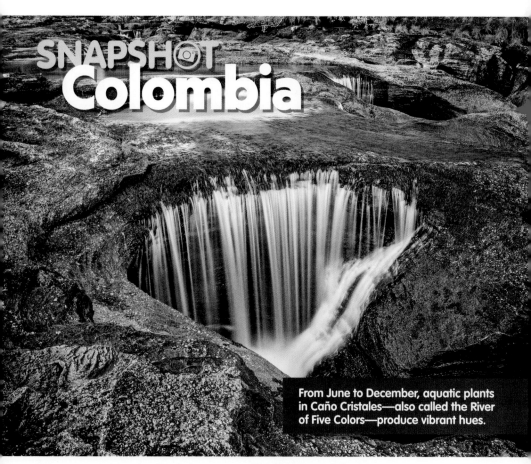

SNAPSHOT
Colombia

From June to December, aquatic plants in Caño Cristales—also called the River of Five Colors—produce vibrant hues.

● Asia ● Europe ● North America ● **South America**

Cuba

Area: 42,803 sq mi (110,860 sq km)
Population: 10,986,000
Capital: Havana, pop. 2,149,000
Currency: Cuban peso (CUP)
Religions: Christian, folk religion
Language: Spanish

Djibouti

Area: 8,958 sq mi (23,200 sq km)
Population: 976,000
Capital: Djibouti, pop. 600,000
Currency: Djiboutian franc (DJF)
Religions: Muslim, Christian
Languages: French, Arabic, Somali, Afar

Cyprus

Area: 3,572 sq mi (9,251 sq km)
Population: 1,308,000
Capital: Nicosia, pop. 269,000
Currency: euro (EUR)
Religion: Eastern Orthodox
Languages: Greek, Turkish, English

Dominica

Area: 290 sq mi (751 sq km)
Population: 75,000
Capital: Roseau, pop. 15,000
Currency: East Caribbean dollar (XCD)
Religions: Roman Catholic, Protestant
Languages: English, French patois

Czechia (Czech Republic)

Area: 30,451 sq mi (78,867 sq km)
Population: 10,706,000
Capital: Prague, pop. 1,323,000
Currency: koruna (CZK)
Religion: Roman Catholic
Languages: Czech, Slovak

Dominican Republic

Area: 18,792 sq mi (48,670 sq km)
Population: 10,791,000
Capital: Santo Domingo, pop. 3,524,000
Currency: Dominican peso (DOP)
Religions: Roman Catholic, Protestant
Language: Spanish

Democratic Republic of the Congo

Area: 905,354 sq mi (2,344,858 sq km)
Population: 111,860,000
Capital: Kinshasa, pop. 16,316,000
Currency: Congolese franc (CDF)
Religions: Roman Catholic, Protestant, other Christian
Languages: French, Lingala, Kingwana, Kikongo, Tshiluba

Denmark

Area: 16,639 sq mi (43,094 sq km)
Population: 5,947,000
Capital: Copenhagen, pop. 1,381,000
Currency: Danish krone (DKK)
Religions: Protestant, Muslim
Languages: Danish, Faroese, Greenlandic, English

3 cool things about DENMARK

1. In use since the Middle Ages, the Danish flag, named the "Dannebrog," is the oldest state flag in the world that's still in use.

2. Denmark includes more than 400 islands.

3. Copenhagen's historic Tivoli Gardens amusement park inspired the design of Disneyland.

COLOR KEY ● Africa ● Australia, New Zealand, and Oceania

Ecuador

Area: 109,483 sq mi
(283,561 sq km)
Population: 17,483,000
Capital: Quito, pop. 1,957,000
Currency: U.S. dollar (USD)
Religions: Roman Catholic, Protestant
Languages: Spanish, Amerindian languages

Egypt

Area: 386,662 sq mi
(1,001,450 sq km)
Population: 109,547,000
Capital: Cairo, pop. 22,183,000
Currency: Egyptian pound (EGP)
Religions: Muslim, Oriental Orthodox
Languages: Arabic, English, French

El Salvador

Area: 8,124 sq mi
(21,041 sq km)
Population: 6,602,000
Capital: San Salvador,
pop. 1,116,000
Currency: U.S. dollar (USD)
Religions: Roman Catholic, Protestant
Language: Spanish

Equatorial Guinea

Area: 10,831 sq mi (28,051 sq km)
Population: 1,738,000
Capital: Malabo, pop. 297,000
Currency: CFA franc BEAC (XAF)
Religions: Roman Catholic, Muslim, Baha'i, animist,
Indigenous beliefs
Languages: Spanish, Portuguese, French, Fang, Bubi

Eritrea

Area: 45,406 sq mi (117,600 sq km)
Population: 6,275,000
Capital: Asmara, pop. 1,073,000
Currency: nakfa (ERN)
Religions: Muslim, Oriental Orthodox, Roman Catholic,
Protestant
Languages: Tigrinya, Arabic, English, Tigre, Kunama,
Afar, other Cushitic languages

Estonia

Area: 17,463 sq mi (45,228 sq km)
Population: 1,203,000
Capital: Tallinn, pop. 454,000
Currency: euro (EUR)
Religions: Eastern Orthodox, Protestant
Languages: Estonian, Russian

Eswatini (Swaziland)

Area: 6,704 sq mi (17,364 sq km)
Population: 1,130,000
Capitals: Mbabane, pop. 68,000;
Lobamba, pop. 90,000
Currency: lilangeni (SZL)
Religions: Roman Catholic, other Christian
Languages: English, siSwati

Ethiopia

Area: 426,372 sq mi
(1,104,300 sq km)
Population: 116,463,000
Capital: Addis Ababa,
pop. 5,461,000
Currency: birr (ETB)
Religions: Oriental Orthodox, Muslim, Protestant
Languages: Oromo, Amharic, Somali, Tigrinya, Afar

It's thought that the FIRST COFFEE BEANS were grown in ETHIOPIA.

Fiji

Area: 7,056 sq mi
(18,274 sq km)
Population: 948,000
Capital: Suva, pop. 178,000
Currency: Fijian dollar (FJD)
Religions: Protestant, Roman Catholic, other
Christian, Hindu, Muslim
Languages: English, Fijian, Fiji Hindi

Finland

Area: 130,558 sq mi
(338,145 sq km)
Population: 5,615,000
Capital: Helsinki, pop. 1,338,000
Currency: euro (EUR)
Religion: Protestant
Languages: Finnish, Swedish

Germany

Area: 137,847 sq mi
(357,022 sq km)
Population: 84,220,000
Capital: Berlin, pop. 3,574,000
Currency: euro (EUR)
Religions: Roman Catholic, Protestant, Muslim
Language: German

France

Area: 248,573 sq mi
(643,801 sq km)
Population: 68,522,000
Capital: Paris, pop. 11,208,000
Currency: euro (EUR)
Religions: Roman Catholic, Muslim
Language: French

Ghana

Area: 92,098 sq mi (238,533 sq km)
Population: 33,846,000
Capital: Accra, pop. 2,660,000
Currency: cedi (GHC)
Religions: Protestant, Roman Catholic, other Christian, Muslim, traditional
Languages: Asante, Ewe, Fante, English

Gabon

Area: 103,347 sq mi (267,667 sq km)
Population: 2,397,000
Capital: Libreville, pop. 870,000
Currency: CFA franc BEAC (XAF)
Religions: Roman Catholic, Protestant, other Christian, Muslim
Languages: French, Fang, Myene, Nzebi, Bapounou/Eschira, Bandjabi

Greece

Area: 50,949 sq mi (131,957 sq km)
Population: 10,498,000
Capital: Athens, pop. 3,154,000
Currency: euro (EUR)
Religion: Eastern Orthodox
Language: Greek

Gambia, The

Area: 4,363 sq mi (11,300 sq km)
Population: 2,469,000
Capital: Banjul, pop. 481,000
Currency: dalasi (GMD)
Religion: Muslim
Languages: English, Mandinka, Wolof, Fula

Grenada

Area: 133 sq mi (344 sq km)
Population: 114,000
Capital: St. George's, pop. 39,000
Currency: East Caribbean dollar (XCD)
Religions: Protestant, Roman Catholic
Languages: English, French patois

Georgia

Area: 26,911 sq mi (69,700 sq km)
Population: 4,936,000
Capital: Tbilisi, pop. 1,082,000
Currency: lari (GEL)
Religions: Eastern Orthodox, Muslim
Language: Georgian

Guatemala

Area: 42,042 sq mi (108,889 sq km)
Population: 17,981,000
Capital: Guatemala City, pop. 3,095,000
Currency: quetzal (GTQ)
Religions: Roman Catholic, Protestant, Indigenous beliefs
Languages: Spanish, Maya languages

COLOR KEY ● Africa ● Australia, New Zealand, and Oceania

Guinea

Area: 94,926 sq mi (245,857 sq km)
Population: 13,607,000
Capital: Conakry, pop. 2,111,000
Currency: Guinean franc (GNF)
Religions: Muslim, Christian
Languages: French, African languages

Guyana

Area: 83,000 sq mi (214,969 sq km)
Population: 792,000
Capital: Georgetown, pop. 110,000
Currency: Guyanese dollar (GYD)
Religions: Hindu, Protestant, Roman Catholic, other Christian, Muslim
Languages: English, Guyanese Creole, Amerindian languages, Indian languages, Chinese

Guinea-Bissau

Area: 13,948 sq mi (36,125 sq km)
Population: 2,079,000
Capital: Bissau, pop. 664,000
Currency: CFA franc BCEAO (XOF)
Religions: Muslim, Christian, animist
Languages: Crioulu, Portuguese, Pular, Mandingo

Haiti

Area: 10,714 sq mi (27,750 sq km)
Population: 11,470,000
Capital: Port-au-Prince, pop. 2,987,000
Currency: gourde (HTG)
Religions: Roman Catholic, Protestant, Vodou
Languages: French, Creole

SNAPSHOT
Germany

In the Middle Ages, townspeople built the old town hall in Bamberg, a city in southern Germany, on an artificial island in the middle of the Regnitz River.

Honduras

Area: 43,278 sq mi
(112,090 sq km)
Population: 9,571,000
Capital: Tegucigalpa,
pop. 1,568,000
Currency: lempira (HNL)
Religions: Roman Catholic, Protestant
Languages: Spanish, Amerindian dialects

Iceland

Area: 39,769 sq mi
(103,000 sq km)
Population: 361,000
Capital: Reykjavík, pop. 216,000
Currency: Icelandic krona (ISK)
Religion: Protestant
Languages: Icelandic, English, Nordic
languages, German

Hungary

Area: 35,918 sq mi (93,028 sq km)
Population: 9,670,000
Capital: Budapest, pop. 1,778,000
Currency: forint (HUF)
Religions: Roman Catholic, Protestant
Languages: Hungarian, English, German

India

Area: 1,269,219 sq mi
(3,287,263 sq km)
Population: 1,399,180,000
Capital: New Delhi, pop. 32,941,000
Currency: Indian rupee (INR)
Religions: Hindu, Muslim
Languages: Hindi, English

SNAPSHOT
Japan

Two Japanese macaques rest in
a hot spring in Honshu, Japan.

COLOR KEY ● Africa ● Australia, New Zealand, and Oceania

Indonesia

Area: 735,358 sq mi
(1,904,569 sq km)
Population: 279,476,000
Capital: Jakarta, pop. 11,249,000
Currency: Indonesian rupiah (IDR)
Religions: Muslim, Protestant
Languages: Bahasa Indonesia, English, Dutch,
local dialects

Iran

Area: 636,371 sq mi
(1,648,195 sq km)
Population: 87,591,000
Capital: Tehran, pop. 9,500,000
Currency: Iranian rial (IRR)
Religion: Muslim
Languages: Persian (Farsi), Turkic dialects, Kurdish

Iraq

Area: 169,235 sq mi
(438,317 sq km)
Population: 41,266,000
Capital: Baghdad, pop. 7,711,000
Currency: Iraqi dinar (IQD)
Religion: Muslim
Languages: Arabic, Kurdish, Turkmen,
Syriac, Armenian

Ireland (Éire)

Area: 27,133 sq mi
(70,273 sq km)
Population: 5,324,000
Capital: Dublin
(Baile Átha Cliath), pop. 1,270,000
Currency: euro (EUR)
Religion: Roman Catholic
Languages: English, Irish (Gaelic)

Israel

Area: 8,970 sq mi (23,232 sq km)
Population: 9,043,000
Capital: Jerusalem, pop. 970,000
Currency: new Israeli shekel (ILS)
Religions: Jewish, Muslim
Languages: Hebrew, Arabic, English

Italy

Area: 116,348 sq mi
(301,340 sq km)
Population: 61,022,000
Capital: Rome, pop. 4,316,000
Currency: euro (EUR)
Religion: Roman Catholic
Languages: Italian, German, French, Slovene

Jamaica

Area: 4,244 sq mi
(10,991 sq km)
Population: 2,821,000
Capital: Kingston, pop.597,000
Currency: Jamaican dollar (JMD)
Religion: Protestant
Languages: English, English patois

Japan

Area: 145,914 sq mi (377,915 sq km)
Population: 123,719,000
Capital: Tokyo, pop. 37,194,000
Currency: yen (JPY)
Religions: Shinto, Buddhist
Language: Japanese

Jordan

Area: 34,495 sq mi
(89,342 sq km)
Population: 11,087,000
Capital: Amman, pop. 2,232,000
Currency: Jordanian dinar (JOD)
Religion: Muslim
Languages: Arabic, English

Kazakhstan

Area: 1,052,089 sq mi
(2,724,900 sq km)
Population: 19,543,000
Capital: Astana pop. 1,291,000
Currency: tenge (KZT)
Religions: Muslim, Eastern Orthodox
Languages: Kazakh (Qazaq), Russian, English

Kenya

Area: 224,081 sq mi (580,367 sq km)
Population: 57,052,000
Capital: Nairobi, pop. 5,325,000
Currency: Kenyan shilling (KES)
Religions: Protestant, Roman Catholic, other Christian, Muslim
Languages: English, Kiswahili, Indigenous languages

Kiribati

Area: 313 sq mi (811 sq km)
Population: 115,000
Capital: Tarawa, pop. 64,000
Currency: Australian dollar (AUD)
Religions: Roman Catholic, Protestant, Mormon
Languages: I-Kiribati, English

Kosovo

Area: 4,203 sq mi (10,887 sq km)
Population: 1,964,000
Capital: Pristina, pop. 219,000
Currency: euro (EUR)
Religion: Muslim
Languages: Albanian, Serbian, Bosnian

Kuwait

Area: 6,880 sq mi (17,818 sq km)
Population: 3,104,000
Capital: Kuwait City, pop. 3,104,000
Currency: Kuwaiti dinar (KWD)
Religions: Muslim, Christian
Languages: Arabic, English

Kyrgyzstan

Area: 77,201 sq mi (199,951 sq km)
Population: 6,123,000
Capital: Bishkek, pop. 1,105,000
Currency: Som (KGS)
Religions: Muslim, Eastern Orthodox
Languages: Kyrgyz, Uzbek, Russian

Laos

Area: 91,429 sq mi (236,800 sq km)
Population: 7,852,000
Capital: Vientiane, pop. 721,000
Currency: kip (LAK)
Religion: Buddhist
Languages: Lao, French, English, ethnic languages

Latvia

Area: 24,938 sq mi (64,589 sq km)
Population: 1,822,000
Capital: Riga, pop. 621,000
Currency: euro (EUR)
Religions: Protestant, Roman Catholic, Eastern Orthodox, Druze
Languages: Latvian, Russian

Lebanon

Area: 4,015 sq mi (10,400 sq km)
Population: 5,331,000
Capital: Beirut, pop. 2,421,000
Currency: Lebanese pound (LBP)
Religions: Muslim, Eastern Catholic
Languages: Arabic, French, English, Armenian

Lesotho

Area: 11,720 sq mi (30,355 sq km)
Population: 2,211,000
Capital: Maseru, pop. 202,000
Currency: loti (LSL)
Religions: Protestant, Roman Catholic, other Christian
Languages: Sesotho, English, Zulu, Xhosa

Liberia

Area: 43,000 sq mi (111,369 sq km)
Population: 5,506,000
Capital: Monrovia, pop. 1,678,000
Currency: Liberian dollar (LRD)
Religions: Christian, Muslim
Languages: English, Indigenous languages

Libya

Area: 679,362 sq mi
(1,759,540 sq km)
Population: 7,253,000
Capital: Tripoli, pop. 1,183,000
Currency: Libyan dinar (LYD)
Religion: Muslim
Languages: Arabic, Italian, English, Berber

Lithuania

Area: 25,212 sq mi
(65,300 sq km)
Population: 2,656,000
Capital: Vilnius, pop. 541,000
Currency: euro (EUR)
Religion: Roman Catholic
Language: Lithuanian

Liechtenstein

Area: 62 sq mi (160 sq km)
Population: 40,000
Capital: Vaduz, pop. 5,000
Currency: Swiss franc (CHF)
Religions: Roman Catholic, Protestant, Muslim
Language: German

Luxembourg

Area: 998 sq mi (2,586 sq km)
Population: 661,000
Capital: Luxembourg,
pop. 120,000
Currency: euro (EUR)
Religion: Roman Catholic
Languages: Luxembourgish, Portuguese,
French, German

SNAPSHOT
Libya

Situated just off the Mediterranean Sea
near downtown Tripoli, the Red Castle was
an important fortress in the Byzantine Empire.

● Asia ● Europe ● North America ● South America

Madagascar

Area: 226,658 sq mi (587,041 sq km)
Population: 28,812,000
Capital: Antananarivo, pop. 3,872,000
Currency: Malagasy ariary (MGA)
Religions: Christian, Indigenous beliefs, Muslim
Languages: French, Malagasy, English

Malawi

Area: 45,747 sq mi (118,484 sq km)
Population: 21,280,000
Capital: Lilongwe, pop. 1,276,000
Currency: Malawian kwacha (MWK)
Religions: Protestant, Roman Catholic, other Christian, Muslim
Languages: English, Chewa, other Bantu languages

Malaysia

Area: 127,355 sq mi (329,847 sq km)
Population: 34,220,000
Capital: Kuala Lumpur, pop. 8,622,000
Currency: ringgit (MYR)
Religions: Muslim, Buddhist, Christian, Hindu
Languages: Bahasa Malaysia (Malay), English, Chinese, Tamil, Telugu, Malayalam, Panjabi, Thai

Maldives

Area: 115 sq mi (298 sq km)
Population: 390,000
Capital: Male, pop. 177,000
Currency: rufiyaa (MVR)
Religion: Muslim
Languages: Dhivehi, English

A new RAINBOW-COLORED species of fish was recently DISCOVERED off the coast of the MALDIVES.

Mali

Area: 478,841 sq mi (1,240,192 sq km)
Population: 21,360,000
Capital: Bamako, pop. 2,929,000
Currency: CFA franc BCEAO (XOF)
Religion: Muslim
Languages: French, Bambara, African languages

Malta

Area: 122 sq mi (316 sq km)
Population: 467,000
Capital: Valletta, pop. 213,000
Currency: euro (EUR)
Religion: Roman Catholic
Languages: Maltese, English

Marshall Islands

Area: 70 sq mi (181 sq km)
Population: 81,000
Capital: Majuro, pop. 31,000
Currency: U.S. dollar (USD)
Religions: Protestant, Roman Catholic, Mormon
Languages: Marshallese, English

Mauritania

Area: 397,955 sq mi (1,030,700 sq km)
Population: 4,245,000
Capital: Nouakchott, pop. 1,492,000
Currency: ouguiya (MRU)
Religion: Muslim
Languages: Arabic, Pulaar, Soninke, Wolof, French

Mauritius

Area: 788 sq mi (2,040 sq km)
Population: 1,309,000
Capital: Port Louis, pop. 149,000
Currency: Mauritian rupee (MUR)
Religions: Hindu, Muslim, Roman Catholic, other Christian
Languages: Creole, English

Mexico

Area: 758,449 sq mi
(1,964,375 sq km)
Population: 129,876,000
Capital: Mexico City,
pop. 22,281,000
Currency: Mexican peso (MXN)
Religions: Roman Catholic, Protestant
Language: Spanish

3 cool things about MEXICO

1. While Spanish is the official language of Mexico, more than 60 languages are spoken.

2. Built on an ancient lake, parts of Mexico City sink some 20 inches (51 cm) every year.

3. Mexico's Great Pyramid of Cholula—a temple honoring Quetzalcoatl, the Aztec god of wind and rain—is the largest known pyramid by volume in the world.

Micronesia, Federated States of

Area: 271 sq mi (702 sq km)
Population: 100,000
Capital: Palikir, pop. 7,000
Currency: U.S. dollar (USD)
Religions: Roman Catholic, Protestant
Languages: English, Chuukese, Kosraean, Pohnpeian, other Indigenous languages

Moldova

Area: 13,070 sq mi
(33,851 sq km)
Population: 3,251,000
Capital: Chișinău,
pop. 488,000
Currency: Moldovan leu (MDL)
Religion: Eastern Orthodox
Languages: Moldovan, Romanian

Monaco

Area: 1 sq mi (2 sq km)
Population: 32,000
Capital: Monaco, pop. 32,000
Currency: euro (EUR)
Religion: Roman Catholic
Languages: French, English, Italian, Monegasque

Mongolia

Area: 603,908 sq mi
(1,564,116 sq km)
Population: 3,255,000
Capital: Ulan Bator,
pop. 1,673,000
Currency: tugrik (MNT)
Religion: Buddhist
Languages: Mongolian, Turkic, Russian

Montenegro

Area: 5,333 sq mi
(13,812 sq km)
Population: 602,000
Capital: Podgorica, pop. 177,000
Currency: euro (EUR)
Religions: Eastern Orthodox, Muslim
Languages: Serbian, Montenegrin

Morocco

Area: 276,662 sq mi
(716,550 sq km)
Population: 37,067,000
Capital: Rabat, pop. 1,959,000
Currency: Moroccan dirham (MAD)
Religion: Muslim
Languages: Arabic, Tamazight, other Berber languages, French

Mozambique

Area: 308,642 sq mi
(799,380 sq km)
Population: 32,514,000
Capital: Maputo, pop. 1,163,000
Currency: metical (MZN)
Religions: Roman Catholic, Protestant, other Christian, Muslim
Languages: Makhuwa, Portuguese, local languages

Myanmar (Burma)

Area: 261,228 sq mi
(676,578 sq km)
Population: 57,970,000
Capital: Nay Pyi Taw,
pop. 723,000
Currency: kyat (MMK)
Religions: Buddhist, Christian
Language: Burmese

Nauru

Area: 8 sq mi (21 sq km)
Population: 10,000
Capital: Yaren, pop. 700
Currency: Australian
dollar (AUD)
Religions: Protestant, Roman Catholic
Languages: Nauruan, English

Namibia

Area: 318,261 sq mi
(824,292 sq km)
Population: 2,777,000
Capital: Windhoek, pop. 477,000
Currency: Namibian dollar (NAD)
Religions: Protestant, Indigenous beliefs
Languages: Indigenous languages, Afrikaans, English

Nepal

Area: 56,827 sq mi
(147,181 sq km)
Population: 30,899,000
Capital: Kathmandu, pop. 1,571,000
Currency: Nepalese rupee (NPR)
Religions: Hindu, Buddhist
Languages: Nepali, Maithili

SNAPSHOT Nepal

Living in the high elevations of the Himalaya of Nepal, these wild goats grow a soft undercoat to keep them warm in the harsh winters.

COLOR KEY ● Africa ● Australia, New Zealand, and Oceania

Netherlands

Area: 16,040 sq mi
(41,543 sq km)
Population: 17,464,000
Capitals: Amsterdam, pop. 1,174,000;
The Hague, pop. 715,000
Currency: euro (EUR)
Religions: Roman Catholic, Protestant, Muslim
Language: Dutch

New Zealand

Area: 103,799 sq mi
(268,838 sq km)
Population: 5,110,000
Capital: Wellington, pop. 422,000
Currency: New Zealand dollar (NZD)
Religions: Roman Catholic, Protestant
Languages: English, Maori

Nicaragua

Area: 50,336 sq mi
(130,370 sq km)
Population: 6,360,000
Capital: Managua, pop. 1,095,000
Currency: cordoba oro (NIO)
Religions: Roman Catholic, Protestant
Language: Spanish

Niger

Area: 489,191 sq mi (1,267,000 sq km)
Population: 25,397,000
Capital: Niamey, pop. 1,437,000
Currency: CFA franc BCEAO (XOF)
Religion: Muslim
Languages: French, Hausa, Djerma

Nigeria

Area: 356,669 sq mi
(923,768 sq km)
Population: 230,843,000
Capital: Abuja, pop. 3,840,000
Currency: naira (NGN)
Religions: Muslim, Roman Catholic, other Christian
Languages: English, Indigenous languages

North Korea

Area: 46,540 sq mi
(120,538 sq km)
Population: 26,072,000
Capital: Pyongyang,
pop. 3,158,000
Currency: North Korean won (KPW)
Religions: Buddhist, Confucianist, Christian,
syncretic Chondogyo
Language: Korean

North Macedonia

Area: 9,928 sq mi
(25,713 sq km)
Population: 2,133,000
Capital: Skopje, pop. 611,000
Currency: Macedonian denar (MKD)
Religions: Macedonian Orthodox, Muslim
Languages: Macedonian, Albanian

Norway

Area: 125,021 sq mi
(323,802 sq km)
Population: 5,598,000
Capital: Oslo, pop. 1,086,000
Currency: Norwegian krone (NOK)
Religion: Protestant
Languages: Bokmal Norwegian, Nynorsk Norwegian

Oman

Area: 119,499 sq mi
(309,500 sq km)
Population: 3,833,000
Capital: Muscat, pop. 1,650,000
Currency: Omani rial (OMR)
Religions: Muslim, Christian, Hindu
Languages: Arabic, English, Baluchi, Swahili, Urdu,
Indian dialects

Pakistan

Area: 307,374 sq mi
(796,095 sq km)
Population: 247,654,000
Capital: Islamabad, pop. 1,232,000
Currency: Pakistan rupee (PKR)
Religion: Muslim
Languages: Punjabi, Sindhi, Saraiki, Urdu, English

Asia ● Europe ● North America ● **South America**

Palau

Area: 177 sq mi (459 sq km)
Population: 22,000
Capital: Ngerulmud, pop. 300
Currency: U.S. dollar (USD)
Religions: Roman Catholic, Protestant, Modekngei
Languages: Palauan, English, Filipino

Philippines

Area: 115,831 sq mi (300,000 sq km)
Population: 116,434,000
Capital: Manila,
pop. 14,667,000
Currency: Philippine peso (PHP)
Religions: Roman Catholic, Protestant, Muslim
Languages: Filipino (Tagalog), English, Indigenous
languages

Panama

Area: 29,120 sq mi (75,420 sq km)
Population: 4,404,000
Capital: Panama City,
pop. 1,977,000
Currency: balboa (PAB)
Religions: Roman Catholic, Protestant
Languages: Spanish, Indigenous languages, English

Poland

Area: 120,728 sq mi
(312,685 sq km)
Population: 37,992,000
Capital: Warsaw, pop. 1,798,000
Currency: zloty (PLN)
Religion: Roman Catholic
Language: Polish

Papua New Guinea

Area: 178,703 sq mi (462,840 sq km)
Population: 9,819,000
Capital: Port Moresby, pop. 410,000
Currency: kina (PGK)
Religions: Protestant, Roman Catholic, other Christian
Languages: Tok Pisin, English, Hiri Motu, other
Indigenous languages

Portugal

Area: 35,556 sq mi
(92,090 sq km)
Population: 10,223,000
Capital: Lisbon, pop. 3,001,000
Currency: euro (EUR)
Religion: Roman Catholic
Languages: Portuguese, Mirandese

Paraguay

Area: 157,048 sq mi
(406,752 sq km)
Population: 7,440,000
Capital: Asunción (Paraguay),
pop. 3,511,000
Currency: Guarani (PYG)
Religions: Roman Catholic, Protestant
Languages: Spanish, Guarani

Qatar

Area: 4,473 sq mi
(11,586 sq km)
Population: 2,532,000
Capital: Doha,
pop. 438,000
Currency: Qatari rial (QAR)
Religions: Muslim, Christian, Hindu
Languages: Arabic, English

Peru

Area: 496,224 sq mi
(1,285,216 sq km)
Population: 32,440,000
Capital: Lima, pop. 11,204,000
Currency: nuevo sol (PEN)
Religions: Roman Catholic, Protestant
Languages: Spanish, Quechua, Aymara

Romania

Area: 92,043 sq mi
(238,391 sq km)
Population: 18,326,000
Capital: Bucharest, pop. 1,776,000
Currency: leu (RON)
Religions: Eastern Orthodox, Protestant
Language: Romanian

Russia

Area: 6,601,665 sq mi (17,098,242 sq km)
Population: 141,699,000
Capital: Moscow, pop. 12,680,000
Currency: Russian ruble (RUB)
Religions: Eastern Orthodox, Muslim
Language: Russian

Note: Russia is in both Europe and Asia, but its capital is in Europe, so it is classified here as a European country.

Samoa

Area: 1,093 sq mi (2,831 sq km)
Population: 208,000
Capital: Apia, pop. 36,000
Currency: tala (SAT)
Religions: Protestant, Roman Catholic, Mormon
Languages: Samoan (Polynesian), English

Rwanda

Area: 10,169 sq mi (26,338 sq km)
Population: 13,401,000
Capital: Kigali, pop. 1,248,000
Currency: Rwandan franc (RWF)
Religions: Protestant, Roman Catholic
Languages: Kinyarwanda, French, English, Kiswahili (Swahili)

San Marino

Area: 24 sq mi (61 sq km)
Population: 35,000
Capital: San Marino, pop. 4,000
Currency: euro (EUR)
Religion: Roman Catholic
Language: Italian

SNAPSHOT
Palau

A saltwater crocodile, which can grow up to 17 feet (5 m) long, lurks below the surface in waters off the coast of Palau.

● Asia ● Europe ● North America ● **South America**

Sao Tome and Principe
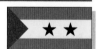
Area: 372 sq mi (964 sq km)
Population: 220,000
Capital: São Tomé, pop. 80,000
Currency: dobra (STN)
Religion: Roman Catholic
Languages: Portuguese, Forro

Saudi Arabia

Area: 830,000 sq mi (2,149,690 sq km)
Population: 35,940,000
Capital: Riyadh, pop. 7,682,000
Currency: Saudi riyal (SAR)
Religion: Muslim
Language: Arabic

Senegal

Area: 75,955 sq mi (196,722 sq km)
Population: 18,385,000
Capital: Dakar, pop. 3,430,000
Currency: CFA franc BCEAO (XOF)
Religion: Muslim
Languages: French, Wolof, other Indigenous languages

Serbia
Area: 29,913 sq mi (77,474 sq km)
Population: 6,693,000
Capital: Belgrade, pop. 1,408,000
Currency: Serbian dinar (RSD)
Religions: Eastern Orthodox, Roman Catholic
Language: Serbian

Seychelles
Area: 176 sq mi (455 sq km)
Population: 98,000
Capital: Victoria, pop. 28,000
Currency: Seychelles rupee (SCR)
Religions: Roman Catholic, Protestant
Languages: Seychellois Creole, English, French

Sierra Leone
Area: 27,699 sq mi (71,740 sq km)
Population: 8,908,000
Capital: Freetown, pop. 1,309,000
Currency: leone (SLL)
Religions: Muslim, Christian
Languages: English, Mende, Temne, Krio

Singapore
Area: 278 sq mi (719 sq km)
Population: 5,975,000
Capital: Singapore, pop. 5,975,000
Currency: Singapore dollar (SGD)
Religions: Buddhist, Christian, Muslim, Taoist, Hindu
Languages: English, Mandarin, other Chinese dialects, Malay, Tamil

Slovakia
Area: 18,933 sq mi (49,035 sq km)
Population: 5,425,000
Capital: Bratislava, pop. 441,000
Currency: euro (EUR)
Religions: Roman Catholic, Protestant
Language: Slovak

Slovenia
Area: 7,827 sq mi (20,273 sq km)
Population: 2,100,000
Capital: Ljubljana, pop. 286,000
Currency: euro (EUR)
Religion: Roman Catholic
Language: Slovenian

Solomon Islands

Area: 11,157 sq mi (28,896 sq km)
Population: 715,000
Capital: Honiara, pop. 82,000
Currency: Solomon Islands dollar (SBD)
Religions: Protestant, Roman Catholic
Languages: Melanesian pidgin, English, Indigenous languages

Somalia

Area: 246,201 sq mi
(637,657 sq km)
Population: 12,694,000
Capital: Mogadishu, pop. 2,610,000
Currency: Somali shilling (SOS)
Religion: Muslim
Languages: Somali, Arabic, Italian, English

South Sudan

Area: 248,777 sq mi
(644,329 sq km)
Population: 12,118,000
Capital: Juba, pop. 459,000
Currency: South Sudanese pound (SSP)
Religions: animist, Christian, Muslim
Languages: English, Arabic, Dinka, Nuer, Bari,
Zande, Shilluk

South Africa

Area: 470,693 sq mi (1,219,090 sq km)
Population: 58,048,000
Capitals: Pretoria (Tshwane),
pop. 2,818,000; Cape Town, pop.
4,890,000; Bloemfontein, pop. 598,000
Currency: rand (ZAR)
Religions: Christian, traditional or animist
Languages: isiZulu, isiXhosa, other Indigenous
languages, Afrikaans, English

Spain

Area: 195,124 sq mi (505,370 sq km)
Population: 47,223,000
Capital: Madrid, pop. 6,751,000
Currency: euro (EUR)
Religion: Roman Catholic
Languages: Castilian Spanish, Catalan,
Galician, Basque

3 cool things about SOUTH AFRICA

1. Boulders Beach, near Cape Town, is home to a protected colony of African penguins.

2. The country's Mponeng gold mine, the world's deepest operating mine, could fit nine Empire State Buildings stacked on top of each other.

3. Vredefort Crater, formed by an asteroid colliding with Earth roughly two billion years ago, is the world's largest known impact crater.

Sri Lanka

Area: 25,332 sq mi
(65,610 sq km)
Population: 23,326,000
Capitals: Colombo, pop. 633,000
Sri Jayewardenepura Kotte, pop. 103,000
Currency: Sri Lankan rupee (LKR)
Religions: Buddhist, Hindu, Muslim, Roman Catholic
Languages: Sinhala, Tamil, English

St. Kitts and Nevis

Area: 101 sq mi (261 sq km)
Population: 55,000
Capital: Basseterre, pop. 14,000
Currency: East Caribbean
dollar (XCD)
Religions: Protestant, Roman Catholic
Language: English

South Korea

Area: 38,502 sq mi
(99,720 sq km)
Population: 51,967,000
Capital: Seoul, pop. 9,988,000
Currency: South Korean won (KRW)
Religions: Protestant, Buddhist, Roman Catholic
Languages: Korean, English

St. Lucia

Area: 238 sq mi (616 sq km)
Population: 168,000
Capital: Castries,
pop. 22,000
Currency: East Caribbean dollar (XCD)
Religions: Roman Catholic, Protestant
Languages: English, French patois

St. Vincent and the Grenadines

Area: 150 sq mi (389 sq km)
Population: 101,000
Capital: Kingstown, pop. 27,000
Currency: East Caribbean dollar (XCD)
Religions: Protestant, Roman Catholic
Languages: English, Vincentian Creole English, French patois

Sudan

Area: 718,723 sq mi (1,861,484 sq km)
Population: 49,198,000
Capital: Khartoum, pop. 6,344,000
Currency: Sudanese pound (SDG)
Religion: Muslim
Languages: Arabic, English, Nubian, Ta Bedawie, Fur

Suriname

Area: 63,251 sq mi (163,820 sq km)
Population: 640,000
Capital: Paramaribo, pop. 239,000
Currency: Surinamese dollar (SRD)
Religions: Protestant, Hindu, Roman Catholic, Muslim
Languages: Dutch, English, Sranan Tongo, Caribbean Hindustani, Javanese

Sweden

Area: 173,860 sq mi (450,295 sq km)
Population: 10,536,000
Capital: Stockholm, pop. 1,700,000
Currency: Swedish krona (SEK)
Religion: Protestant
Language: Swedish

Switzerland

Area: 15,937 sq mi (41,277 sq km)
Population: 8,564,000
Capital: Bern, pop. 441,000
Currency: Swiss franc (CHF)
Religions: Roman Catholic, Protestant, other Christian, Muslim
Languages: German (Swiss German), French, Italian, Romansch

Syria

Area: 71,870 sq mi (186,142 sq km)
Population: 22,934,000
Capital: Damascus, pop. 2,585,000
Currency: Syrian pound (SYP)
Religions: Muslim, Eastern Orthodox, Oriental Orthodox, Eastern Catholic, other Christian
Languages: Arabic, Kurdish, Armenian, Aramaic, Circassian, French, English

Tajikistan

Area: 55,637 sq mi (144,100 sq km)
Population: 9,246,000
Capital: Dushanbe, pop. 987,000
Currency: Tajikistani somoni (TJS)
Religion: Muslim
Languages: Tajik, Uzbek

MOUNTAINS cover more than 90 PERCENT of TAJIKISTAN.

Tanzania

Area: 365,754 sq mi (947,300 sq km)
Population: 65,643,000
Capitals: Dodoma, pop. 262,000
Currency: Tanzanian shilling (TZS)
Religions: Christian, Muslim
Languages: Kiswahili (Swahili), Kiunguja, English, Arabic, local languages

Thailand

Area: 198,117 sq mi (513,120 sq km)
Population: 69,795,000
Capital: Bangkok, pop. 11,070,000
Currency: baht (THB)
Religion: Buddhist
Languages: Thai, English

COLOR KEY ● Africa ● Australia, New Zealand, and Oceania

Timor-Leste (East Timor)

Area: 5,743 sq mi (14,874 sq km)
Population: 1,476,000
Capital: Díli, pop. 281,000
Currency: U.S. dollar (USD)
Religion: Roman Catholic
Languages: Tetun Prasa, Mambai, Makasai, Portuguese, Indonesian, English

Togo

Area: 21,925 sq mi (56,785 sq km)
Population: 8,704,000
Capital: Lomé, pop. 1,982,000
Currency: CFA franc BCEAO (XOF)
Religions: Christian, folk religion, Muslim
Languages: French, Ewe, Mina, Kabye, Dagomba

Tonga

Area: 288 sq mi (747 sq km)
Population: 105,000
Capital: Nuku'alofa, pop. 23,000
Currency: pa'anga (TOP)
Religions: Protestant, Mormon, Roman Catholic
Languages: Tongan, English

Trinidad and Tobago

Area: 1,980 sq mi (5,128 sq km)
Population: 1,407,000
Capital: Port of Spain, pop. 545,000
Currency: Trinidad and Tobago dollar (TTD)
Religions: Protestant, Roman Catholic, Hindu, Muslim
Languages: English, Creole, Caribbean Hindustani, Spanish, Chinese

Tunisia

Area: 63,170 sq mi (163,610 sq km)
Population: 11,976,000
Capital: Tunis, pop. 2,475,000
Currency: Tunisian dinar (TND)
Religion: Muslim
Languages: Arabic, French, Berber

Türkiye (Turkey)

Area: 302,535 sq mi (783,562 sq km)
Population: 83,593,000
Capital: Ankara, pop. 5,397,000
Currency: Turkish lira (TRY)
Religion: Muslim
Languages: Turkish, Kurdish

Turkmenistan

Area: 188,456 sq mi (488,100 sq km)
Population: 5,691,000
Capital: Ashgabat, pop. 902,000
Currency: Turkmenistani manat (TMT)
Religions: Muslim, Eastern Orthodox
Languages: Turkmen, Russian

Tuvalu

Area: 10 sq mi (26 sq km)
Population: 12,000
Capital: Funafuti, pop. 7,000
Currency: Australian dollar (AUD)
Religion: Protestant
Languages: Tuvaluan, English, Samoan, Kiribati

No point on TUVALU IS HIGHER THAN 16.4 FEET (5 M) above sea level.

Uganda

Area: 93,065 sq mi (241,038 sq km)
Population: 47,730,000
Capital: Kampala, pop. 3,846,000
Currency: Ugandan shilling (UGX)
Religions: Protestant, Roman Catholic, Muslim
Languages: English, Ganda (Luganda), local languages, Swahili, Arabic

Ukraine

Area: 233,032 sq mi
(603,550 sq km)
Population: 43,306,000
Capital: Kyiv, pop. 3,017,000
Currency: hryvnia (UAH)
Religions: Eastern Orthodox, Eastern Catholic, Roman Catholic, Protestant
Languages: Ukrainian, Russian

United Kingdom

Area: 94,058 sq mi
(243,610 sq km)
Population: 68,138,000
Capital: London, pop. 9,648,000
Currency: pound sterling (GBP)
Religions: Protestant, Roman Catholic
Languages: English, Scots, Scottish Gaelic, Welsh, Irish, Cornish

United Arab Emirates

Area: 32,278 sq mi (83,600 sq km)
Population: 9,973,000
Capital: Abu Dhabi,
pop. 1,567,000
Currency: UAE dirham (AED)
Religions: Muslim, Christian
Languages: Arabic, English, Hindi, Malayam, Urdu, Pashto, Tagalog, Persian

United States

Area: 3,796,741 sq mi
(9,833,517 sq km)
Population: 339,665,000
Capital: Washington, D.C.,
pop. 672,000
Currency: U.S. dollar (USD)
Religions: Protestant, Roman Catholic
Languages: English, Spanish, Native American languages

SNAPSHOT
Vatican City

St. Peter's Basilica, at the center of Vatican City, is one of the largest religious buildings in the world.

COLOR KEY ● Africa ● Australia, New Zealand, and Oceania

Uruguay

Area: 68,037 sq mi
(176,215 sq km)
Population: 3,416,000
Capital: Montevideo, pop. 1,774,000
Currency: Uruguayan peso (UYU)
Religions: Roman Catholic, other Christian
Language: Spanish

Uzbekistan

Area: 172,742 sq mi
(447,400 sq km)
Population: 31,361,000
Capital: Tashkent,
pop. 2,603,000
Currency: Uzbekistan sum (UZS)
Religions: Muslim, Eastern Orthodox
Languages: Uzbek, Russian, Tajik

Vanuatu

Area: 4,706 sq mi (12,189 sq km)
Population: 313,000
Capital: Port-Vila, pop. 53,000
Currency: Vatu (VUV)
Religions: Protestant, Roman Catholic
Languages: local languages, Bislama, English, French

Vatican City

Area: 0.2 sq mi (0.4 sq km)
Population: 1,000
Capital: Vatican City, pop. 1,000
Currency: euro (EUR)
Religion: Roman Catholic
Languages: Italian, Latin, French

Venezuela

Area: 352,144 sq mi
(912,050 sq km)
Population: 30,518,000
Capital: Caracas, pop. 2,972,000
Currency: bolivar soberano (VES)
Religion: Roman Catholic
Languages: Spanish, Indigenous languages

Vietnam

Area: 127,881 sq mi
(331,210 sq km)
Population: 104,799,000
Capital: Hanoi, pop. 5,253,000
Currency: dong (VND)
Religions: Buddhist, Roman Catholic
Languages: Vietnamese, English, French, Chinese, Khmer, Mon-Khmer, Malayo-Polynesian

Yemen

Area: 203,850 sq mi
(527,968 sq km)
Population: 31,566,000
Capital: Sanaa, pop. 3,292,000
Currency: Yemeni rial (YER)
Religion: Muslim
Language: Arabic

DRAGON'S BLOOD TREES, which only grow in YEMEN, can LIVE FOR 1,000 YEARS.

Zambia

Area: 290,587 sq mi
(752,618 sq km)
Population: 20,216,000
Capital: Lusaka, pop. 3,181,000
Currency: Zambian kwacha (ZMW)
Religions: Protestant, Roman Catholic
Languages: Bembe, Nyanja, Tonga, other Indigenous languages, English

Zimbabwe

Area: 150,872 sq mi
(390,757 sq km)
Population: 15,419,000
Capital: Harare, pop. 1,578,000
Currency: Zimbabwean dollar (ZWL)
Religions: Protestant, Roman Catholic, other Christian
Languages: Shona, Ndebele, English, Indigenous languages

THE POLITICAL UNITED STATES

9:00 AM PACIFIC TIME

Cape Flattery

Seattle
Olympia • Tacoma
WASHINGTON
Spokane
Portland
Yakima
Lewiston
Great Falls
Columbia
Salem
Columbia
Eugene
OREGON
Boise
Idaho Falls
Medford
Klamath Falls
Snake
Pocatello

10:00 AM
MOUNTAIN TIME

Minot
MONTANA
Butte • Helena
Billings
Cody
Yellowstone L.
Great Falls
Missouri

NORTH DAKOTA
Bismarck
Aberdeen
SOUTH DAKOTA
Pierre
Rapid City
Missouri

WYOMING
Casper
Cheyenne
Laramie
Fort Collins
N. Platte

NEBRASKA
Grand Island
Platte
S. Platte

Eureka
Redding
Reno
Carson City
Sacramento
Lake Tahoe
San Francisco • Oakland
San Jose
Salinas
Fresno
Bakersfield
Point Conception
Los Angeles
Long Beach
San Diego

Great Salt Lake
Ogden
Salt Lake City
Provo
NEVADA
Great Basin
Mojave
Las Vegas
St. George
Desert
Salton Sea
Riverside
Grand Canyon
Flagstaff
ARIZONA
Phoenix • Mesa
Yuma
Tucson

UTAH
Grand Junction
Lake Powell
Colorado
COLORADO
Denver • Boulder
Colorado Springs
Pueblo

Santa Fe
Albuquerque
NEW MEXICO
Rio Grande
Las Cruces
Roswell
El Paso

KANSAS
Dodge City
Wichita
Arkansas

OKLAH
Oklahoma City
Lawton
Amarillo
Wichita Falls
Lubbock
Red
Fort Worth
Midland • Abilene
Odessa
Waco
TEXAS
Austin
San Antonio
Corpus Christi
Laredo
Rio Grande
Brownsville

7:00 AM
HAWAII-ALEUTIAN TIME

Brooks Range
Yukon
Alaska Range
Juneau
Anchorage
Alaska Peninsula
ALEUTIAN ISLANDS
ALASKA
0   400 Miles
0   400 Kilometers

8:00 AM
ALASKA TIME

Kaua'i
Ni'ihau   O'ahu
Honolulu   Moloka'i
Lāna'i   Maui
HAWAI'I   Kaho'olawe   Hawai'i
Hilo
0   150 Miles
0   150 Kilometers

7:00 AM
HAWAII-ALEUTIAN TIME

The Hawaiian Islands and parts of Arizona do not follow Daylight Savings Time.

The United States is made up of 50 states joined like a giant quilt. Each is unique, but together they make a national fabric held together by a constitution and a federal government. State boundaries set apart internal political units within the country. The national capital—Washington, D.C.—is marked by a star in a double circle. The capital of each state is marked by a star in a single circle.

TIME ZONES: Earth is divided into 24 time zones, each about 15 degrees of longitude wide, reflecting the distance Earth turns from west to east each hour. The U.S. is divided into six time zones, indicated by red dotted lines on the map.

THE PHYSICAL UNITED STATES

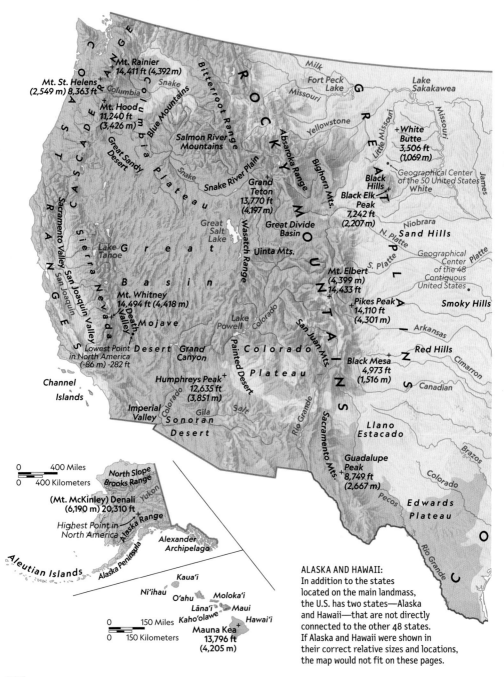

Mt. Rainier 14,411 ft (4,392 m)

Mt. St. Helens (2,549 m) 8,363 ft

Mt. Hood 11,240 ft (3,426 m)

CASCADE RANGE

COAST RANGE

Columbia

Snake

Blue Mountains

Columbia Plateau

Great Sandy Desert

BITTERROOT RANGE

Salmon River Mountains

Snake

Snake River Plain

ROCKY

Milk

Fort Peck Lake

Missouri

Yellowstone

Absaroka Range

Grand Teton 13,770 ft (4,197 m)

Great Salt Lake

Wasatch Range

Uinta Mts.

Bighorn Mts.

Great Divide Basin

GREAT

Little Missouri

Missouri

Lake Sakakawea

White Butte 3,506 ft (1,069 m)

Black Hills

Black Elk Peak 7,242 ft (2,207 m)

Geographical Center of the 50 United States

White

James

Niobrara

N. Platte

Sand Hills

Geographical Center of the 48 Contiguous United States

Platte

Sierra Nevada

Sacramento Valley

San Joaquin

San Joaquin Valley

Lake Tahoe

Great Basin

Mt. Whitney 14,494 ft (4,418 m)

Death Valley

Mojave

S. Platte

Mt. Elbert (4,399 m) 14,433 ft

Pikes Peak 14,110 ft (4,301 m)

Smoky Hills

Arkansas

MOUNTAINS

Lake Powell

Colorado

San Juan Mts.

Colorado

Lowest Point in North America (-86 m) -282 ft

Channel Islands

Desert

Grand Canyon

Painted Desert

Plateau

Humphreys Peak 12,635 ft (3,851 m)

Colorado

Imperial Valley

Sonoran Desert

Gila

Salt

Rio Grande

Sacramento Mts.

Plateau

Black Mesa 4,973 ft (1,516 m)

Red Hills

Cimarron

Canadian

Llano Estacado

Brazos

Guadalupe Peak 8,749 ft (2,667 m)

Colorado

Pecos

Edwards Plateau

Rio Grande

0 ——— 400 Miles
0 ——— 400 Kilometers

North Slope

Brooks Range

Yukon

(Mt. McKinley) Denali (6,190 m) 20,310 ft

Highest Point in North America

Alaska Range

Alexander Archipelago

Aleutian Islands

Alaska Peninsula

Kaua'i

Ni'ihau

O'ahu

Moloka'i

Lāna'i

Maui

Kaho'olawe

Hawai'i

0 ——— 150 Miles
0 ——— 150 Kilometers

Mauna Kea 13,796 ft (4,205 m)

ALASKA AND HAWAII:
In addition to the states located on the main landmass, the U.S. has two states—Alaska and Hawaii—that are not directly connected to the other 48 states. If Alaska and Hawaii were shown in their correct relative sizes and locations, the map would not fit on these pages.

Stretching from the Atlantic Ocean in the east to the Pacific Ocean in the west, the United States is the third largest country (by area) in the world. Its physical diversity ranges from mountains to fertile plains to dry deserts. Shading on the map indicates changes in elevation, while colors show different vegetation patterns.

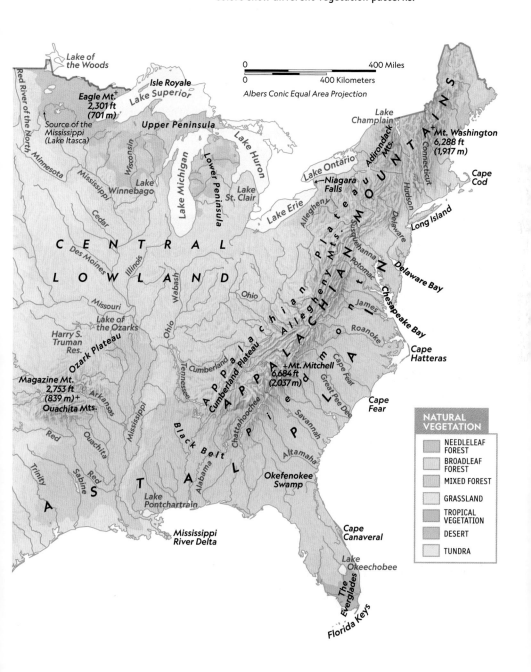

0   400 Miles
0   400 Kilometers
Albers Conic Equal Area Projection

Lake of the Woods
Isle Royale
Lake Superior
Eagle Mt. 2,301 ft (701 m)
Source of the Mississippi (Lake Itasca)
Upper Peninsula
Red River of the North
Minnesota
Mississippi
Wisconsin
Cedar
Lake Winnebago
Lake Michigan
Lower Peninsula
Lake Huron
Lake St. Clair
Lake Champlain
Adirondack Mts.
Mt. Washington 6,288 ft (1,917 m)
Connecticut
Hudson
Cape Cod
Lake Ontario
Niagara Falls
Lake Erie
Allegheny
Plateau Mts.
Delaware
Long Island
Delaware Bay
Des Moines
Illinois
Wabash
Ohio
Allegheny
Susquehanna
Potomac
Chesapeake Bay
Missouri
Lake of the Ozarks
Harry S. Truman Res.
Ozark Plateau
Ohio
Tennessee
Cumberland
Cumberland Plateau
James
Roanoke
Cape Hatteras
Magazine Mt. 2,753 ft (839 m)
Ouachita Mts.
Arkansas
Mississippi
Mt. Mitchell 6,684 ft (2,037 m)
Cape Fear
Great Pee Dee
Cape Fear
Red
Ouachita
Black Belt
Chattahoochee
Savannah
Altamaha
Trinity
Sabine
Red
Lake Pontchartrain
Alabama
Okefenokee Swamp
Mississippi River Delta
Cape Canaveral
Lake Okeechobee
The Everglades
Florida Keys

CENTRAL LOWLAND

APPALACHIAN MOUNTAINS

COASTAL PLAIN

NATURAL VEGETATION

- NEEDLELEAF FOREST
- BROADLEAF FOREST
- MIXED FOREST
- GRASSLAND
- TROPICAL VEGETATION
- DESERT
- TUNDRA

THE STATES

From sea to shining sea, the United States of America is a nation of diversity. In the 249 years since its creation, the nation has grown to become home to a wide range of peoples, industries, and cultures. The following pages present a general overview of all 50 states in the United States.

The country is generally divided into five large regions: the Northeast, the Southeast, the Midwest, the Southwest, and the West. Though loosely defined, these zones tend to share important similarities, including climate, history, and geography. The color key below provides a guide to which states are in each region.

The flag of each state and highlights of demography and industry are also included. These details offer a brief overview of each state.

In addition, each state's official flower and bird are identified.

Color Key by Region

Alabama

Nickname: Heart of Dixie
Area: 52,420 sq mi (135,767 sq km)
Population: 5,074,000
Capital: Montgomery; population 199,000
Statehood: December 14, 1819; 22nd state
State flower/bird: Camellia/yellowhammer (northern flicker)

Alaska

Nickname: Last Frontier
Area: 665,384 sq mi (1,723,337 sq km)
Population: 734,000
Capital: Juneau; population 32,000
Statehood: January 3, 1959; 49th state
State flower/bird: Alpine forget-me-not/ willow ptarmigan

Arizona

Nickname: Grand Canyon State
Area: 113,990 sq mi (295,234 sq km)
Population: 7,359,000
Capital: Phoenix; population 1,625,000
Statehood: February 14, 1912; 48th state
State flower/bird: Saguaro cactus blossom/ cactus wren

Arkansas

Nickname: Natural State
Area: 53,179 sq mi (137,732 sq km)
Population: 3,046,000
Capital: Little Rock; population 202,000
Statehood: June 15, 1836; 25th state
State flower/bird: Apple blossom/ mockingbird

California

Nickname: Golden State
Area: 163,695 sq mi (423,967 sq km)
Population: 39,029,000
Capital: Sacramento; population 525,000
Statehood: September 9, 1850; 31st state
State flower/bird: California poppy/ California quail

The BEAR on CALIFORNIA'S STATE FLAG was modeled after a REAL-LIFE GRIZZLY NAMED MONARCH.

Colorado

Nickname: Centennial State
Area: 104,094 sq mi (269,601 sq km)
Population: 5,840,000
Capital: Denver; population 711,000
Statehood: August 1, 1876; 38th state
State flower/bird: Rocky Mountain columbine/ lark bunting

Connecticut

Nickname: Constitution State
Area: 5,543 sq mi (14,357 sq km)
Population: 3,626,000
Capital: Hartford; population 121,000
Statehood: January 9, 1788; 5th state
State flower/bird: Mountain laurel/American robin

> The world's LARGEST pair of GOOGLY EYES—some 12 feet (3.6 m) tall—were made in NORWALK, CONNECTICUT.

Delaware

Nickname: First State
Area: 2,489 sq mi (6,446 sq km)
Population: 1,018,000
Capital: Dover; population 39,000
Statehood: December 7, 1787; 1st state
State flower/bird: Peach blossom/blue hen chicken

Florida

Nickname: Sunshine State
Area: 65,758 sq mi (170,312 sq km)
Population: 22,245,000
Capital: Tallahassee; population 197,000
Statehood: March 3, 1845; 27th state
State flower/bird: Orange blossom/mockingbird

Georgia

Nickname: Peach State
Area: 59,425 sq mi (153,910 sq km)
Population: 10,913,000
Capital: Atlanta; population 496,000
Statehood: January 2, 1788; 4th state
State flower/bird: Cherokee rose/brown thrasher

Hawaii

Nickname: Aloha State
Area: 10,932 sq mi (28,313 sq km)
Population: 1,440,000
Capital: Honolulu; population 346,000
Statehood: August 21, 1959; 50th state
State flower/bird: Pua aloalo/nene (Hawaiian goose)

Idaho

Nickname: Gem State
Area: 83,569 sq mi (216,443 sq km)
Population: 1,939,000
Capital: Boise; population 237,000
Statehood: July 3, 1890; 43rd state
State flower/bird: Syringa/mountain bluebird

Illinois

Nickname: Prairie State
Area: 57,914 sq mi (149,995 sq km)
Population: 12,582,000
Capital: Springfield; population 113,000
Statehood: December 3, 1818; 21st state
State flower/bird: Violet/northern cardinal

Indiana

Nickname: Hoosier State
Area: 36,420 sq mi (94,326 sq km)
Population: 6,833,000
Capital: Indianapolis; population 882,000
Statehood: December 11, 1816; 19th state
State flower/bird: Peony/northern cardinal

Iowa

Nickname: Hawkeye State
Area: 56,273 sq mi (145,746 sq km)
Population: 3,201,000
Capital: Des Moines; population 212,000
Statehood: December 28, 1846; 29th state
State flower/bird: Wild prairie rose/American goldfinch

Kansas

Nickname: Sunflower State
Area: 82,278 sq mi (213,100 sq km)
Population: 2,937,000
Capital: Topeka; population 126,000
Statehood: January 29, 1861; 34th state
State flower/bird: Wild native sunflower/ western meadowlark

3 wild things about KANSAS

1. Around 90 tornadoes touch down in Kansas each year.

2. Cawker City, Kansas, is home to a giant ball of twine, which weighs more than an adult elephant.

3. A 1,000-pound (454 kg) meteorite nicknamed the "Space Wanderer" was discovered on a farm near Greensburg, Kansas.

Kentucky

Nickname: Bluegrass State
Area: 40,408 sq mi (104,656 sq km)
Population: 4,512,000
Capital: Frankfort; population 29,000
Statehood: June 1, 1792; 15th state
State flower/bird: Goldenrod/northern cardinal

Louisiana

Nickname: Pelican State
Area: 52,378 sq mi (135,659 sq km)
Population: 4,590,000
Capital: Baton Rouge; population 222,000
Statehood: April 30, 1812; 18th state
State flower/bird: Magnolia/brown pelican

Maine

Nickname: Pine Tree State
Area: 35,380 sq mi (91,633 sq km)
Population: 1,385,000
Capital: Augusta; population 19,000
Statehood: March 15, 1820; 23rd state
State flower/bird: White pine cone and tassel/ black-capped chickadee

Maryland

Nickname: Old Line State
Area: 12,406 sq mi (32,131 sq km)
Population: 6,165,000
Capital: Annapolis; population 41,000
Statehood: April 28, 1788; 7th state
State flower/bird: Black-eyed Susan/ Baltimore oriole

Massachusetts

Nickname: Bay State
Area: 10,554 sq mi (27,336 sq km)
Population: 6,982,000
Capital: Boston; population 655,000
Statehood: February 6, 1788; 6th state
State flower/bird: Mayflower/ black-capped chickadee

Michigan

Nickname: Wolverine State
Area: 96,714 sq mi (250,487 sq km)
Population: 10,034,000
Capital: Lansing; population 113,000
Statehood: January 26, 1837; 26th state
State flower/bird: Apple blossom/ American robin

Minnesota

Nickname: North Star State
Area: 86,936 sq mi (225,163 sq km)
Population: 5,717,000
Capital: Saint Paul; population 307,000
Statehood: May 11, 1858; 32nd state
State flower/bird: Pink and white lady slipper/ common loon

Mississippi

Nickname: Magnolia State
Area: 48,432 sq mi (125,438 sq km)
Population: 2,940,000
Capital: Jackson; population 150,000
Statehood: December 10, 1817; 20th state
State flower/bird: Magnolia/mockingbird

Missouri

Nickname: Show-Me State
Area: 69,707 sq mi (180,540 sq km)
Population: 6,178,000
Capital: Jefferson City; population 43,000
Statehood: August 10, 1821; 24th state
State flower/bird: White hawthorn blossom/
eastern bluebird

Montana

Nickname: Treasure State
Area: 147,040 sq mi (380,831 sq km)
Population: 1,123,000
Capital: Helena; population 33,000
Statehood: November 8, 1889; 41st state
State flower/bird: Bitterroot/
western meadowlark

Nebraska

Nickname: Cornhusker State
Area: 77,348 sq mi (200,330 sq km)
Population: 1,968,000
Capital: Lincoln; population 293,000
Statehood: March 1, 1867; 37th state
State flower/bird: Goldenrod/
western meadowlark

Nevada

Nickname: Silver State
Area: 110,572 sq mi (286,380 sq km)
Population: 3,178,000
Capital: Carson City; population 59,000
Statehood: October 31, 1864; 36th state
State flower/bird: Sagebrush/
mountain bluebird

New Hampshire

Nickname: Granite State
Area: 9,349 sq mi (24,214 sq km)
Population: 1,395,000
Capital: Concord; population 44,000
Statehood: June 21, 1788; 9th state
State flower/bird: Purple lilac/purple finch

New Jersey

Nickname: Garden State
Area: 8,723 sq mi (22,591 sq km)
Population: 9,262,000
Capital: Trenton; population 90,000
Statehood: December 18, 1787; 3rd state
State flower/bird: Violet/eastern goldfinch

The incandescent **LIGHT BULB** was **INVENTED** by **THOMAS EDISON** in Menlo Park, New Jersey.

New Mexico

Nickname: Land of Enchantment
Area: 121,590 sq mi
(314,917 sq km)
Population: 2,113,000
Capital: Santa Fe; population 88,000
Statehood: January 6, 1912; 47th state
State flower/bird: Yucca/greater roadrunner

New York

Nickname: Empire State
Area: 54,555 sq mi
(141,297 sq km)
Population: 19,677,000
Capital: Albany; population 99,000
Statehood: July 26, 1788; 11th state
State flower/bird: Rose/eastern bluebird

 Midwest **Southwest**  West

North Carolina

Nickname: Tar Heel State
Area: 53,819 sq mi (139,391 sq km)
Population: 10,699,000
Capital: Raleigh; population 469,000
Statehood: November 21, 1789; 12th state
State flower/bird: Flowering dogwood/ northern cardinal

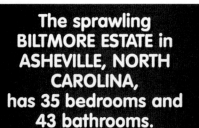

The sprawling **BILTMORE ESTATE** in **ASHEVILLE, NORTH CAROLINA,** has 35 bedrooms and 43 bathrooms.

North Dakota

Nickname: Peace Garden State
Area: 70,698 sq mi (183,108 sq km)
Population: 779,000
Capital: Bismarck; population 74,000
Statehood: November 2, 1889; 39th state
State flower/bird: Wild prairie rose/ western meadowlark

Ohio

Nickname: Buckeye State
Area: 44,826 sq mi (116,098 sq km)
Population: 11,756,000
Capital: Columbus; population 907,000
Statehood: February 19, 1803; 17th state
State flower/bird: Scarlet carnation/ northern cardinal

Oklahoma

Nickname: Sooner State
Area: 69,899 sq mi (181,037 sq km)
Population: 4,020,000
Capital: Oklahoma City; population 688,000
Statehood: November 16, 1907; 46th state
State flower/bird: Oklahoma rose/ scissor-tailed flycatcher

Oregon

Nickname: Beaver State
Area: 98,379 sq mi (254,799 sq km)
Population: 4,240,000
Capital: Salem; population 178,000
Statehood: February 14, 1859; 33rd state
State flower/bird: Oregon grape/ western meadowlark

Pennsylvania

Nickname: Keystone State
Area: 46,054 sq mi (119,280 sq km)
Population: 12,972,000
Capital: Harrisburg; population 50,000
Statehood: December 12, 1787; 2nd state
State flower/bird: Mountain laurel/ ruffed grouse

Rhode Island

Nickname: Ocean State
Area: 1,545 sq mi (4,001 sq km)
Population: 1,094,000
Capital: Providence; population 190,000
Statehood: May 29, 1790; 13th state
State flower/bird: Violet/ Rhode Island red

South Carolina

Nickname: Palmetto State
Area: 32,020 sq mi (82,933 sq km)
Population: 5,283,000
Capital: Columbia; population 138,000
Statehood: May 23, 1788; 8th state
State flower/bird: Yellow jessamine/ Carolina wren

South Dakota

Nickname: Mount Rushmore State
Area: 77,116 sq mi (199,729 sq km)
Population: 910,000
Capital: Pierre; population 14,000
Statehood: November 2, 1889; 40th state
State flower/bird: American pasque/ ring-necked pheasant

Tennessee

Nickname: Volunteer State
Area: 42,144 sq mi (109,153 sq km)
Population: 7,051,000
Capital: Nashville; population 679,000
Statehood: June 1, 1796; 16th state
State flower/bird: Iris/mockingbird

Texas

Nickname: Lone Star State
Area: 268,596 sq mi (695,662 sq km)
Population: 30,030,000
Capital: Austin; population 964,000
Statehood: December 29, 1845; 28th state
State flower/bird: Bluebonnet/mockingbird

BEAUMONT, TEXAS, is home to a 24-foot (7.3-m)-tall FIRE HYDRANT painted like a DALMATIAN.

Utah

Nickname: Beehive State
Area: 84,897 sq mi (219,882 sq km)
Population: 3,381,000
Capital: Salt Lake City; population 200,000
Statehood: January 4, 1896; 45th state
State flower/bird: Sego lily/California gull

Vermont

Nickname: Green Mountain State
Area: 9,616 sq mi (24,906 sq km)
Population: 647,000
Capital: Montpelier; population 8,000
Statehood: March 4, 1791; 14th state
State flower/bird: Red clover/hermit thrush

Virginia

Nickname: Old Dominion
Area: 42,775 sq mi (110,787 sq km)
Population: 8,684,000
Capital: Richmond; population 227,000
Statehood: June 25, 1788; 10th state
State flower/bird: American dogwood/ northern cardinal

Washington

Nickname: Evergreen State
Area: 71,298 sq mi (184,661 sq km)
Population: 7,786,000
Capital: Olympia; population 56,000
Statehood: November 11, 1889; 42nd state
State flower/bird: Coast rhododendron/ American goldfinch

West Virginia

Nickname: Mountain State
Area: 24,230 sq mi (62,756 sq km)
Population: 1,775,000
Capital: Charleston; population 48,000
Statehood: June 20, 1863; 35th state
State flower/bird: Rhododendron/ northern cardinal

Wisconsin

Nickname: Badger State
Area: 65,496 sq mi (169,635 sq km)
Population: 5,893,000
Capital: Madison; population 269,000
Statehood: May 29, 1848; 30th state
State flower/bird: Wood violet/ American robin

Wyoming

Nickname: Equality State
Area: 97,813 sq mi (253,335 sq km)
Population: 581,000
Capital: Cheyenne; population 65,000
Statehood: July 10, 1890; 44th state
State flower/bird: Indian paintbrush/ western meadowlark

THE TERRITORIES

The United States has 14 territories— political divisions that are not states. Three of these are in the Caribbean Sea, and the other 11 are in the Pacific Ocean.

St. John, U.S. Virgin Islands

Convention Center, San Juan, Puerto Rico

Talofofo Falls, Guam

U.S. CARIBBEAN TERRITORIES

Puerto Rico
Area: 5,325 sq mi (13,791 sq km)
Population: 3,222,000
Capital: San Juan; population 2,440,000
Languages: Spanish, English

U.S. Virgin Islands
Area: 733 sq mi (1,898 sq km)
Population: 105,000
Capital: Charlotte Amalie; population 52,000
Languages: English, Spanish, French

U.S. PACIFIC TERRITORIES

American Samoa
Area: 581 sq mi (1,505 sq km)
Population: 45,000
Capital: Pago Pago; population 3,000
Language: Samoan, English

Guam
Area: 571 sq mi (1,478 sq km)
Population: 169,000
Capital: Hagåtña (Agana); population 147,000
Languages: English, Filipino, Chamorro, other Pacific island and Asian languages

Northern Mariana Islands
Area: 1,976 sq mi (5,117 sq km)
Population: 51,000
Capital: Capital Hill; population 51,000
Languages: Philippine languages, Chinese, Chamorro, English

Other U.S. Territories
Baker Island, Howland Island, Jarvis Island, Johnston Atoll, Kingman Reef, Midway Islands, Palmyra Atoll, Wake Island, Navassa Island (in the Caribbean)

Figures for capital cities vary widely between sources because of differences in the way areas are defined and other projection methods.

THE U.S. CAPITAL

District of Columbia
Area: 68 sq mi (177 sq km)
Population: 672,000

Abraham Lincoln, who was president during the Civil War and an opponent of slavery, is remembered in the Lincoln Memorial, located at the opposite end of the National Mall from the U.S. Capitol Building.

The Lincoln Memorial celebrated its 100th anniversary in 2022.

COLOR KEY   ● Territories ● Northeast

weird but true!

Check out these outrageous U.S.A. facts.

Texas's **largest wind farm is 4.5 times** the size of Manhattan, New York.

A Wisconsin **corn maze** was **designed** in the shape of a **trilobite**, an **arthropod** that crawled seafloors **250 million years ago.**

In California's Mono Lake, limestone formations called **tufa towers** are three stories tall.

The **Angel Oak** Tree near Charleston, South Carolina, shades an area the size of **three and a half basketball courts.**

Each American eats more than 40 quarts (38 L) of popcorn every year, on average.

Salamanders in the United States can **range in size** from a **paper clip** to longer than a **baseball bat.**

La Casa Estrecha— **The Narrow House** in San Juan, Puerto Rico—is just over **five feet** (1.6 m) wide.

10 NEAT FACTS ABOUT NATIONAL PARKS

Ruins from Maya **settlements** more than 1,000 years old are found at **Tikal National Park in Guatemala.**

Bryce Canyon National Park in **Utah, U.S.A.,** is filled with **hoodoos—** limestone spires created by weather and erosion.

SERENGETI NATIONAL PARK IN TANZANIA SEES THE ANNUAL MIGRATION OF HUNDREDS OF THOUSANDS OF WILDEBEESTS, ZEBRAS, AND GAZELLES. IT IS CONSIDERED TO HAVE ONE OF THE PLANET'S OLDEST ECOSYSTEMS.

Italy's Etna National Park holds one of the **MOST ACTIVE VOLCANOES** on Earth. Mount Etna has been in a state of near-continuous eruption **FOR HALF A MILLION YEARS!**

Kaieteur Falls in **GUYANA'S Kaieteur National Park** are five times higher than Niagara Falls.

Edelweiss is a protected flower that grows thousands of feet above sea level in the **Swiss National Park** in **Switzerland;** it is the subject of a song in the movie *The Sound of Music.*

You can take an elevator down 750 feet (229 m) into a cave at **Carlsbad Caverns National Park in New Mexico, U.S.A.**

Saguaro National Park in Arizona, U.S.A., has 25 species of cactus, including the teddy-bear cholla cactus and the pinkflower hedgehog cactus.

India's Kaziranga National Park is home to **2,000 one-horned rhinos;** rhinos can **run 25 miles an hour** (40 km/h).

THE PETIT TRAIN D'ARTOUSTE, THE LITTLE RAILWAY IN **FRANCE'S PYRÉNÉES NATIONAL PARK, TAKES TOURISTS UP 6,562 FEET** (2,000 M) FOR MOUNTAIN VIEWS. IT IS ONE OF EUROPE'S HIGHEST RAILWAYS.

Bet You Didn't Know!

7 cool facts about castles

1 The castle barber was also the DENTIST.

2 Neuschwanstein Castle in Germany was the inspiration for Disneyland's SLEEPING BEAUTY CASTLE.

3 The first castles were built about A THOUSAND YEARS AGO.

4 England's Windsor Castle is about 200 TIMES LARGER than a typical house in the United States.

5 Ireland's Blarney Castle has a stone that VISITORS KISS for luck.

6 The number of people who lived in some castles could have FILLED a small village.

7 Supplies were often smuggled into castles through SECRET TUNNELS.

WILD VACATION

Totally Wild Hotel

GIRAFFE MANOR

WHERE Kenya, Africa

WHY IT'S COOL Ever have the feeling you're being watched? That's because a giraffe might be at your hotel window! Giraffe Manor is home to about 10 Rothschild's giraffes that roam the property. And they're definitely not shy: Some of the giraffes may stick their heads into your second-story bedroom window or eat right off the breakfast table. When they want a snack, the giraffes have been known to pluck flowers from the manor's vases. Mpingo and Olerai, two of the youngest giraffes, are sometimes seen playfully running through the national park that borders the hotel. But no one thinks that these permanent residents are a pain in the neck!

GET UP CLOSE!

COOL THINGS ABOUT KENYA

Kenya is about the same size as Texas, U.S.A.

The bones of one of the earliest human ancestors found to date were discovered in Kenya's Turkana Basin.

The elephants in Kenya's Tsavo East National Park cover themselves in iron oxide–rich soil, which turns them red.

THINGS TO DO IN KENYA

Cheer on dozens of camels—some running the wrong way—at the International Camel Derby in the town of Maralal.

Bird-watch on the shores of Lake Nakuru, where hundreds of thousands of bright pink flamingos flock each year.

Swim in glowing waters at a beach in Kilifi. (The secret is the tiny bioluminescent animals living there!)

WHAT WEIRD DESTINATION IS RIGHT FOR YOU?

Lake Hillier, Middle Island, Western Australia

Researchers think that bacteria in this pink lake give it its rosy color. But because the island is used only for research, your visit will be from the air.

Spotted Lake, British Columbia, Canada

The water of this lake evaporates in summer, leaving behind small mineral pools of varying colors. They're best viewed from far enough away that you can see all the quirky circles at once.

Do you like your weirdness from a distance?

Skylodge Adventure Suites, Cusco, Peru

Get cozy in your transparent bedroom capsule 1,000 feet (305 m) up—hanging from the side of a cliff in Peru's Sacred Valley.

Bonne Terre Mine, Missouri, U.S.A.

Scuba dive to your heart's content in this flooded underground lead mine—now the world's largest freshwater dive resort.

Or do you prefer your weirdness up close?

INTERNATIONAL PEDAL POWER

Want to go on a bike ride? With some one billion bicycles on the road worldwide, bikes are one of the most popular ways to get around. Strap on your helmet and pedal your way around 10 of the most bike-friendly cities in Europe.

1. UTRECHT, NETHERLANDS

2. MÜNSTER, GERMANY

3. ANTWERP, BELGIUM

4. COPENHAGEN, DENMARK

5. AMSTERDAM, NETHERLANDS

6. MALMÖ, SWEDEN

7. BERN, SWITZERLAND

8. BREMEN, GERMANY

9. HANOVER, GERMANY

10. STRASBOURG, FRANCE

91.5% of American households have a car, but only **half** have a **bike.**

EUROPE

THE COLOR OF THE BOX BEHIND EACH NUMBER MATCHES THE COLOR OF ITS LOCATION TAG.

Bizarre EVENTS

Aside from being the fastest, competitors can also pick up prizes for having the cleanest and most realistic-looking outhouses.

MEXICO CITY'S SUMMER CELEBRATION

WHAT: Kermit Salutes Statue
WHERE: Mexico City, Mexico
WHY IT'S BIZARRE: It's easy being green when you're the star of the parade. A giant Kermit the Frog balloon floated by the capital's famous Angel of Independence monument as part of a parade to welcome summer. The Muppet was joined by the likes of Mickey Mouse and Spider-Man. Who knew frogs could fly?

OUTHOUSE RACE

WHAT: Skiing Toilet
WHERE: Anchorage, Alaska, U.S.A.
WHY IT'S BIZARRE: This event brings new meaning to "potty training." Alaska's most populous city hosts a winter festival each year to celebrate the state's history. A crowd favorite is the outhouse race in which residents paint outhouses, or outdoor bathrooms, before pushing them through town on skis. Wonder if the prize is a golden plunger?

INTERNATIONAL PILLOW FIGHT DAY

WHAT: Attack of the Feathers
WHERE: Budapest, Hungary
WHY IT'S BIZARRE: Feathers fly as a massive crowd bops each other with pillows. Many cities participate in the April event, held to encourage people to get off their rumps and play.

Down pillows are discouraged in some cities because they make too much of a mess.

THE ORIGINAL 7 WONDERS of the WORLD

More than 2,000 years ago, many travelers wrote about sights they had seen on their journeys. Over time, seven of those places made history as the "wonders of the ancient world." There are seven because the Greeks, who made the list, believed the number seven to be magical.

THE PYRAMIDS OF GIZA, EGYPT
BUILT: ABOUT 2600 B.C.
MASSIVE TOMBS OF EGYPTIAN PHARAOHS LIE INSIDE THIS ANCIENT WONDER—THE ONLY ONE STILL STANDING TODAY.

HANGING GARDENS OF BABYLON, IRAQ
BUILT: DATE UNKNOWN
LEGEND HAS IT THAT THIS GARDEN PARADISE WAS PLANTED ON AN ARTIFICIAL MOUNTAIN, BUT MANY EXPERTS SAY IT NEVER REALLY EXISTED.

TEMPLE OF ARTEMIS AT EPHESUS, TÜRKİYE
BUILT: SIXTH CENTURY B.C.
THIS TOWERING TEMPLE WAS BUILT TO HONOR ARTEMIS, THE GREEK GODDESS OF THE HUNT.

STATUE OF ZEUS, GREECE
BUILT: FIFTH CENTURY B.C.
THIS 40-FOOT (12-M) STATUE DEPICTED THE KING OF THE GREEK GODS.

MAUSOLEUM AT HALICARNASSUS, TÜRKİYE
BUILT: FOURTH CENTURY B.C.
THIS ELABORATE TOMB WAS BUILT FOR KING MAUSOLUS.

COLOSSUS OF RHODES, RHODES (AN ISLAND IN THE AEGEAN SEA)
BUILT: FOURTH CENTURY B.C.
THE 110-FOOT (34-M) STATUE HONORED THE GREEK SUN GOD HELIOS.

LIGHTHOUSE OF ALEXANDRIA, EGYPT
BUILT: THIRD CENTURY B.C.
THE WORLD'S FIRST LIGHTHOUSE, IT USED MIRRORS TO REFLECT SUNLIGHT FOR MILES OUT TO SEA.

THE NEW 7 WONDERS of the WORLD

Why name new wonders of the world? Most of the original ancient wonders no longer exist. To be eligible for the new list, the wonders had to be human-made before the year 2000 and in preservation. They were selected through a poll of more than 100 million voters!

TAJ MAHAL, INDIA
COMPLETED: 1648
THIS LAVISH TOMB WAS BUILT AS A FINAL RESTING PLACE FOR MUMTAZ MAHAL, THE BELOVED WIFE OF EMPEROR SHAH JAHAN.

PETRA, SOUTHWEST JORDAN
COMPLETED: ABOUT 200 B.C.
SOME 30,000 PEOPLE ONCE LIVED IN THIS ROCK CITY CARVED INTO CLIFF WALLS.

MACHU PICCHU, PERU
COMPLETED: ABOUT 1450
OFTEN CALLED THE "LOST CITY IN THE CLOUDS," MACHU PICCHU IS PERCHED 7,710 FEET (2,350 M) HIGH IN THE ANDES.

THE COLOSSEUM, ITALY
COMPLETED: A.D. 80
WILD ANIMALS—AND HUMANS—FOUGHT EACH OTHER TO THE DEATH BEFORE 50,000 SPECTATORS IN THIS ARENA.

CHRIST THE REDEEMER STATUE, BRAZIL
COMPLETED: 1931
TOWERING ATOP CORCOVADO MOUNTAIN, THIS STATUE IS TALLER THAN A 12-STORY BUILDING AND WEIGHS ABOUT 2.5 MILLION POUNDS (1.1 MILLION KG).

CHICHÉN ITZÁ, MEXICO
COMPLETED: 10TH CENTURY
ONCE THE CAPITAL CITY OF THE ANCIENT MAYA EMPIRE, CHICHÉN ITZÁ IS HOME TO THE FAMOUS PYRAMID OF KUKULCÁN.

GREAT WALL OF CHINA, CHINA
COMPLETED: 1644
THE LONGEST HUMAN-MADE STRUCTURE EVER BUILT, IT WINDS OVER AN ESTIMATED 4,500 MILES (7,200 KM).

QUIZ WHIZ

Is your geography knowledge off the map? Quiz yourself to find out!

Write your answers on a piece of paper. Then check them below.

1 Scientists sent a robot to follow penguins in _____ so they could learn how climate change affects animals there.

a. Iceland
b. Russia
c. Argentina
d. Antarctica

2 Roughly how many one-horned rhinos live inside India's Kaziranga National Park?

a. 20
b. 200
c. 2,000
d. 20,000

3 **True or false?** The world's largest lily pads, found in Bolivia, grow to be as wide as a garage door.

4 Ireland's Blarney Castle has a stone that visitors _____ for luck.

a. hug
b. kiss
c. toss
d. kick

5 The water of Canada's _____ evaporates in the summer, leaving behind small mineral pools.

a. Leopard Lake
b. Dalmatian Lake
c. Polka Lake
d. Spotted Lake

Not **STUMPED** yet? Check out the *NATIONAL GEOGRAPHIC KIDS QUIZ WHIZ* collection for more fun **GEOGRAPHY** questions!

ANSWERS: 1. d; 2. c; 3. True; 4. b; 5. d

HOMEWORK HELP

Finding Your Way Around

LATITUDE AND LONGITUDE lines help us determine locations on Earth. Every place on Earth has a special address called absolute location. Imaginary lines called lines of latitude run west to east, parallel to the Equator. These lines measure distance in degrees north or south from the Equator (0° latitude) to the North Pole (90° N) or to the South Pole (90° S). One degree of latitude is approximately 70 miles (113 km).

Lines of longitude run north to south, meeting at the poles. These lines measure distance in degrees east or west from 0° longitude (prime meridian) to 180° longitude. The prime meridian runs through Greenwich, England.

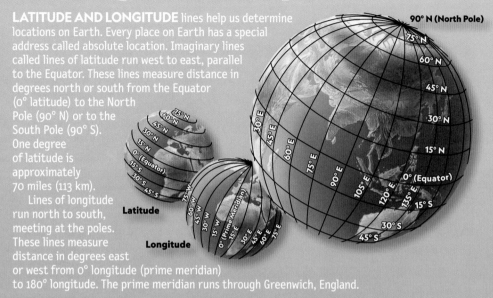

Latitude

Longitude

ABSOLUTE LOCATION. Suppose you are using latitude and longitude to play a game of global scavenger hunt. The clue says the prize is hidden at absolute location 30° S, 60° W. You know that the first number is south of the Equator, and the second is west of the prime meridian. On the map at right, find the line of latitude labeled 30° S. Now find the line of longitude labeled 60° W. Trace these lines with your fingers until they meet. Identify this spot. The prize must be located in northern Argentina (see arrow, right).

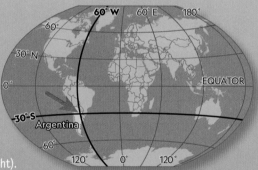

CHALLENGE!

1. Look at the map of Africa on pp. 280–281. Which country can you find at 10° S, 20° E?

2. Look at the map of Asia on pp. 288–289. Which country can you find at 20° N, 80° E?

3. On the map of Europe on pp. 296–297, which country is found at 50° N, 30° E?

4. Look at the map of North America on pp. 300–301. Which country can you find at 20° N, 100° W?

ANSWERS: 1. Angola; 2. India; 3. Ukraine; 4. Mexico

GAME ANSWERS

Shivering Shapes
page 130
1. narwhals
2. Atlantic puffin
3. royal penguin
4. polar bear

What in the World?
page 132

Top row: fish, bird eggs, cheetah
Middle row: deer, frog, mushroom
Bottom row: beetle, lily, squid

Find the Hidden Animals
page 134
1. C, 2. A, 3. D, 4. E, 5. B

Stump Your Parents
page 136
1. C, 2. C, 3. B, 4. B, 5. A, 6. A, 7. A, 8. D, 9. C, 10. C

Signs of the Times
page 137
Signs 1 and 6 are fake.

What in the World?
page 138

Top row: cloud, rope, leaf
Middle row: flower, islands, potato
Bottom row: marine worm, ravioli,
                      door handle

What in the World?
page 141

Top row: ruler, water fountain, eraser
Middle row: ballpoint pen, school bus,
                      combination lock
Bottom row: scissors, backpack,
                      pencil sharpener

Stump Your Parents
page 142
1. A, 2. A, 3. C, 4. B, 5. B, 6. D, 7. B, 8. B, 9. C, 10. D

Find the Hidden Animals
page 144
1. D, 2. A, 3. E, 4. B, 5. C

What in the World?
page 145

Top row: doughnut, guitar, Swiss cheese
Middle row: rabbit hole, inner tube,
                      keyhole
Bottom row: cereal, honeycomb,
                      golf hole

Want to Learn More?

Find more information about topics in this book in these National Geographic Kids resources.

Weird But True! series

Just Joking series

5,000 Awesome Facts (About Everything!) series

1,000 Facts series

Critter Chat
Rosemary Mosco
May 2022

Ultimate Book of the Future
Stephanie Warren Drimmer
June 2022

Break Down
Mara Grunbaum
August 2022

Weird But True! World 2024
National Geographic Kids
August 2023

The Ultimate Book of Reptiles
Ruchira Somaweera and Stephanie Warren Drimmer
August 2023

Not-So-Common Cents
Sarah Wassner Flynn
January 2023

That's Fact-tastic!
National Geographic Kids
February 2023

How to Survive in the Age of Dinosaurs
Stephanie Warren Drimmer
April 2023

Abbreviations:
AL: Alamy Stock Photo; AS: Adobe Stock; BI: Bridgeman Images; DS: Dreamstime; GI: Getty Images; IS: iStockphoto; MP: Minden Pictures; NGIC: National Geographic Image Collection; SS: Shutterstock; WHHA: White House Historical Association

All Maps
By National Geographic

Front Cover
Franco Tempesta/National Geographic Partners, LLC

Spine
Franco Tempesta/National Geographic Partners, LLC

Back Cover
(Earth), ixpert/SS; (butterfly), Steven Russell Smith/AL; (penguin), USO/IS/GI; (Icarus), Javier Espila; (dinosaur), Franco Tempesta/National Geographic Partners, LLC

Front Matter (2-7)
2-3, Sylvain Cordier/Biosphoto; 5,(A) AP Photo/Sunday Alamba; 5,(B), Robert Clark/NGIC; 5,(C) Manoj Shah/GI; 5,(D) elen31/AS; 5 (E), Science RF/AS; 6,(UP LE) Thomas Barwick/GI; 6,(UP RT) Alexander Raths/AS; 6,(UP CTR LE) Stefan Cioata/GI; 6,(UP CTR RT) Jim Paillot; 6,(LO CTR LE) Surender/AS; 6,(LO CTR RT) Hurst Photo/SS; 6,(LO LE) Sollina Images/GI; 6 (LO RT), Karrrtinki/AS; 7,(UP LE) KOTO/AS; 7,(UP RT), JAXA/ISS/NASA; 7,(UP CTR LE) Damocean/GI; 7, (UP CTR RT) Ivan Kmit/AS; 7,(LO CTR LE) freeartist/AL; 7,(LO LE) Artur Debat/GI

Your World 2025 (8-17)
8-9, AP Photo/Sunday Alamba; 10 (UP), Angela Weiss/AFP/GI; 10 (LO), dennisjacobsen/AS; 11 (UP), Susannah Ireland/Reuters; 11 (LO), U.S. Navy; 12 (UP,INSET), The AGE/GI; 12 (UP), Phil Walter/GI; 12 (LO LE), Charles Helm/SWNS; 12 (LO RT), Charles Helm/SWNS; 13 (UP), Sanjay Kanojia/GI; 13 (CTR), Abir Sultan/EPA-EFE/SS; 13 (LO LE), Christopher Furlong/GI; 13 (LO RT), Amir Cohen/Reuters; 14 (UP LE), Alex Wong/GI; 14 (UP RT), Amanda Andrade-Rhoades/The Washington Post/GI; 14 (LO), Sezeryadigar/GI; 15 (UP), Audun Rikardsen/NGIC; 15 (CTR), Audun Rikardsen/NGIC; 15 (LO), Bai Xuefei/Xinhua/GI; 16 (A), Jak Wonderly; 16 (B), Mike Flippo/SS; 16 (C), nate samui/SS; 16 (D), Vladimir Sukhachev/SS; 16 (E), Jackson Pearson/AS; 16 (F), Eric Isselée/AS; 16 (G), photastic/SS; 16,(H) Somchai Som/SS; 16 (I), radko68/AS; 17 (UP RT) Matthew Modoono/Northeastern University; 17 (CTR RT), Matthew Modoono/Northeastern University; 17 (CTR LE), Chrispo/AS; 17,(LO), Amanda Quezada

Greatest Breakthroughs (18-33)
18-19, Robert Clark/NGIC; 20, ktsdesign/AS; 21 (UP), Kaspars Grinvalds/AS; 21 (CTR), Michael Rosskothen/AS 21 (LO), Franco Tempesta/National Geographic Partners; 22 (UP), Smith Collection/Gado/GI; 22 (CTR), David McNew/Mario Tama/GI; 22 (LO), Vera Kuttelvaserova/AS 23 (UP), ArgitopIA/AS; 23 (CTR RT), NG Maps; 23 (LO LE) Robert Clark/NGIC; 24 (UP), Robert Clark/NGIC; 24 (UP,INSET) Mark Thiessen/National Geographic Partners, LLC; 24 (LO), Mathabela Tsikoane; 25 (UP), Lee Berger; 25 (CTR), Mark Thiessen/NGIC; 25 (LO LE), Lee Berger; 25 (LO

RT), Robert Clark/NGIC; 26-27 (ALL), Lee Berger; 28 (UP), NASA GSFC/CIL/Adriana Manrique Gutierrez; 28 (LO LE), NASA/JPL-Caltech (K. Miller/IPAC); 28 (LO RT), NASA/Chris Gunn; 29 (UP LE), NASA/Desiree Stover; 29 (UP RT), rsooll/SS; 29 (CTR), NASA/ESA/CSA/STScI; 29 (LO LE), NASA/Chris Gunn; 29 (LO RT), NASA/JPL/Space Science Institute; 30-31, Lori Epstein/Nat Geo Staff; 32 (UP LE), ktsdesign/AS; 32 (CTR RT), Vera Kuttelvaserova/AS; 32 (LO RT), NASA GSFC/CIL/Adriana Manrique Gutierrez; 32 (LO LE), Mathabela Tsikoane; 33 (UP RT), Alb0003/SS

Amazing Animals (34-85)
34-35, Manoj Shah/GI; 36 (UP), PetlinDmitry/SS; 36 (LO), Claire Simeone/The Marine Mammal Center; 37 (UP), Newstead Country Preschool; 37 (LO), Zaheer Ali; 38 (UP), Lisa Basile Ellwood/SS; 38 (CTR LE), Brian E Kushner/SS; 38 (CTR RT), AP Photo/Barry Reeger; 38 (LO), OceanFishing/GI; 39 (UP), Dean MacAdam; 39 (CTR), Dean MacAdam; 39 (LO), Dean MacAdam; 40 (UP RT), Wild Wonders of Europe/Zankl/Nature Picture Library; 40 (UP LE) Vicki Jauron/Babylon and Beyond Photography/GI; 40 (LO LE), KenCanning/GI; 41 (UP LE), Suzi Eszterhas/MP; 41 (UP RT), Richard McManus/GI; 41 (CTR LE), sergioboccardo/GI; 41 (LO), Vitalii Kalutskyi/GI; 42 (UP), Joseph Tepper; 42 (CTR), slow-motiongli/AS; 42 (LO LE), Joe Blossom/AL; 42 (LO RT), Karel Zahradka/SS; 43 (UP RT), Fiona McAllister Photography/GI; 43 (CTR LE), Christian Musat/SS; 43 (CTR RT), Roni Kurniawan/EyeEm/GI; 43 (LO), creativenature/AS; 44 (UP), Dani Vincek/SS; 44 (CTR), DioGen/SS; 44 (LO), Nick Garbutt; 45 (UP RT), Kant Liang/EyeEm/GI; 45 (UP RT), reptiles4all/SS; 45 (CTR), Hiroya Minakuchi/MP; 45 (CTR RT), FP media/SS; 45 (LO), Ziva_K/IS/GI; 46 (CTR), Dan Costa/University of California Santa Cruz; 46 (LO), Sara Labrousse WAPITI cruise JR16004; 47, Florida Power and Light; 48-49, Blue Ridge Wildlife Center; 50, Fred Olivier/NPL/MP; 51 (UP), Jay Dickman/GI; 51 (LO), Breck P. Kent/Animals Animals/Earth Scenes/NGIC; 52 (UP), Blue Planet Archive/Scubazoo/Jason Isley; 52 (LO LE), Niels van Gijn/GI; 52 (LO RT), talseN/SS; 53 (UP LE), Tom McHugh/Science Source; 53 (UP RT), Christian Ziegler/MP/NGIC; 53 (CTR LE), Helen E. Grose/DS; 53 (CTR RT), Auscape/GI; 53 (LO), Alex Mustard/Nature Picture Library; 54 (UP RT), Paul Nicklen/GI; 54 (UP CTR), Paul Nicklen/NGIC; 54 (LO CTR), Flip Nicklin/MP; 54 (LO RT), Russ Kinne/age fotostock; 54 (BACKGROUND), Paul Nicklen/NGIC; 55, Emily M. Eng/NG Staff; 56 (UP), WaterFrame/AL; 56 (CTR), Andy Murch/Blue Planet Archive; 56 (LO), David Gruber; 57 (UP), Masa Ushioda/Blue Planet Archive; 57 (CTR), Saul Gonor/Blue Planet Archive; 57 (LO), Richard Carey/AS; 58, Edward Myles/MP; 59 (UP), Claudio Contreras/MP; 59 (LO), Claudio Contreras/MP; 60, Stefanie Schweers/Zoo Krefeld; 61 (UP), Kildare Animal Foundation; 61 (LO), Kildare Animal Foundation; 62 (UP), Suzi Eszterhas/MP; 62 (CTR LE), Sumio Harada/MP; 62 (CTR RT), Charlie Summers/MP; 62 (LO), Jeff Foott/MP; 63 (UP LE), Konrad Wothe/MP; 63 (UP RT), Gary Bell/Oceanwide/MP; 63 (UP CTR), Robert Canis/MP; 63 (CTR LE), Sarah Cusser; 63 (CTR RT), Steven Kazlowski/MP; 63 (LO), Hiroya Minakuchi/MP; 64 (UP), Andrew Walmsley/Nature Picture Library; 64 (LO), Andrew Walmsley/Nature Picture Library/AL; 65, Michael Durham/MP; 66-67, Alejandro Mesa; 68, Andy Rouse/Nature Picture Library; 69 (snow leopard fur), Eric Isselee/SS; 69 (lion), Eric Isselée/SS; 69 (tiger), Eric Isselée/SS; 69 (leopard), Eric Isselée/SS; 69 (jaguar), DLILLC/Corbis/GI; 69 (lion fur), Eric Isselée/SS; 69 (leopard fur), WitR/SS; 69

(tiger fur), Kesu/SS; 69 (jaguar fur), worldswild-lifewonders/SS; 69 (snow leopard), Eric Isselee/SS; 70 (LE), Gerard Lacz/Science Source; 70 (CTR), FionaAyerst/GI; 70 (RT), Suzi Eszterhas/MP; 71 (UP), Henner Damke/AS; 71 (CTR LE), Nick Garbutt/MP; 71 (LO LE), Kris Wiktor/SS; 71 (LO RT), Jak Wonderly/NGIC; 72-73, Nichole Sobecki/NGIC; 74 (UP LE), age fotostock/SuperStock; 74 (UP RT), smrm1977/GI; 74 (LO LE), Eva Blanco/EyeEm/GI; 74 (LO RT), Corbis/SuperStock; 75 (UP), Ocean Walker; 75 (UP CTR), Ole Jorgen Liodden/Nature Picture Library; 75 (LO CTR), Rolf Kopfle/Ardea; 75 (LO RT), Falcon1708/DS; 76 (UP), Chris Butler/Science Source; 76 (LO), Christian Jegou/Science Source; 76 (LO), Pixeldust Studios/NGIC; 77 (A), Christian Jegou/Science Source; 77 (B), Laurie O'Keefe/Science Source; 77 (C), Chris Butler/Science Source; 77 (D), Christian Jegou/Science Source; 77 (E), Chase Studio/Science Source; 78 (UP), Christian Ziegler; 78 (LO LE), John Flynn/Rodolfo Salas Gismondi; 78 (LO RT), Anjali Goswami/Rodolfo Salas Gismondi; 79 (UP LE), John Flynn/Rodolfo Salas Gismondi; 79 (UP RT), Rodolfo Salas Gismondi; 79 (LO LE), Rodolfo Salas Gismondi; 79 (LO RT), Rodolfo Salas Gismondi; 80 (UP), Franco Tempesta; 80 (LO), Franco Tempesta; 81 (ALL), Franco Tempesta/National Geographic Partners, LLC; 82, Davide Bonadonna; 83 (UP), Davide Bonadonna; 83 (LO), Davide Bonadonna; 84 (UP), OceanFishing/GI; 84 (CTR), Dean MacAdam; 84 (LO), Franco Tempesta/National Geographic Partners, LLC; 85, GOLFX/SS

Space and Earth (86-107)
86-87, elen31/AS; 88, NASA/Goddard/SDO; 89, Alexander Rieber/EyeEm/GI; 90-91, David Aguilar; 92 (Eris), David Aguilar; 92 (Pluto), NASA/JHUAPL/SwRI; 92 (Haumea), David Aguilar; 93 (UP), L. Medeiros/Institute for Advanced Study, D. Psaltis/Georgia Tech, T. Lauer/NSF's NOIRLab, F. Ozel/Georgia Tech; 93 (LO), Joe Rocco; 94 (UP LE), Evan Dalen/Stocksy/AS; 94 (UP RT), cosmicvue/AS; 94 (LO LE), Peter/AS; 94 (LO RT), Tandem Stock/AS; 95 (UP), Mark Garlick/Science Source; 95 (CTR), Keenpress/NGIC; 95 (LO), Science RF/AS; 96, Mondolithic Studios Inc; 97, Allexxandar/IS/GI; 98 (UP), NGIC; 98 (LO), Joe Rocco; 99 (gneiss), Dirk Wiersma/Science Source; 99 (halite), Theodore Clutter/Science Source; 99 (andesite), MarekPhotoDesign/AS; 99 (UP), Ralph Lee Hopkins/NGIC; 99 (granite), Iosmandarinas/SS; 99 (mica), Yeso58 Montree Nanta/SS; 99 (limestone), Charles D. Winters/Science Source; 100 (UP LE), raiwa/IS; 100 (UP RT), MarcelC/IS; 100 (CTR RT), Anatoly Maslennikov/SS; 100 (LO LE), Albert Russ/SS; 100 (LO RT), IS; 101 (topaz), Igorkali/DS; 101 (calcite), Kazakovmaksim/DS; 101 (corundum), oldeez/DS; 101 (apatite), Ingemar Magnusson/DS; 101 (orthoclase), Joel Arem/Science Source; 101 (gold), didyk/IS; 101 (gypsum), Meetchum/DS; 101 (fluorite), Albertruss/DS; 101 (diamond), 123dartist/DS; 101 (microcline), Mark A. Schneider/Science Source; 101 (talc), Ben Johnson/Science Source; 102, Frank Ippolito; 103 (LO RT), NG Maps; 103 (UP LE), Gary Fiegehen/All Canada Photos/Alamy; 103 (UP RT), Salvatore Gebbia/NGIC; 103 (CTR LE), NASA/JSC; 103 (CTR RT), Diane Cook & Len Jenshel/NGIC; 104, Robert Madden/NGIC; 105 (UP LE), Peng Zhuang/DS; 105 (UP RT), Jorge Santos/agefotostock/AL; 105 (LO), Don C. Powell/Yellowstone National Park Ranger Naturalist Service/Library of Congress; 106,(UP LE) Charles D. Winters/Science Source; 106 (UP RT), Joe Rocco; 106 (LO LE), Peng Zhuang/DS; 106 (LO RT), raiwa/IS; 107, pixhook/E+/GI

Awesome Exploration (108–127)

108-109, Thomas Barwick/GI; 110 (UP LE), Anna Sedneva/AS; 110 (UP RT), Allyson Shaw; 110 (CTR RT), khuruzero/AS; 110 (LO LE), Ursula Page/AS; 110 (LO RT), Monty Rakusen/GI; 111 (UP), kotijelly/GI; 111 (CTR), Alexander Raths/AS; 111 (LO), Skip Brown/NGIC; 112 (UP LE), Sreerag Krishnan; 112 (UP RT), Anton van Niekerk; 112 (UP CTR LE), Tselane Rebotile Rachuene; 112 (UP CTR), Matt Pretorius; 112 (CTR LE), Ha Hoang; 112 (LO), Anton van Niekerk; 113 (UP LE), Matt Biddulph; 113 (UP CTR), Matt Biddulph; 113 (UP RT), Randall Scott/NGIC; 113 (CTR), Nora Shawki; 113 (CTR RT), Nora Shawki; 113 (LO LE), Hagai Nativ/The Morris Kahn Marine Research Station; 113 (LO RT), Dror Vardimon/Ashdod Maritime Education Center; 114 (ALL), Joel Sartore/National Geographic Photo Ark/NGIC; 115 (UP LE), Joel Sartore/National Geographic Photo Ark/NGIC; 115 (UP RT), Michel and Christine Denis-Huot/MP; 115 (CTR LE), Suzi Eszterhas/MP; 115 (LO CTR RT), Pete Oxford/MP; 115 (LO LE), Joel Sartore/National Geographic Photo Ark/NGIC; 115 (LO RT), Glenn Bartley/MP; 116 (UP RT), Pablo Cerqueira; 116 (CTR LE), Washington Wachira; 116 (CTR RT), Washington Wachira; 116 (LO), Washington Wachira; 117 (UP LE), Marcelo Sturaro & Pedro Peloso; 117 (fish), Luiz Rocha/California Academy of Sciences; 117 (lizard), Eric N. Smith, Ph.D.; 117 (tree), Lorna Mackinnon/RBG KEW; 117 (dinosaur), Sergey Krasovskiy/Stocktrek Images/Science Source; 117 (CTR LE), Pedro Peloso; 117 LO LE), Pedro Peloso; 117 (LO CTR), Adriano Maciel; 117 (LO RT), Mirian Tsuchiya; 118 (UP), Steve Winter/NGIC; 118 (LO), Jay Fleming; 119 (UP), Paul Nicklen/NGIC; 119 (LO), Birgitte Wilms/MP; 120 (LE), Gabby Wild; 120 (UP RT), Rebecca Hale/NG Staff; 120 (LO RT), Theo Allofs/MP; 121, Nicolas McComber/GI; 122 (UP), Frank Hurley/Royal Geographical Society via GI; 122 (CTR), Frank Hurley/Scott Polar Research Institute, University of Cambridge/GI; 122 (LO), Frank Hurley/Scott Polar Research Institute, University of Cambridge/GI; 123 (UP LE), Falklands Maritime Heritage Trust; 123 (UP RT), Falklands Maritime Heritage Trust; 124 (UP), Mark Thiessen/National Geographic Partners, LLC; 124 (CTR), Lee Berger; 124 (LO), Robert Clark/NGIC; 125 (A), bestv/SS; 125 (B), BearFotos/SS; 125 (C), Ajn/DS; 125 (D), Twin Design/SS; 125 (E), MR Vector/AS; 125 (F), charles taylor/SS; 126 (LE), Frank Hurley/Scott Polar Research Institute, University of Cambridge/GI; 126 (UP LE), Joel Sartore/National Geographic Photo Ark/NGIC; 126 (UP RT), khuruzero/AS; 126 (LO RT), Luiz Rocha/California Academy of Sciences; 127, Grady Reese/IS

Fun and Games (128–147)

128-129, Stefan Cioata/GI; 130 (UP LE), Flip Nicklin/MP; 130 (UP RT), Guy Bryant/AS; 130 (LO LE), Galaxiid/GI; 130 (LO RT), Wayne Lynch/AllCanadaPhotos/AS; 131 (UP RT), Fiona M. Donnelly/SS; 131 (skunk), bobloblaw/GI; 131 (salamander), Nigel Bean/MP; 131 (mole), Ken Catania; 131 (owl), Gerry Ellis/MP; 131 (kit lessons), Don Johnston_WU/AL; 131 (owl chicks), Diane McAllister/MP; 131 (baby salamander), Custom Life Science Images/AL; 131 (skunk spray), Yuval Helfman/AL; 131 (emojis), Turgay Malikli/SS; 131 (skunk log), Cordier Sylvain/hemis.fr/AL; 132 (fish), Jones & Shimlock/Jaynes Gallery/DanitaDelimont; 132 (eggs), Duncan Usher/Foto Natura/MP; 132 (cheetah), Lookingforcats/SS; 132 (deer), Lars Persson/Naturbild/Corbis; 132 (frog), Thomas Marent/ARDEA; 132 (mushroom), Per Grunditz/EyeEm/GI; 132 (beetle), Pascal Goetgheluck/ARDEA; 132 (flower), IndexStock/SuperStock; 132 (squid), Jones-Shimlock/Jaynes Gallery/DanitaDelimont; 133 (UP), Dan Sipple; 133 (LO), Dan Sipple; 134 (A), Piotr Naskrecki/MP; 134 (B), Pete Oxford/MP; 134 (C), Gary Bell/Oceanwide/MP; 134 (D), Thomas Marent/MP; 134 (E), Mark Carwardine/MP; 135 (UP RT), Zizza Gordon-Panama Wildlife/AL; 135 (anteater), Michael and Patricia Fogden/MP; 135 (eagle), Lee Dalton/AL; 135 (ocelot), Pete Oxford/MP; 135 (anaconda), gerard lacz/AL; 135 (seed pod), Akima Futura/AL; 135 (anaconda smelling), Tony Crocetta/MP; 136 (UP LE), Jean-Pierre Clatot/AFP/GI; 136 (UP RT), Gerry Ellis/MP; 136 (CTR LE), Warpaintcobra/GI; 136 (CTR RT), weisschr/GI; 136 (LO LE), Vsevolod Vlasenko/GI; 136 (LO RT), Theo Allofs/MP; 137 (one), Igor Stevanovic/AL; 137 (two), Nick Scott plaques/sign photos/AL; 137 (three), Westend61/GI; 137 (four), Norbert Wu/Corbis; 137 (five), Reinhard Krull/GI; 137 (six), azmanq/SS; 137 (seven), I L/DS; 138 (clouds), Yuji Sakai/GI; 138 (rope), Roman Sigaev/SS; 138 (leaf), MIMAGES/Alamy; 138 (flower), Loskutnikov/SS; 138 (islands), Pablo Scapinachis/Arquiplay77/DS; 138 (potato), Ira Heuvelman-Dobrolyub/GI; 138 (worm), Chris Newbert/MP; 138 (ravioli), Ron Sumners/Sumnersgraphicsinc/DS; 138 (door), Samantha Carrirolo/GI; 139 (UP), Jim Paillot; 139 (LO), Jim Paillot; 140 (UP RT), Steven Gnam; 140 (wolverine), Steven Gnam; 140 (falcon), Shattil and Rozinski/MP; 140 (caribou), Mark Raycroft/MP; 140 (ground squirrel), Donald M. Jones/MP; 140 (emojis), Turgay Malikli/SS; 140 (swimming caribou), Donald M. Jones/MP; 140 (climbing wolverine), Steven Gnam/NGIC; 140 (gyrfalcon nest), Ian McCarthy/MP; 141 (ruler), Stockbyte/Photolibrary; 141 (water fountain), Rob Casey/GI; 141 (eraser), Dynamic Graphics/Creatas Images/Jupiterimages; 141 (pen), Christopher Scott/Alamy; 141 (bus), Stockagogo Photos/SS; 141 (lock), HomeStudio/SS; 141 (scissors), Image Source Black/Jupiterimages; 141 (backpack), Fuse/Corbis; 141 (pencil sharpener), PhotosIndia/AL; 142 (UP RT), Mitsuaki Iwago/MP; 142 (UP LE), tom pfeiffer/AL 142 (CTR LE), Burcu Atalay Tankut/GI; 142 (CTR RT), pelooyen/AS; 142 (LO LE), HeresTwoPhotography/AS; 142 (LO CTR), mr_piboon/GI; 142 (LO RT), AJ Pics/AL; 143 (UP), Jason Tharp; 143 (UP CTR), James Yamasaki; 143 (LO), Jason Tharp; 144 (A), Vicki Jauron, Babylon and Beyond Photography/GI; 144 (B), Nick Garbutt/MP; 144 (C), Roland Seitre/MP; 144 (D), Sirachai Arunrugstichai/GI; 144 (E), Tui De Roy/MP; 145 (doughnut), Pablo631/DS; 145 (guitar), Christian Bridgwater/Rigsby8131/DS; 145 (cheese), Eyewave/DS; 145 (rabbit hole), Yin Jian Ng/Zen/DS; 145 (inner tube), Tombaky/DS; 145 (keyhole), Eutoch/DS; 145 (cereal), PhotoPaper/SS; 145 (honeycomb), Mihail Orlov/Oma/DS; 145 (golf hole), Chris.g.wood/DS; 146-147, Strika Entertainment

Laugh Out Loud (148–163)

148-149, Surender/AS; 150 (UP LE), franticoo/SS; 150 (CTR LE), Paranamir/SS; 150 (CTR RT), Paranamir/SS; 150 (LO LE), gorosan/SS 150 (LO RT), Sandra van der Steen/SS; 151 (UP LE), Loic Poidevin/Nature Picture Library; 151 (UP RT), fabrice cahez/Nature Picture Library; 151 (LO), Hermann Brehm/Nature Picture Library; 152, Paul/AS; 154 (UP), Tambako the Jaguar/GI; 154 (LO), Karine Aigner/Staff; 155 (ALL), Chris Ware; 157 (UP LE), bidala/AS; 157 (UP RT), Julio Ricco/AS; 157 (CTR LE), supamas/AS; 157 (CTR), Jagodka/SS; 157 (CTR RT), sommai/AS; 157 (LO LE), Hurst Photo/SS; 157 (LO RT), Fernando Gregory/DS; 158, JoffreyM/SS; 159 (ALL), Jean Galvão; 160 (UP LE), Sudpoth Sirirattanasakul/SS; 160 (UP RT), exopixel/SS; 160 (CTR LE), posteriori/SS; 160 (CTR), Warongdech/SS; 160 (CTR RT), VGstockstudio/SS; 160 (LO), VGstockstudio/SS; 161 (LO LE), Anan Kaewkhammul/SS; 161 (LO RT), GoodFocused/SS; 161 (BACKGROUND), Victor Lapaev/SS; 162 (UP LE), tsuneomp/SS; 162 (UP RT), Anastasia_Panait/SS; 162 (propellers), Lyudmila Suvorova/SS; 162 (CTR LE), Photodisc; 162 (CTR LE background), ABCDstock/AS; 162 (CTR RT), Valentyna Chukhlyebova/SS; 162 (LO), Meinzahn/DS; 163 (UP LE), Dwi/AS; 163 (UP RT), Ryan/AS; 163 (CTR), rob2588/AS 163 (CTR RT), National Geographic Partners, LLC; 163 (LO LE), LN team/SS; 163 (LO RT), Andrea Izzotti/AS

Culture Connection (164–187)

164-165, Sollina Images/GI; 166 (A), CreativeNature/SS; 166 (B), Karrrtinki/AS; 166 (C), Kevin Foy/AL; 166 (D), vectorfusionart/AS; 166 (E), bildfokus/AS; 166 (F), Ju_see/AS; 166 (G), New Africa/AS; 167 (UP), Dinodia Photos; 167 (CTR), Zee/Alamy; 167 (LO), wacpan/SS; 168 (UP), Scott Keeler/Tampa Bay Times/Zuma Wire/AL; 168 (LO), Marie1969/SS; 169 (UP LE), VisitBritain/John Coutts/GI; 169 (UP RT), lev radin/SS; 169 (CTR LE), CR Shelare/GI; 169 (CTR RT), Viviane Ponti/GI; 169 (LO LE), epa european pressphoto agency b.v./AL; 169 (LO RT), Carol M. Highsmith/Library of Congress Prints and Photographs Division; 170 (throughout page), MaeW/SS; 171, Nalidsa/AL; 172, phive/SS; 172 (banner on page), StockImageFactory/SS; 173, Subir Basak/GI; 174 (UP LE), Gail Shumway/GI; 174 (UP RT), Steven Mark Needham/Corbis; 174 (LO LE), Nicolas Leser/Media Bakery; 174 (LO RT), James L. Stanfield/NGIC; 175 (UP LE), Biwa Studio/GI; 175 (CTR LE), StockFood/Foodfolio; 175 (CTR RT), age fotostock/SuperStock; 175 (LO), Exactostock/SuperStock; 176-177, Joe Rocco; 178 (UP LE), US Mint; 178 (UP RT), Stack's Bowers Galleries; 178 (CTR LE), US Mint; 178 (CTR RT), Milan/AS; 178 (LO LE), Yevgen Romanenko/GI; 178 (LO RT), Universal History Archive/Universal Images Group/GI 179 (UP LE), hueberto/GI; 179 (UP RT), pamela_d_mcadams/GI; 179 (UP CTR LE), marino bocelli/SS; 179 (UP CTR RT), © Bank of England; 179 (LO CTR LE), Mohamed Osama/DS; 179 (LO CTR RT), Nataly Studio/SS; 179 (LO LE), Colin Hampden-White 179 (LO RT), Kelley Miller/NGS Staff; 180 (UP RT), Ho Trung Lam; 180 (UP LE), Nguyen Dai Duong; 180 (LO LE), Mark Thiessen/National Geographic Partners; 180 (LO RT), Randall Scott/NGIC; 181 (UP LE), Jeremy Fahringer; 181 (UP RT), Mark Thiessen/NGIC; 181 (UP CTR LE), Robert Massee; 181 (UP CTR RT), Catherine Cofré; 181 (LO CTR LE), K. Bista; 181 (LO CTR RT), Mark Thiessen/NG Staff; 181 (LO LE), Jeevan Sunuwar Kirat; 181 (LO RT), Jeevan Sunuwar Kirat; 182, Nevena Tsvetanova/AL; 183 (UP), Lefteris_/GI; 183 (CTR), Bodor Tivadar/SS; 183 (LO), IanDagnall Computing/AL; 184 (UP), Randy Olson; 184 (LO LE), Martin Gray/NGIC; 184 (LO RT), Sam Panthaky/AFP/GI; 185 (UP), Abed Omar Qusini/Reuters; 185 (LO LE), Reza/NGIC; 185 (LO RT), Richard Nowitz/NGIC; 186 (UP), Bodor Tivadar/SS; 186 (UP LE), StockFood/Foodfolio; 186 (LO LE), Subir Basak/GI; 186 (LO RT), Milan/AS; 187 (UP LE), spatuletail/SS; 187 (UP RT), PictureLake E+/GI; 187 (CTR), cifotart/SS; 187 (LO), zydesign/SS

Science and Technology (188–211)

188-189, KOTO/AS; 190 (UP RT), Nippon News/

Aflo Co. Ltd./Alamy Live News; 190 (UP LE), JAXA/ISS/NASA; 190 (LO), Photo Japan/AL; 191 (UP LE), Christopher Jue- Nippon News/Aflo Co. Ltd./AL; 191 (UP RT), The Asahi Shimbun/GI; 191 (CTR LE), Ger Bosma/AL; 191 (CTR RT), r.kathesi/SS; 191 (LO LE), Makstorm/SS; 191 (LO RT), CB2/ZOB/WENN/Newscom; 192 (UP), Carnival Cruise Line; 192 (LO), BitOGenius; 193 (UP LE), OrCam Technologies; 193 (UP CTR), Cutecircuit; 193 (UP RT), The Sound Shirt by CuteCircuit Allows Hearing Impaired People to Feel Music; 193 (LO LE), Y-Brush; 193 (LO RT), Shenzhen Elephant Robotics Technology Co., Ltd; 194, Ted Kinsman/Science Source; 195 (protists), sgame/SS; 195 (1), Sebastian Kaulitzki/SS; 195 (2), Eye of Science/Science Source; 195 (3), Volker Steger/Christian Bardele/Photo Researchers Inc.; 195 (fungi), ancelpics/GI; 195 (plants), puwanai/SS; 195 (animals), kwest/SS; 196 (A), imageBROKER GmbH & Co. KG/NielsDK/AL; 196 (B), Richard Gardner/SS; 196 (C), Mark Moffett/MP; 196 (D), Katuhiko Motonaga; 196 (E), Ed Reschke/GI; 196 (F), Neil Lucas/MP; 196 (G), KPG-Payless2/SS; 197 (UP), David Tipling/MP; 197 (LO LE), Zen Rial/GI; 197 (LO CTR LE), Natural Garden Images/AL; 197 (LO CTR), jspix/imageBROKER/GmbH & Co. KG/AL; 197 (LO CTR RT), Paroli Galperti/REDA &CO srl/AL; 197 (LO RT), John Keates/AL; 198, SciePro/SS; 199 (CTR), Andrey_Kuzmin/SS; 200 (UP), Eric Isselee/SS; 200 (CTR), Alessandro Grandini/AS; 200 (LO), radub85/AS; 201 (UP LE), juan moyano/AL; 201 (UP RT), William West/AFP via GI; 201 (LO LE), VikramRaghuvanshi/GI; 201 (LO RT), Pasieka/Science Source; 202 (UP), WavebreakMediaMicro/AS; 202 (UP CTR), Rost9/SS; 202 (CTR RT), alswart/AS; 202 (CTR), Maxximmm/DS; 204 (UP), Patrick Endres/agefotostock; 204 (LO), allstars/SS; 205 (UP LE), Suzi Eszterhas/MP; 205 (UP RT), Chris Radburn/PA Images/AL; 205 (LO), Stefan Christmann/MP; 206-207, Mondolithic Studios; 208-209, Mondolithic Studios Inc; 210 (UP LE), JAXA/ISS/NASA; 210 (UP RT), David Tipling/MP; 210 (LO LE), Eye of Science/Science Source; 210 (LO RT), Neil Lucas/MP; 211, Klaus Vedfelt/GI

Wonders of Nature (212–235)

212-213, Damocean/GI; 214 (LE), AVTG/IS; 214 (RT), Brad Wynnyk/SS; 215 (UP LE), Rich Carey/SS; 215 (UP RT), Richard Walters/IS; 215 (LO LE), Karen Graham/IS; 215 (LO RT), Michio Hoshino/MP/NGIC; 216 (inset), Carsten Peter/SS; 216-217, Frank Krahmer/Corbis; 217 (ALL), Carsten Peter/NGIC; 218 (LE), cbpix/SS; 218 (RT), Mike Hill/Photographer's Choice/GI; 218-219 (BACKGROUND), Chris Anderson/SS; 218-219 (globes), NG Maps; 219 (CTR LE), Will Meinderts/Buiten-beeld/MP; 219 (CTR RT), Paul Nicklen/NGIC; 219 (LO RT), Jan Vermeer/MP; 220 (UP), Reinhard Dirscherl/GI; 220 (CTR RT), THP Creative/SS; 220 (LO LE), Gerald Nowak/GI; 221 (UP LE), doble-d/GI; 221 (UP RT), cordimages/GI; 221 (CTR LE), Fudio/GI; 221 (CTR RT), Bicho_raro/GI; 221 (LO LE), Kat Ka/SS; 221 (LO RT), ipeggas/GI; 221 (LO RT), Corbis/VCG/GI; 222 (UP), tobi-asjo/GI; 222 (LO), NG Maps; 223 (UP), Chasing Light-Photography by James Stone/GI; 223 (RT), James Balog/NGIC; 224 (UP LE), Wead/AS; 224 (A), Farinoza/DS; 224 (B), Valt Ahyppo/SS; 224 (C), reptiles4all/SS; 224 (D), Farinoza/DS; 224 (CTR RT), USFS Photo/AL; 224 (LO LE), Jim Reed/Science Source; 225 (UP LE), Nature and Science/AL; 225 (UP RT), Ivan Kmit/AS; 225 (CTR LE), OAR/National Undersea Research Program/World History Archive/AL; 225 (CTR RT), AP Photo/Norman Transcript/Mike Harmon; 225 (LO), Arctic-Images/Corbis; 226 (UP), Stuart Armstrong; 226 (LO), Franco Tempesta; 227 (1), Leonid Tit/SS; 227

(2), Frans Lanting/NGIC; 227 (3), Lars Christensen/SS; 227 (4), Daniel Loretto/SS; 227 (LO), Richard Peterson/SS; 228, Andrew Mayovskyy/SS; 229, arnold_oblistil/AS; 230, 3dmotus/SS; 231 (UP LE), Lori Mehmen/Associated Press; 231 (LO LE), Jim Reed; 231 (EFo), Susan Law Cain/SS; 231 (EF1), Brian Nolan/IS; 231 (EF2), Susan Law Cain/SS; 231 (EF3), Judy Kennamer/SS; 231 (EF4), jam4travel/SS; 231 (EF5), jam4travel/SS; 232 (A), U.S. Geological Survey; 232 (B), Drew Downs/Usgs/Zuma Press; 232 (C), AP Photo/The Yomiuri Shimbun; 232 (D), KYODO/Reuters; 233 (UP), Jouan Rius/MP; 233 (LO), Currumbin Wildlife Hospital; 234 (UP LE), Drew Downs/Usgs/Zuma Press; 234 (UP RT), Arctic-Images/Corbis; 234 (LO LE), AVTG/IS; 234 (LO RT), Paul Nicklen/NGIC

History Happens (236–267)

236-237, freeeartist/AL; 238-239, Gloria Felix; 240 (UP), Alice Brereton; 240 (LO), Alice Brereton; 241 (UP LE), Victor R. Boswell, Jr/NGIC; 241 (UP CTR), Aristidis Vafeiadakis/ZUMA Press; 241 (UP RT), Brett Seymour/ARGO via Greek Culture Ministry/AP Photo; 241 (CTR LE), Derek McLennan & Martin McSweeney/Reuters/Newscom; 241 (CTR RT), Xinhua/eyevine/Redux; 241 (LO LE), Franck Goddio/Hilti Foundation, photo: Jérôme Delafosse; 241 (LO CTR), Baz Ratner/Reuters; 241 (LO RT), Anglia Press Agency Ltd./REX; 241 (BACKGROUND), Israel Antiquities Authority/Xinhua News Agency/Newscom; 242 (LO LE), Robross/DS; 242 (LO RT), RJ Lerich/SS; 242-243 (UP CTR), Kenneth Garrett/NGIC; 243 (UP RT), Art of Life/SS; 243 (CTR RT), Michael DeFreitas/robertharding/AL; 244 (UP RT), Carmen Sanchez; 244 (CTR), Andrey Burmakin/SS; 244 (LO LE), Lisheng Chang/Wirestock/AS; 245 (UP RT), Carmen Sanchez; 245 (CTR), Edgars Sermulis/stoatphoto/AS; 245 (LO RT), Seregam/SS; 246 (UP LE), Sara Woolley-Gomez; 246 (LO RT), Sara Woolley-Gomez; 247 (UP CTR), Granger, All rights reserved; 247 (UP RT), Iunstream/AL; 247 (LO RT), Sara Woolley-Gomez; 248 (UP RT), Fine Art/VCG Wilson/Corbis/GI; 248 (LE), Miguel Medina/Stringer/GI; 248 (LO RT), Thomas Haupt/Westend61 GmbH/AL; 249 (UP), Nick Garbutt/MP; 249 (CTR RT), Turkish Presidency of National Palaces Administration/Anadolu Agency/GI; 249 (LO), Martha Avery/Asian Art & Archaeology, Inc./Corbis/GI; 250, Vera/AS; 251 (LO), akg-images; 252 (UP), Scott Rothstein/SS; 253 (UP), SS; 253 (CTR), Zack Frank/SS; 253 (LO), Gary Blakely/SS; 254 (UP), grandriver/E+/GI; 254 (CTR), Stan Honda/AFP via GI; 254 (LO), grandriver/E+/GI; 255 (ALL), WHHA; 256 (ALL), WHHA; 257 (ALL), WHHA; 258 (ALL), WHHA; 259 (Clinton), WHHA; 259 (Trump), Shealah Craighead/The White House; 259 (Biden), David Lienemann/The White House; 259 (Ford), WHHA; 259 (Carter), WHHA; 259 (Reagan), WHHA; 259 (Bush), WHHA; 259 (George W. Bush), WHHA; 259 (cow), Elisabeth Aardema/SS; 259 (Obama), Pete Souza/The White House; 260-261 (UP), SS; 260-261 (LO), piotr_pabijan/SS; 262 (INSET), Science Source/GI; 262 (UP), Bettmann/Corbis/GI; 263 (UP), Charles Kogod/NGIC; 263 (LO), Saul Loeb/AFP via GI; 264, Bettmann Archive/GI; 265 (UP LE), Kent Nishimura/Los Angeles Times via GI; 265 (LO), Hanna Franzen/EPA-EFE/SS; 265, Justin Milhouse; 266 (UP CTR), Fine Art/VCG Wilson/Corbis/GI; 266 (UP LE), RJ Lerich/SS; 266 (CTR RT), Israel Antiquities Authority/Xinhua News Agency/Newscom; 266 (LO LE), Sara Woolley-Gomez; 266 (LO RT), Edgars Sermulis/stoatphoto/AS; 267, Christopher Furlong/GI

Geography Rocks (268–353)

268-269, Artur Debat/GI; 270-271, NG Maps;

272-273, NG Maps; 274, NG Maps; 275 (UP), Mark Thiessen/National Geographic Partners; 275 (LO), NASA; 276 (ALL), NG Maps; 277 (UP LE), Thomas J. Abercrombie/NGIC; 277 (UP CTR), Maria Stenzel/NGIC; 277 (UP RT), Gordon Wiltsie/NGIC; 277 (LO CTR), Bill Hatcher/NGIC; 277 (LO LE), James P. Blair/NGIC; 277 (LO RT), Carsten Peter/NGIC; 277 (BACKGROUND), Fabiano Rebeque/Moment/GI; 278, Michel & Christine Denis-Huot/Biosphoto; 279 (UP RT), AdemarRangel/GI; 279 (CTR RT), imageBROKER/SS; 279 (LO RT), David Havel/SS; 279 (CTR LE), Robert Gess; 279 (LO LE), Chris Philpot; 280-281, NG Maps; 282, heckepics/GI; 283 (UP RT), Achim Baque/SS; 283 (CTR LE), Daniel P. Zitterbart/Woods Hole Oceanographic Institution; 283 (CTR RT), Flipser/SS; 283 (LO LE), Chris Philpot; 283 (LO RT), Antony Gilbert; 284-285, NG Maps; 286, Tim on Tour/AS; 287 (UP), Grant Rooney Premium/AL; 287 (CTR LE), rudiernst/AS; 287 (CTR RT), Nate Allen/EyeEm/GI; 287 (LO LE), Chris Philpot; 287 (LO RT), R.M. Nunes/AS; 288-289, NG Maps; 290, Dave Watts/Nature Picture Library; 291 (UP RT), Andrew Watson/John Warburton-Lee Photography Ltd/GI; 291 (CTR LE), Adwo/AS; 291 (CTR RT), Michael Frese/University of Canberra; 291 (LO LE), Chris Philpot; 291 (LO RT), Witte-Art/AS; 292-293, NG Maps; 294, Andy Trowbridge/Nature Picture Library; 295 (UP RT), Roy Pedersen/SS; 295 (CTR LE), drhfoto/AS; 295 (CTR RT), tanuha2001/SS; 295 (LO RT), Alice Zoo; 296-297, NG Maps; 298, Yaacov Dagan/AL; 299 (UP), Dina Julayeva/SS; 299 (CTR LE), Javier Trueba/MSF/Science Source; 299 (CTR RT), Kitchin and Hurst/All Canada Photos/AL; 299 (LO), Jim West/AL; 300-301, NG Maps; 302, Ecuadorpostales/SS; 303 (UP), Soberka Richard/hemis.fr/GI; 303 (CTR LE), buteo/AS; 303 (CTR RT), Sarmat/AS; 303 (LO LE), NG Maps; 303 (LO RT), Jacek Warsaw PL/AS; 304-305, NG Maps; 308, Steven M Lang/SS; 311, JorgeIvan/AS; 315, elxeneize/AS; 316, Ketkarn sakultap/AS; 319, Mohamed I Khalid/SS; 322, bbtomas/AS; 325, Giordano Cipriani/GI; 330, TTstudio/AS; 332-333, NG Maps; 334-335, NG Maps; 342 (UP), SeanPavonePhoto/IS/GI; 342 (CTR LE), TexPhoto/E+/GI; 342 (CTR RT), Harold G Herradura/GI; 342 (LO), PhotoDisc; 343 (UP LE), dszc/GI; 343 (UP CTR), Treinen Farm Corn Maze and Pumpkin Patch; 343 (UP RT), George Lamson/SS; 343 (CTR LE), Pat Canova/AL; 343 (LO LE), StockImageFactory/SS; 343 (LO CTR), Gary Meszaros/GI; 343 (LO RT), RandomHartz/SS; 344 (UP LE), Leonid Andronov/AS; 344 (UP RT), Jenifoto/SS; 344 (LO LE), Crea il tuo web/AS; 344 (LO RT), gudkovandrey/AS; 345 (UP LE), Stefan/AS; 345 (CTR LE), Jaahnlieb/DS; 345 (CTR RT), KK/AS; 345 (LO), photlook/AS; 346, Noppasin/SS; 347 (BOTH), The Safari Collection; 348 (UP), Auscape International Pty Ltd/AL; 348 (CTR LE), CB2/ZOB/Supplied by WENN/Newscom; 348 (CTR LE), Bruce Obee/Newscom; 348 (CTR RT), Alastair Pollock Photography/GI; 349, NG Maps; 350 (UP LE), Susana Gonzalez/Corbis; 350 (UP RT), Design Pics Inc/AL; 350 (LO), Laszlo Balogh/Reuters; 351 (A), sculpies/GI; 351 (B), Archives Charmet/BI; 351 (C), Archives Charmet/BI; 351 (D), Archives Charmet/BI; 351 (E), BI; 351 (F), Archives Charmet/BI; 351 (G), DEA Picture Library/GI; 351 (H), Holger Mette/SS; 351 (I), Holger Mette/SS; 351 (J), Jarno Gonzalez Zarraonandia/SS; 351 (K), David Iliff/SS; 351 (L), ostill/SS; 351 (M), Hannamariah/SS; 351 (N), Jarno Gonzalez Zarraonandia/SS; 352 (UP LE), KK/AS; 352 (UP RT), Daniel P. Zitterbart/Woods Hole Oceanographic Institution; 352 (CTR LE), Sarmat/AS; 352 (LO RT), Bruce Obee/Newscom; 353, NG Maps

359

NATIONAL GEOGRAPHIC and Yellow Border Design are trademarks of the
National Geographic Society, used under license.

Since 1888, the National Geographic Society has funded more than
14,000 research, conservation, education, and storytelling projects around
the world. National Geographic Partners distributes a portion of the funds
it receives from your purchase to National Geographic Society to support
programs including the conservation of animals and their habitats.
To learn more, visit natgeo.com/info.

For more information, visit nationalgeographic.com,
call 1-877-873-6846, or write to the following address:

National Geographic Partners, LLC
1145 17th Street N.W.
Washington, DC 20036-4688 U.S.A.

More for kids from National Geographic: natgeokids.com

National Geographic Kids magazine inspires children to explore their world
with fun yet educational articles on animals, science, nature, and more.
Using fresh storytelling and amazing photography, *Nat Geo Kids* shows kids
ages 6 to 14 the fascinating truth about the world—and why they should care.
natgeo.com/subscribe

For rights or permissions inquiries, please contact National Geographic
Books Subsidiary Rights: bookrights@natgeo.com

Designed by Kathryn Robbins and Ruthie Thompson

The publisher would like to thank the team that made this book possible:
Rose Davidson, project editor; Christina Sauer and Ariane Szu-Tu, editors;
Sarah Wassner Flynn, writer; Lori Epstein, photo manager; Michelle Harris,
researcher; Mike McNey, map production; Michael J. Horner, map editor;
Molly Reid, production editor; and Lauren Sciortino and David Marvin,
associate designers.

Trade paperback ISBN: 978-1-4263-7602-3
Reinforced library binding ISBN: 978-1-4263-7609-2

Printed in the United States of America
24/WOR/1